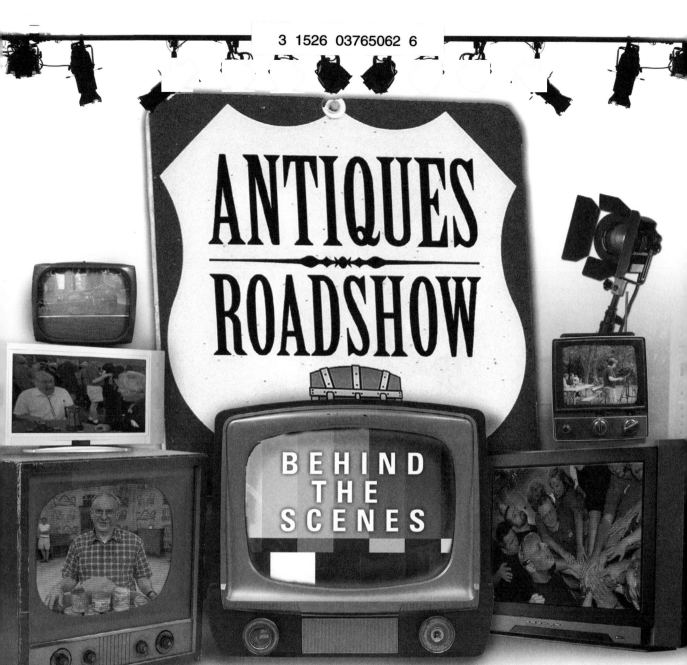

ANTIQUES ROADSHOW

BEHIND THE SCENES

An Insider's Guide to PBS's #1 Weekly Show

Marsha Bemko

A Touchstone / Stonesong Press Book
Published by Simon & Schuster
New York London Toronto Sydney

Touchstone
A Division of Simon & Schuster, Inc.
1230 Avenue of the Americas
New York, NY 10020

First Touchstone trade paperback edition December 2009
Published by arrangement with the Stonesong Press

TOUCHSTONE and colophon are registered trademarks
of Simon & Schuster, Inc.

For information about special discounts for bulk purchases, please
contact Simon & Schuster Special Sales at 1-866-506-1949
or business@simonandschuster.com.

The Simon & Schuster Speakers Bureau can bring authors to your live event.
For more information or to book an event contact the Simon & Schuster Speakers
Bureau at 866-248-3049 or visit our website at www.simonspeakers.com.

Designed by Mada Design and produced by the Stonesong Press, LLC

Manufactured in the United States of America

10 9 8 7 6 5 4 3 2 1

Library of Congress Cataloging-in-Publication Data
  Bemko, Marsha (Marsha Komins), 1955–
  Antiques Roadshow behind the scenes : an insider's guide to PBS's #1 weekly show/Marsha
Bemko.
    p.   cm.
  "A Fireside Book."
  "A Stonesong Press Book."
  Includes bibliographical references and index.
  1. Antiques roadshow (Television program : U.S.) 2. Antiques—United States.
3. Collectibles—United States. I. Title.
  NK1125 .B445 2010
  745.1—dc22   2009021847
ISBN 978-1-4391-0330-2
ISBN 978-1-4391-4913-3 (ebook)

Antiques Roadshow is a trademark of the BBC and is produced for PBS
by WGBH/Boston under license from BBC Worldwide.

PBS's #1 Weekly Show—Source: Nielsen NTI Special TV Ratings
for PBS Live+7 AA% regular programs '97/'98 through '07/'08 seasons.

Please see page 181 for photograph credits.

Dedicated to treasure hunters everywhere

ACKNOWLEDGMENTS

With all the people who contribute to making *Antiques Roadshow*, I'm bound to leave someone out and for this I apologize in advance.

Before I get to professional nods, I must start with my husband, Paul. In a superhuman feat, he humors my belief that he was my soldier in that bakery generations ago who took longer than expected to rescue me and proves daily that his love is true and pure. To my beautiful daughters, Michelle and Brittany, who gracefully tolerate Mom's career, and my son, Morgan, who has always been a loving voice.

The staff is the soul of *Roadshow*; they are what make coming to work each day a treat. Bless Sam Farrell for reviewing every page and making excellent suggestions; Adam Monahan for endlessly checking the facts; Sarah Elliott, Jill Giles, Amy Santamaria, and Jeff Cronenberg for their review and rewrites. The rest of my longtime staff, who teach me to be a better person and producer: Brian Beenders, Kelsey Bresnahan, Luke Crafton, Erika Denn, Nina Farouk, Tiffany Henery-Brown, and Christina Pan. And my publicist, Judy Matthews: on top of being a gifted writer, her advice is solid.

The crew is dedicated and their contributions priceless. Our longtime veterans come back every year to sacrifice their summer and join the tour. Chas Norton, our lighting director, is so much more than the title explains, which doesn't reflect his year-round devotion or his attention to detail, including his invaluable assistance in preparing sections of this book.

My sincere thanks to Judy Linden, our editor at Stonesong; she navigated the waters to make one cohesive whole. To writers Dorothy Harris and Joe Rosson: they are brave souls who toured with us and weeded through complicated details to understand and articulate our story.

To our appraisers: All of them give so much and so graciously to *Antiques Roadshow*, WGBH, and PBS. Without their intelligence and contributions of time—and their willingness to pick up their own expenses—it would be a very different *Roadshow*. And to all those appraisers who don't appear in this book, my apologies. With about 150 experts, including everyone was impossible.

WGBH is like my second home. I will always be indebted to Peter S. McGhee for believing in me and guiding my career. Margaret Drain, my vice president and supporter: her advice and gentle toughness is the juice I need. Mary Cahill Farella helped make the book possible. Peter B. Cook: thanks for teaching me *Roadshow*.

To everyone at PBS, in particular John F. Wilson for his advice and friendship, and to all the PBS stations for their coproduction help at every stop we make.

Thank you to Lara Spencer, my first host as executive producer. We cried together the day she told me she had to leave for another job but have stayed close and I treasure our friendship. To Mark L. Walberg, our host since Season 10 and my dear friend since that first week in Providence, Rhode Island. You make traveling fun, and the time we spend together is my favorite part of the day—especially in hotels with Louise, balconies, and great views.

And of course, thank you to our guests who come to the events to be part of our cast. To the 110 folks in each city who volunteer their time: we really couldn't do it without you. Ultimately, the biggest thanks to you, our audience: without viewers like you, we wouldn't be here.

CONTENTS

FOREWORD

I had just gotten off the plane in Wichita, Kansas and I was starving. After a short ride to the hotel and check-in, I began to figure out dinner. I knew what I wouldn't be eating—anything I could have at home or at a national chain. That is my first hard and steadfast *Roadshow* rule: Never eat a meal you can get at home.

As if a prayer had been answered, I looked out of my hotel window to discover Lawrence-Dumont Stadium just across the river. The minor league Wichita Wingnuts were warming up and local fans were filing in from all directions. I could even hear the PA announcer inviting people to stay after the game for a fireworks show. I'd found my dinner spot.

With a quick text, my associate producer Adam, cameraman Bob, and audio man Charlie, met me in the hotel lobby, and off we went to enjoy a warm Kansas summer night at the ballpark. It was truly a "field of dreams." We bought seats at the door, met all the locals, ate hot dogs, drank beer, and watched the Wingnuts' manager throw a temper tantrum that had him ejected from the game. It made the national news and we were there in the third row! You see, wherever we go, we get to see great American history—sometimes as it's happening.

This is what I love about *Antiques Roadshow*. As we crisscross America, executive producer Marsha Bemko and I, and the rest of the gang, have found ourselves in numerous, uniquely American moments like this one. It may be

Roadshow host Mark Walberg on the set in Palm Springs in 2008.

that we are seekers of local flavor. Or maybe it's that *Antiques Roadshow* feels like a traveling summer camp—working hard and having fun with people you really enjoy. That has been my experience since I signed on as host in 2005—although when they first contacted me, I thought it must've been a mistake.

{ **LOOKING BACK, I'M THE LUCKIEST GUY AROUND.** }

My agent called, saying that the *Antiques Roadshow* people were looking for a new host and wanted to see me. I met Marsha and her associate at a restaurant. During our conversation, Marsha asked me, "Why do you think you would be a good host for *Antiques Roadshow?*"

I was silent for a long moment before replying, "Quite honestly, I haven't a clue. You called me!" I could feel the heat come into my face. But I gathered myself and said something that is still true today. "You already have a hundred and fifty of the greatest experts on the show. You sure don't need another one. I can be a curious and eager student—asking the same questions the viewers are asking and enjoying what America tunes in to experience." Luckily, Marsha had an idea of what she needed in a host and she thought I might do a good job. Thank goodness for that!

Looking back, I'm the luckiest guy around. I not only scored a great new job on an incredible show but also gained a family of true friends, with Marsha being number one. I am the fourth host, and *Roadshow* audiences are very specific about what they like to watch. Like we say on the air, "The antiques are the stars!" During those early days, I didn't want to do anything to upset the viewers' *Roadshow* experience. I was just hoping that they would accept me as a competent new host and ultimately embrace me as part of the family. I've described that first taping city as feeling like what it must feel like to get married before meeting your new in-laws—awkward, but no turning back now!

It didn't take long for our production unit to get in a great groove and for me to grow into the role of host. We've got the best team I've ever worked with: Sarah, Adam, Louise, Bob, and Charlie—and I'm proud to see our field productions on TV.

Things also have changed as I tape all the stand-ups (intros, promos, sign-offs, etc.) on the appraisal floor in the convention centers. In my first season, I would walk from one appraisal table to another during breaks and no one would even notice. I was just another face in the 5,000-plus-person crowd.

These days it's a bit different. People are so excited to meet all of us. I love talking to everybody, and I love hearing their stories. It makes me feel honored that I "made the cut" as the host. And even though I'm usually done shooting at 4:00 PM on appraisal day, you can almost always find me hanging around until 7:00 or so looking over the appraisers' shoulders and trying to pick up some tips. I'll sit down at the Glass, Pottery, Sports, or Silver table and try to hone my amateur appraising skills. The experts are all so willing to teach, but I'm a novice student. They start with the basic question "Can you tell me if this is old or new?" That's about how far I've gotten up the appraiser ladder!

At *Roadshow*, we say you either have—or don't have—the collector's "disease." I don't and that's a very good thing. Everywhere I go, I see something so fascinating that I vow to start collecting that genre. First it was Colt pistols, then guitars, beer steins, Navajo jewelry, and tractor seats. When I started considering needlepoint samplers, I knew I had a problem! If I collected everything I found interesting I surely would go broke.

The vibe on the set has, and probably always will be, the purest form of positive energy, and it's completely intoxicating. It stems from the genuine excitement shared by the people both on-and offscreen: the producers, camera operators, volunteers, appraisers, guests… I could go on and on. There isn't a single person present who doesn't get romanced by the stories behind the items brought to *Roadshow* and by the appraisers' contributions to these stories. These conversations are the threads that connect the objects of history to the everyday life to which we can all relate. These stories give history humanity. And I believe the keepers of these stories are the true historians.

You'll be wowed by the stories in this book. You'll be surprised to learn how the production comes together and what happens when appraisal day is done. Most importantly—for me

at least—you'll see that we are much more than coworkers and colleagues. We really are one big (somewhat dysfunctional!) family—eclectic, yes, but so connected. Having worked in commercial television for over twenty years, I can assure you that the *Roadshow* experience isn't like any other TV production. Marsha Bemko infuses our days with an infectious passion and camaraderie that spreads through the entire staff, into the control room, out through the hundreds of volunteers, and into the words of our appraisers. People who watch *Roadshow* depend on a certain quality, and Marsha makes sure those expectations are met in every episode. And when the shows are all taped and the summer tour is over, it's our friendship that I take back home—and it's our friendship that grows with every new city we visit.

Within these pages is the inside scoop that even I didn't know. I guarantee you will find *Antiques Roadshow: Behind the Scenes* a truly memorable experience, just like my night at the ballpark in Wichita.

—Mark L. Walberg

Mark Walberg (left), a student of local flavor, stands with appraiser Rafael Eledge.

Cameraman Randy Gray and Marsha Bemko look for the perfect shot.

INTRODUCTION

One of the proudest aspects of my life—besides being a parent—is being at the helm of *Antiques Roadshow*, arguably the most popular, long-running television series to ever appear on PBS. There is a quote I heard years ago—unfortunately, I am no longer sure who said it or when—but it maintained that there are just three "brands" in the field of antiques: eBay, Sotheby's (or was it Christie's?), and *Antiques Roadshow*. Each week, about 10 million viewers tune in to watch *Roadshow*, and with such a large audience, no matter where I go, people know about our show. On the rare occasion when they don't, they tend to ask something like, "Is that the show where people find out if they have something worth a lot of money?"

"Well, sometimes they do, and sometimes they don't," is my typical answer. One observation about our lucky guests with items that are worth five and six figures (a fairly uncommon occurrence) is that if the object was inherited, usually the owner does not want to sell it. The sentimental value exceeds the monetary worth by a wide margin. However, for those truly lucky guests who have paid a small sum for a very valuable object or perhaps rescued a treasure from the trash, making a quick and easy profit almost always is an option to be considered. But remember this: Someone out there actually sold the item for a pittance—or threw it away—without knowing its significant worth. As executive producer of *Antiques Roadshow*, one of my goals is to make certain that unfortunate person is not you! In other words, our show is more about education than it is about money.

Officially, I am the executive producer of *Roadshow*, which means that I am the ultimate decision-maker about virtually everything that happens on the show. That said, television is a team sport, and the staff and crew of *Antiques Roadshow* are superb, with in-the-trenches, hands-on roles of putting the show together and making it happen. It almost takes a village to produce *Antiques Roadshow*. When we go on the road for taping, we take with us fifteen full-and part-time, year-round staff, plus four summertime freelancers. In addition, there are twenty-five crew members from Boston and beyond backed up by an additional fifteen drawn from the local area. The local PBS station provides 110 volunteers, each of whom receive an official *Antiques Roadshow* shirt and the right to bring an item to be appraised—a very coveted perk. There are about seventy-five appraisers who donate their travel and services to

The *Roadshow* Crew—it almost takes a village to produce each episode.

HOW TO GET TICKETS TO ANTIQUES ROADSHOW

* Tickets are free! But there is a two-ticket limit per household either when obtained online or by sending in a postcard.

* Tickets are available to adults who are residents of either the United States or Canada.

* The application process usually begins in January and closes in April. Check our Web site pbs.org/antiques for specifics.

* Name, mailing address, and a valid e-mail address are necessary to apply online.

* From the applications received, 3,200 pairs of tickets will be issued, another 250 pairs will be given to the local PBS station to distribute for promotional and fund-raising purposes, plus another 250 pairs for complimentary purposes, and another 100 pairs to be distributed to local community organizations for a total of 3,800 pairs of tickets altogether. The recipients of the 3,200 pairs of tickets will be selected by random drawing, and it does not matter if an application is made early or at the deadline. Everyone has an equal chance of being selected.

* E-mail notification to successful applicants will be sent in May, and tickets will be mailed approximately three weeks prior to the event date.

be part of the show and a top-notch security staff (whose numbers cannot be divulged), which vigilantly insures the safety of our guests and staff during every taping event.

Our taping events happen on our summer tour, which is an exciting and invigorating time for me even though I have often called it "my own private hell." But this is really just a bit of drama born from the demands of the day and the utter exhaustion that comes after a minimum of twelve hours of taping, which starts before 8:00 in the morning and can go well into the night. When it's all over, however, I do love all the excitement and rushing around the floor from appraiser to appraiser seeing what they have to show me and making The Picks of the items that will ultimately be taped. I never tire of hearing peoples' stories, the fascinating glimpses into history, the enthusiasm of the crowd waiting to see the appraisers, all the hubbub and commotion, and the excitement of both the appraisers and the guests over the treasures we see. This can be a very emotional experience for those who come to *Roadshow*—sometimes there are tears of joy and other times tears of disappointment.

This past year, one of our appraisers, Don Cresswell, was pitching an 1885 print to me in the hopes that we might tape it. The guest who owned the print was accompanied by his daughter and they told me the picture had been a prized possession of his wife's. She loved the *Roadshow*, had applied for tickets, gotten them, and couldn't wait to come. Sadly, she died six months before *Roadshow* came to town, and her husband was presenting the print to us in her honor.

I replied, "Oh, that is so sad," and we hugged. When I stepped back, our eyes met and I felt his deep and abiding pain. We were both silent, and I hoped that if neither one of us talked, I could gulp the tears down. No such luck. Tears fell down both our faces, and then the daughter started. We all hugged, and thankfully, a guest who had been watching the whole thing ran up with a handful of tissues to stem the flood. I have cried while watching footage before, but never in front of a guest. That was the first, and so far the only, time.

For each city we visit, we receive thousands of requests

for tickets—sometimes tens of thousands of requests. In the beginning, we didn't issue tickets and admitted guests on a first-come-first-served basis. At one of our earlier tapings, our now-head of security had to turn away more than 6,000 people, many of whom had waited in line all day to come in and see an appraiser. He reports that he was concerned there would be a riot and that he might have had to control an angry mob. Now we distribute tickets with hourly appointment times, but still, we cannot possibly see everyone who wants to come to *Antiques Roadshow* (I wish we could!). For every event, we provide a total of 3,800 pairs of tickets. That breaks down to 3,200 pairs of tickets distributed to the public, along with an additional 250 pairs that are allotted to the local PBS station to help them with fund-raising and to generate a little excitement; another 100 pairs to be distributed to local community organizations; and 250 pairs for appraiser, staff, and corporate underwriter comps.

On the day of the event, we have between seventy-five and eighty experts (drawn from a pool of about 150) ready to meet the 5,000 to 6,000 people who show up. Despite all the in-

MARSHA'S MUSINGS

We tried using a professional ticket distributor, but between the cost and our random-selection process it was more efficient to distribute tickets ourselves. Besides, now every attendee gets a specially designed *Roadshow* ticket as a memento.

tensity surrounding the acquisition of tickets, about 20 percent of the people who have tickets do not show up. I cannot imagine why there are so many no-shows, but according to the ticketing experts we consulted, this is about normal for events with free tickets.

Starting around 6:00 AM on the day of the event, those guests holding 8:00 AM tickets (that is, first-entry tickets) begin to arrive, and we try to let them in a little early, usually around 7:30 or 7:45. We have people of all ages and physical conditions, from very young children to older folks in wheelchairs, all waiting eagerly to get into the building to see the appraisers. The children are usually clutching a little treasure. But what they are hoping for, like most of the adults, is to be on television.

Between 5,000 and 6,000 guests bring treasures large and small to each event.

In these pages, I tell the inside story of the making of *Antiques Roadshow* and share my insights with all those who love *Roadshow*. In the chapter "Success, Setbacks, and Serendipity," I tell the largely unpublished and unknown story of how *Roadshow* began, and in another chapter we will go "On the Road with *Roadshow*" and explore every aspect of a day's taping.

One of the most exciting parts of the chapter, "What to Bring to *Antiques Roadshow*," is a discussion of selecting the items that will be taped for possible inclusion in a future episode. We follow the teams (one headed by myself) that are making what we call "The Picks," and just a hint: It is the appraiser's enthusiasm and the story that goes along with the item that can make all the difference between being on television and not making the cut.

I also outline what happens after the taping is done, how we put the show together, and the ways we meticulously fact-check in order to try and eliminate mistakes—such as the one an appraiser made when she said that a miniature portrait painting on porcelain from the late 1700s or early 1800s had been painted in "West Virginia." Well, West Virginia per se did not exist until the time of the Civil War, so using the state name was an anachronism.

What the appraiser meant to say was that the piece had been painted in "western Virginia." It was a seemingly small error, a three-letter little slip of the tongue, but it was a mistake that had to be corrected. After all, in addition to teaching the public about art, antiques, and collectibles, we're also teaching history, and accuracy is extremely important. Fortunately, we did manage to turn "west" into "western" Virginia on the tape, which allowed us to air the segment after all.

Behind the Scenes tells a lot of stories from the appraisers' points of view so you can get to know them better. Our experts explore what to bring and what not to bring to *Antiques Roadshow*, and some of them share their stories about how they became appraisers, how they developed their special interests—and how those of you with a passion for antiques and history might be able to follow a similar path.

I'm very committed to providing information readers can take away with them. For example, this book includes an appendix that lists all the reference books as well as other books of interest, associations and collectors clubs, and interesting Web sites we use as we travel around the country.

Still another chapter, "Antiques Across America," explores some of the best and most interesting items we have found in our journeys around the country since 1996—*Roadshow*'s first summer tour. There is a lot of "WOW!" and "Imagine finding that in your attic or at a flea market!" But there also are rare glimpses into family histories and fascinating explorations of America's past.

In addition, I know viewers are interested in what happens after the lights go off and *Roadshow* leaves town. What do our guests do with their objects? Do they sell them, and are they happy with the results? Do some items go to museums? Or is the information obtained at *Roadshow* used to ensure that future generations will understand the monetary value and importance of an object when it is passed down in their family? And if so, is the piece properly preserved for posterity? One of the chapters I like best is "Missing Masterpieces"—what they are and if they turn up at *Antiques Roadshow*. The appraisers let you in on what they consider to be masterpieces, what they personally have seen while sitting at a *Roadshow* table, and what "missing" masterpiece they are hunting for and would like to see come through the door at a future *Roadshow* event. There is also key information on how you can recognize such a piece if you should be lucky enough to happen upon it. Sometimes, a masterpiece can be rather unassuming. In Tucson, Arizona, in 2001, while on our sixth tour, a gentleman brought in a Navajo blanket to be appraised. It was brown, blue, and white, and if it were displayed near many other Navajo blankets, with their bright colors and intricate design, most laypeople would dismiss it as being much too plain and drab to have a substantial value.

This seemingly plain blanket turned out to be one of the most monetarily valuable items ever brought to *Roadshow*. It was a first-phase Ute-style blanket (so named because the Ute Indians favored this Navajo design) made circa 1820, and was judged to be worth between $350,000 and $500,000 at the time. Needless to say, the owner was weak-kneed and flabbergasted at the unexpected good news.

The blanket held the honor of being the most valuable find until our visit to Palm Springs, California, during Season 13, when a guest brought in an early Clyfford Still painting. The blanket moved to third place in Season 14 when we taped our first million-dollar appraisal—but more on *that* later.

I have a lot to cover in the following pages, so sit back, turn the page, and learn all you ever wanted to know about the inside workings of *Antiques Roadshow*—from its ultimate insider.

This simple Navajo blanket was valued between $350,000 and $500,000!

The first American *Roadshow* took place in Concord, Massachusetts, in 1996 with appraisers. Titi Halle (middle) and Jo Kris (right)

SUCCESS, SETBACKS & SERENDIPITY

The original *Antiques Roadshow* was first broadcast

in the United Kingdom in 1979 and was the brainchild of the British Broadcasting Corporation (BBC), which is the world's largest broadcasting company. This was a very British show that was often taped outdoors with very proper appraisers conversing charmingly and politely with guests, who were often somewhat reserved in their reaction to the information they were receiving.

Roadshow did not come to the United States until almost seventeen years later when it debuted on PBS in 1997 (from tapings that occurred on the 1996 summer tour). The journey of this extremely popular show across the Atlantic was a surprisingly difficult one, and only the vision of one man, Peter S. McGhee, made the trip possible at all.

But first there was Dan Farrell.

The story of the *Roadshow*'s journey from England to America has never been fully told—at least not in print—and many people who work on the American version of *Roadshow* today are not familiar with the twists and turns in the saga. *Antiques Roadshow* in America almost did not happen, and what follows is a short exploration of how the *Roadshow* finally did make it to the United States and onto our television screens.

ANTIQUES ROADSHOW: TAKE ONE

Dan Farrell was in the film business in London. As he puts it, he took charge of "special financial effects," meaning that he was involved more in the money end of the business as opposed to the production of motion pictures or television programs. He had a banking background and was not passionately interested in antiques at all.

"Antiques were always a part of my life," he explains, "because they were always around in my family home, in my grandmother's home, and in the homes of my aunts." The antiques were really "just there," the way a sofa is just there or the table at which a family eats is just there. To Farrell, antiques were very much like stage props that the inhabitants of the house sit on or use as needed. They were not something that he thought about very much.

"I was not a collector," he states. "But my wife and I would spend pleasant New England afternoons driving around looking at the antiques in the various shops. It was a weekend diversion, not a hobby or avocation.

"Then while I was living in London, I happened to turn on the television and there was *Antiques Roadshow.* It was new at the time, and I was fascinated by it. I knew that many great American television shows were based on British originals. *All in the Family*, for example, was based on *Till Death Us Do Part,* while *Three's Company* was inspired by *Man About the House.*"

It would be hard to imagine bigger television hits than these, and the early eighties was the dawn of cable network television in the

Peter S. McGhee had an amazing influence on American television. *Frontline, American Experience, Rock & Roll* and many other landmark series on PBS were created and produced under his watch. He championed the idea to put *Antiques Roadshow* on PBS. Aida Moreno, the show's first executive producer, deserves credit for the startup of the series. She and her team developed many procedures still in use today.

United States. Farrell reasoned that there might be a place on the newly expanding American television for *Antiques Roadshow*, and thought, "Maybe this is something I should take back to the States.

"I approached an agent in London who got me in contact with the BBC to see if a deal could be reached. The arrangements were made and the BBC expressed their willingness to sell me the North American rights to *Antiques Roadshow.* So, I got together the lawyers and the agents and crafted an agreement that the BBC accepted.

"The original agreement was signed in October 1981. The document was just a couple of pages, hardly more than a good-sized letter. I acquired the North American rights in perpetuity to the *Roadshow* format. When Norman Lear and the other producers of American television sitcoms based on British shows acquired the rights, they got somewhat more than I did, including such things as scripts, characters, and plot ideas.

GOING FOR A SONG

According to Simon Shaw, the current series editor of the British version of *Antiques Roadshow, Roadshow* had its beginning as an outgrowth of a program called *Going for a Song.* "There was a meeting for ideas to update the program" Shaw said. "The production had been receiving a lot of letters saying, 'I've got one of those... how much is it worth?' Someone at the meeting mentioned that auction houses did 'sweeps' where they sent two or three experts to a town for a day or two to discreetly value people's items and wondered if this would translate into a program." From this meeting, *Antiques Roadshow* would grow and become something of a phenomenon on the BBC. Perhaps it was a bit surprising to some, but the show was a dramatic success: 15 million viewers watched it in the UK every week at the height of its popularity. Most importantly, its audience crossed all demographic barriers. Christopher Lewis, the second executive producer of the British *Antiques Roadshow,* reasons that *Roadshow* was a hit because it was "a kind of a game show in which everybody has a prize to begin with and the 'contestants' are just trying to find out if it is worth anything." Farrell agrees and contends that, "*Roadshow* is, in fact, a kind of treasure hunt."

"Today, many people are astounded that I got the rights in perpetuity, but maybe nobody was paying much attention at the time. I did not pay a great deal of money and remember, I was using my own money and buying it just for myself. The BBC may have thought that any money at all was money they did not have, for a product they didn't have any prospects of selling to anyone else."

"When I got back to the United States," Farrell continues, "I made an effort to get it on the air. I called up the new cable channels with a mass market and got a friendly reception until I mentioned that the show was about antiques. At that point, you could almost see it through the phone: Their eyes glazed over and all interest was lost. They thought that not enough Americans were interested in the subject matter, and that those who were, did not fit into the correct demographic.

Dan Farrell is the man who believed in the American version of *Antiques Roadshow* when no one else did.

"Over the next thirteen years," Farrell says, "I made a few dents, but could get no traction. Then, I was approached by the New York office of the BBC who said they wanted to become involved in getting an American version of *Antiques Roadshow* on the air. Part of our problem in my view was that we only had the British version of *Roadshow* to show to the American television people, and we really needed to show the program in the American idiom."

At this point, Farrell approached Skinner, the major Boston auction house, to propose that he and his team do a taping at one of Skinner's discovery-day sessions. "This was about 1994. I decided to bring someone in to host, and I asked Monty Hall of *Let's Make a Deal* fame to come to Boston and do the job. He was a friend and he agreed to do it just for his expenses.

"All we wanted to do was make a short reel to show *Antiques Roadshow* in the American style," Farrell remembers. "We were only going to tape for three or four hours and produce a tape that was ten or fifteen minutes long." It was to be a kind of pitch piece and was never intended to be a pilot or appear on the air in any way. Today, no one at the *Roadshow* has seen this tape, and it is something of a legend and mystery to all those currently involved with the show—except, of course, Dan Farrell, who is the current consulting producer.

Shortly thereafter Farrell tells another curve in the story: The BBC backed out of their commitment to the project, and he ended up with the cost of the reel, which was approximately $18,000. Then the BBC asked to see the tape, and Farrell refused. Subsequently, the BBC offered to pay part of the cost. Farrell allowed them to see it and was paid about half of his investment.

"The relationship with the BBC had kind of soured," Farrell says, "but the deal between me and the BBC to make the tape with Skinner was about to expire, and when it did all rights reverted to me. I frankly did not know what to do next."

ANTIQUES ROADSHOW: TAKE TWO

At this point, the second truly important figure in the saga, Peter S. McGhee, enters the story. Like Farrell, McGhee was often in London. He was vice president of national programming for WGBH, the flagship station for PBS, based in Boston, and as part of his duties, McGhee frequently traveled to England and the rest of Western Europe seeking production partnerships with British and other European broadcasters. This had led to successful coproductions of such milestone programs as *Vietnam: A Television History*, which had both French and British partners, and as mentioned earlier, the iconic *Rock & Roll*.

Like Farrell, McGhee watched British television while in London, and his favorite show by far was the BBC's *Antiques Roadshow*. The programs were oh-so British, a little staid perhaps and even a bit stuffy at times, but there was something about the program that was intriguing to McGhee and very entertaining.

To be sure, it was educational. It was that rare television program that could teach such things as history and cultural dynamics, but make the process engaging by solving mysteries such as, "Is it old?" "Is it a fake?" and perhaps more compellingly, "Is it monetarily valuable?"

Viewers got intriguing peeks inside private lives and family histories, and in the end, the disclosure of value often brought a bit of reserved surprise and maybe a little "gee-whiz" response from both the owner of the object being appraised and those watching the festivities on the telly. It also caused those at home to wonder if that old horror they got from Great-Aunt Agnes might be worth something after all.

Back in Boston, McGhee decided to see if the British *Antiques Roadshow* could be brought to the United States. He sent Aida Moreno, who later became the first executive producer, to England to see if WGBH could produce a similar show.

Moreno went to England and reported back that the show could not be produced the same way as the British show. It was just too cumbersome and expensive. According to Moreno, the British operation was like "night and day" when compared to the way that the American version of the *Roadshow* eventually would be done. "The only similarity was that both shows had appraisers appraising antiques and collectibles. How we did our business was completely different."

One of the primary and most costly differences concerned the setup: The British version of *Roadshow* took two to three days. Moreno explained, "The lighting staff had to come in and build a grid to hang the lights. Then other people had to construct the set, and they used huge wooden panels. This took a lot of time and money and it just would not work here. For logistics and efficiency we decided we had to be able to do it all in one day. We also decided we had to work indoors and have weatherproof venues."

It was determined that, by doing it this way, *Antiques Roadshow* could be much more efficient and cost-effective. I will discuss how this was done in chapter 3, "On the Road with *Roadshow*." Suffice it to say, at this point a way was found to make everything lightweight and portable so that the set and lighting could be quickly and easily assembled and dismantled, and *Antiques Roadshow* could go from a completely empty space to being ready to tape in just one day. It was quite an achievement.

With these problems addressed, legal inquiries began. The BBC, which was accustomed to doing projects with WGBH, was agreeable,

Peter McGhee was responsible for bringing *Antiques Roadshow* to PBS.

but they quickly hit a roadblock when they discovered that they had sold the North American rights to *Antiques Roadshow* in perpetuity to Farrell some fifteen years before.

As revealed earlier, Farrell had had no luck marketing *Antiques Roadshow* in the U.S., but Farrell's luck changed when he "heard it through the antiques grapevine that WGBH was interested in the show.

"At this point, some fifteen years into the project," Farrell continues, "I was grateful that anyone was interested in the show. I had learned about WGBH's interest from Sam Pennington, founder of the influential *Maine Antique Digest (M.A.D.)*, but I had purposefully stayed away from PBS as a possible home for *Antiques Roadshow* because I was interested in making money."

Pennington had learned about WGBH's interest from Moreno. She had called him wanting him to send her some back copies of the *Maine Antique Digest* so she could learn more about antiques and the antiques business. Moreno told Pennington about the *Roadshow* project, and Pennington said something like "Sounds like something this guy has been trying to do for years."

Moreno knew of Dan Farrell but had been unable to reach him; Pennington offered to put the two of them together to discuss their mutual interest in the project. "Within a week," Moreno says, "we started to talk." Farrell sent the paperwork to Moreno, and it was clear that he owned the North American format rights to *Roadshow.* Then it came down to what Farrell wanted from WGBH, and at the top of that list was that Farrell wanted to work on the show. He had never done a television show before but he knew art and antiques so he thought he could make a continuing contribution.

This worked for Moreno too; she wanted someone familiar with the world of antiques so Farrell became consulting producer of the American *Antiques Roadshow.* In the beginning, Farrell assisted obtaining the initial pool of appraisers. "I introduced Moreno to Skinner and Christie's." Farrell also contacted dealer and appraiser organizations to help find further experts for the show.

ASSEMBLING THE TEAM

According to *Roadshow*'s then-senior producer, Peter B. Cook, "The British *Roadshow* had been on the air for fifteen years, and they had established a cadre of qualified people to work with them. We had the daunting task of assembling a group of qualified experts who were willing to do it on their own nickel, without pay and paying their own expenses."

In addition, the new show needed a host. Farrell encouraged Chris Jussel, his friend and fellow antiques aficionado, to come and audition. According to Farrell, "Chris knew the antiques business, he was charming, he had run antiques shows, and he was well known in the business." He and others came to audition, but Jussel got the job after he relaxed a bit in front of the camera. "As far as I was concerned," Farrell remembers, "he had the job after he looked into the camera and said with a twinkle in his eye, 'There is an old saying in the antiques business—the only person who cares what your grandmother had was

your grandfather.'"

Aida Moreno put it another way: "We weren't looking for someone who already had

> **{ AT THIS POINT, SOME FIFTEEN YEARS INTO THE PROJECT... I WAS GRATEFUL THAT ANYONE WAS INTERESTED IN THE SHOW... }**

experience in front of a camera, because we knew that could be taught. What we needed was someone who, first, knew his stuff and had the respect of the antiques community — credibility was key. And second, we needed someone whose schedule was flexible enough to allow him (or her) to invest the time we needed to make the show a success. That first year, we traveled to thirteen cities over eighteen weeks. Before that, there was TV training—'host school'—to attend, and afterward there were the demands of the promotion plan leading up to and during the broadcasts. So it was an enormous commitment of time. Chris had the credibility, the personality, and the time we needed from a host to launch that first season."

Peter Cook added, "Chris Jussel had serious credentials, and he was the person who seemed to have the respect of the people we were dealing with. In the early days we needed credibility, and although he had no experience in front of the camera, he was willing to learn, was low-key, and had the esteem of the people in the business. He was an easy choice."

It might be assumed that it was smooth sailing from here, but that wasn't the case. PBS was not really sold on the idea of a show on antiques and did not want to run *Antiques Roadshow* in prime time. PBS thought it was just another "how-to" show, which meant they thought it should run in the afternoons with the other similar shows in the lineup. PBS also thought that a half-hour rather than a full-hour format would be more appropriate.

But WGBH believed in the program and McGhee put heavy pressure to get PBS to finally agree to run the first season of *Antiques Roadshow* in a prime-time slot. He wanted PBS to designate it for "common carriage," meaning that most PBS stations would carry it at a certain time on a certain day. This designation was fairly new at PBS at the time. PBS refused.

Common carriage is important for attracting major national sponsorships: Shows are able to maximize sponsorship revenues when they can promise national exposure on a specific day and time on most PBS stations around the country. Common carriage tends to create a stable viewership because people around the country know when a program is going to broadcast. This, in turn, helps the underwriters understand who is watching the program and seeing their all-important message.

It took a few episodes in the first season for *Antiques Roadshow* to really catch on, but the buzz around the country built to a roar as the season progressed. People who seldom tuned into PBS were talking about it around the office watercooler, a sure sign of a show's success. Viewers would stop their friends on the street, chat about the incredible items they had seen on *Antiques Roadshow*, and wonder if

Chris Jussel was the original host of the American version of *Antiques Roadshow.*

they might have some treasure that might allow for an early retirement. The show was such a big hit that in the second season, *Roadshow* got common carriage and moved to Monday nights at 8:00 PM, where it has stayed ever since.

THE EARLY DAYS OF *ROADSHOW*

In its first year of production, *Antiques Roadshow* visited thirteen cities, and the tapings occasionally occurred in spaces that would now be completely unsuitable. The overwhelming need today is to provide for adequate crowd control (although not that much was needed in the very early days).

Unlike the British *Antiques Roadshow*, the American version did not (and will not) tape outdoors, although Moreno says that she did not entirely rule that out in the beginning. This is because the taping takes place all day at a whirlwind pace and can run from 7:45 AM to 7:00 PM (there have even been some instances when taping has continued for longer, but seldom past 8:30 at night). If taping is done outdoors, the production becomes much less efficient, and there is just no time to do that with the number of people waiting with their treasures to be taped.

The first taping was done in Concord, Massachusetts, in the summer of 1996. It was held in the old armory building, which was rather small, and the production unit had to secure its own generator to cover the extra power needs.

According to then-executive producer Aida

Moreno, "Only about three hundred people showed up, but we still got to tape about thirty items, which was far more than was needed to make a good one-hour program. None of the appraisers had ever done this before, and I had to teach them television. We had TV school every Friday before each shoot, and they learned how to hold things, how to point a certain way to show off areas of interest for the camera, how to converse with the guests, and how to do 'pick-ups.'"

"Pick-ups" are shots and/or conversations about the items done after the main part of the taping is completed. They are used as good quality close-ups or for additional information in the final version that appears on television.

"In that first year," says Aida Moreno, "we got thirteen hours of television out of thirteen cities, the next year we got sixteen hours out of eight cities. That first year was not always easy. In our third city, College Park, Maryland, tragedy struck when a longtime, much respected WGBH cameraman named Greg Macdonald died suddenly on the Thursday night before the Friday setup. It was very traumatic. Greg was one of our favorites and his sudden death cast a pall over the event." Fourteen years later, Greg's death remains a very painful memory for the longtime *Roadshow* crew.

REMEMBRANCES OF *ROADSHOW*'S FIRST SEASON

Gloria Lieberman, who is vice president and director of jewelry at Skinner, has been with the *Roadshow* from the very beginning. She was even there when Dan Farrell created the original pitch tape at Skinner's Bolton, Massachusetts, gallery, with Monty Hall. "Monty Hall," Lieberman remembered, "was much more casual in

MARSHA'S MUSINGS

Some years ago, I revisited the idea of doing a show outdoors in hopes of finding a wider choice of venues (there just aren't that many convention centers in this country). But about this time, I had the fortunate experience of catching the BBC production of *Antiques Roadshow* while visiting Canada. After witnessing their complications with sound and light I recognized we could do a show outdoors only if we were making just one episode of television from every event. The BBC spent an enormous amount of time chasing the sun and avoiding outdoor ambient sound (e.g., airplanes).

"Chasing the sun" means that the changing position of the sun can cause serious lighting difficulties: too light, too dark, too much glare. As a result, the camera position has to be changed frequently, which takes too much time and is too much trouble with so many people waiting to be taped. Also, if it should rain on taping day, it would be a disaster all the way around.

his approach. I believe I did a pair of jade earrings for taping, and we did it standing up."

What she remembers about Concord is, "It was hot, very hot. It must have been ninety-five degrees and the armory was not air-conditioned. I remember that about seven hundred people showed up—don't hold me to that, it may have

Monty Hall with Gloria Lieberman, appraiser and vice president and director of jewelry at Skinner, appear at the preliminary taping.

been fewer—and I appraised an Art Nouveau broach that was actually appraised again on a much later episode of *Roadshow*. In Concord, none of us knew what to expect; it could be great or it could be awful.

"The day was much shorter for that show than it is today. The appraisers did not start at 7:00 AM as we do now, and it did not take the entire day as it does now. In Concord, we saw what I expected to see. There were no new things brought. Many of the people who came to the jewelry table had the things that we now expect to see at every show: pocket watches, cameos, engagement rings, and strands of pearls. You can always depend on those items showing up at every location.

"The first taping was very scary. I had never been on television before except on one of those dance shows that taped in New York City. I won some luggage on the show, but this did not prepare me to tape an appraisal for *Antiques Roadshow*. We had all done Aida Moreno's 'television school' and tried our best to follow the rules, but were just not sure how it would all turn out."

Caroline Ashleigh of Caroline Ashleigh Associates, Birmingham, Michigan, was not at the first *Roadshow* taping, but she was at a later one in Season 1 in Southfield, Michigan, a northern suburb of Detroit. "The event was held in a very small convention center," Ashleigh remembers, "and there was nowhere near the crowds we are accustomed to today. Many of the people who came were familiar with the British *Roadshow* and wanted to know if we were part of that.

"After it was over, a number of appraisers got together and the general consensus was this was really fun to do, but each one of us was asking, 'Do you think it is going to succeed?' *Roadshow* seemed like such a great idea, and we thought we really needed to promote it to make it succeed."

Appraiser and auction company owner Ken Farmer's first experience was in Durham, North Carolina, which was the ninth taping location of the first season. Since Concord, Massachusetts, interest in *Roadshow* had been building, but it was still quite anemic compared with the next summer's tour.

When Farmer was asked to participate on *Roadshow,* he said that he marked the date in his calendar but was not excited about the event. Farmer said, "I was told I would be doing free appraisals for PBS and that I would have fun. I was not all that excited and did not think much about it. In fact, I almost did not go."

The line at our first taping in Concord, Massachusetts in 1996: It's much shorter than it would be today if we didn't distribute tickets beforehand.

SEASON ONE

BROADCAST YEAR: 1997
HOST: Chris Jussel
TOUR: 1996
CITIES: Concord, MA (6/1), Philadelphia, PA (6/15), College Park, MD (6/29), Seattle, WA (7/13), Denver, CO (7/20), Albuquerque, NM (7/27), Southfield (8/3), San Antonio, TX (8/17), Durham, NC (8/24), Minneapolis, MN (9/7), Kansas City, MO (9/14), Greenwich, TK (9/28), Chicago, IL (10/5)

Come appraisal day, the normal complement of appraisers was on hand, but no real crowd to speak of. The people of Durham and the surrounding area had never heard of *Antiques Roadshow* and no episode had aired yet. There was no buzz, no anticipation like there would be in later years. Farmer remembers that only about 1,000 people showed up, and "it was not enough to keep us busy all day."

According to Farmer, "At those first few shows, the guests had no idea what was going on and most of us—the staff and appraisers—didn't either. But after the shows aired, the second season was quite different. That is when the overwhelming crowds started coming and *Roadshow* became a megahit."

ANTIQUES ROADSHOW'S LOST TREASURE

Peter Cook remembers wondering at those early *Roadshow* events if the crew should go out on the streets to bring people into the show.

Ironically, he says that one of the most valuable—perhaps *the* most valuable item ever brought into *Roadshow* until Season 14—turned up in the afternoon of the first taping in Concord. Unfortunately, that taped segment could not be used and the story now is almost completely unknown.

The piece was actually a set of documents that the present owner's father had collected over many years. They came contained in manila envelopes that had rusted clasps and some moisture damage, but the contents were spectacular. The guest's father had collected documents and manuscripts signed by America's presidents, their vice presidents, and their cabinet members. The collection ranged from George Washington through the 1920s, but stopped about the time of Franklin Delano Roosevelt. However, it included an FDR document signed when he was assistant secretary of the navy under Woodrow Wilson.

One of the most exciting items was a twenty-page handwritten manuscript by Theodore Roosevelt that concerned "Camping in the Adirondacks," which is where Roosevelt was when he heard that President William McKinley was gravely injured and not expected to live. The large number of manila envelopes was a treasure trove of American history and the appraiser was Wendell Garrett, then senior vice president for Sotheby's Americana.

"At the time," Garrett said, "we did not have a Books and Manuscripts table so I was called upon to do the appraisal. I felt that these documents were worth around one million dollars at the time, and was very upset—and I still am a

Season 1: A Dutch Répoussé copper kindling bucket is appraised by Stephen Fletcher (far right).

little—when it was decided that we could not air them." What was the reason? Well, the property was owned by a brother and sister, and the brother would not consent for the items to be broadcast. Pity.

SEASON TWO: A NEW BEGINNING

Moreno remembers the morning of the first show of the second season, which was in Pittsburgh, Pennsylvania. "I got up early in the morning and went to my hotel room window and opened the drapes. I could see the convention center from my windows. Although it was very early in the morning, there were thousands of people wrapped around the building. They were down the block and around the corner and there were police cars, mounted patrolmen, and helicopters overhead; I could not imagine why they were there. I wondered, what the heck is this? Must be some kind of rock star in town.

"I got dressed and went down. Then I realized that all those people were lined up to get tickets for *Roadshow*. It was the most amazing sight I had ever seen. I was wearing my *Roadshow* shirt and suddenly lots of people were asking me things like 'Can we get in?' and 'Can we have that shirt?'

"I walked into the hall and couldn't see the concrete floor because there were so many people standing on it. 'Oh my God! What have we done?' was my first reaction, and then it was the thrill of success. In the first year of the show, I would pray for more people. But from the first taping in the second season, I found myself praying for fewer!"

THE INFAMOUS "WATERMELON" SWORD INCIDENT

One of the most famous (and infamous) *Roadshow* appraisals happened in Seattle dur-

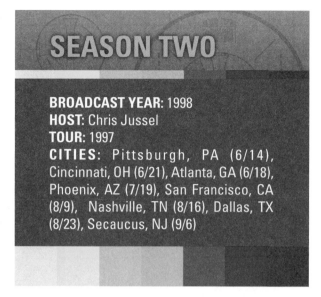

SEASON TWO

BROADCAST YEAR: 1998
HOST: Chris Jussel
TOUR: 1997
CITIES: Pittsburgh, PA (6/14), Cincinnati, OH (6/21), Atlanta, GA (6/18), Phoenix, AZ (7/19), San Francisco, CA (8/9), Nashville, TN (8/16), Dallas, TX (8/23), Secaucus, NJ (9/6)

ing these early seasons—actually during Season 1—but according to Peter Cook, it did not start to haunt the program until several years later.

The watermelon sword was a great piece with a charming story, and initially everyone looked upon its appraisal as one of the highlights of the first season. For a time, the watermelon sword was even used in televised *Roadshow* promotions. Here's what happened:

Someone identifying himself as "Steve" came into *Roadshow* in Seattle with a Confederate Civil War–era sword. He reported it had been found in the family attic and that he had used it as a child to cut a watermelon.

It was a stunning story that allowed *Roadshow* viewers to visualize a little boy hacking away at a watermelon with a sword that previously had been used during the time of America's greatest crisis and bloodiest internal conflict. George Juno, one of *Roadshow*'s most popular appraisers at the time, gave the appraisal on air. He delivered the upbeat opinion that the sword was worth $35,000, and Steve expressed overwhelming surprise and pleasure at the value. The whole thing made for great television—but unfortunately, it was all a hoax.

What follows is taken from an FBI Web site because this unhappy event needs to be discussed as impartially as possible. According to the FBI Art Theft Program, Juno was working with Russ Pritchard III, another popular *Roadshow* appraiser, and the two men were Confederate Civil War sword, which they [Pritchard and Juno] supplied to him. On July 20, 1996, the three men staged a phony *Antiques Roadshow* session for a later broadcast…"

What resulted was a wonderful appraisal that no one thought much about until the beginning of the year 2000, when Peter Cook was just tak-

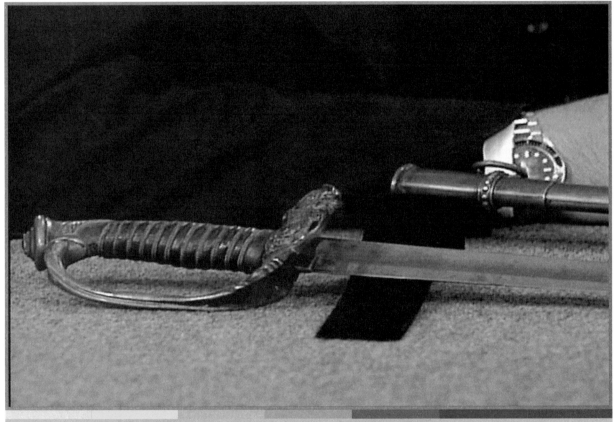

The infamous "watermelon sword" that launched an investigation with the FBI.

"…engaged in the business of appraising, purchasing, and selling military-related artifacts through their business, American Ordnance Preservation Association (AOPA)."

The Web site continues: "Pritchard III and Juno used the *Antiques Roadshow* to enhance their reputation as appraisers of military artifacts. In July 1996, the two men met with a man named 'Steve' to rehearse a story about a

ing over as executive producer from Aida Moreno. Then the proverbial storm broke. (Actually, the clouds had been gathering for some time as Pritchard and Juno found themselves involved in court cases revolving around other events, other items, and other swords.)

When the show aired in early 1997, and according to the FBI, the "descendants of Major Samuel J. Wilson, a Union officer in the

Civil War, contacted AOPA after watching the 'Watermelon Sword' episode; they asked the Association to appraise a sword once used by their ancestor. Russ Pritchard III and George Juno gave it a value of $8,000 and persuaded the family to sell them the sword."

This in itself is a highly unethical act, as professional appraisers are not allowed to purchase items they have appraised, owing to the very real possibility of a conflict of interest. The FBI Art Theft Program goes on to disclose, "The Wilson family had no intention of selling the sword prior to the meeting with the appraisers but, because they believed their descendant would have a place of honor for all time, the family sold it."

It is reported in other sources that the Wilson family thought the sword would go to a museum, "But," the FBI relates, "instead of giving the sword to the museum, George Juno used it as collateral to secure a loan. Then he helped a family member sell the Wilson sword to a private collector for $20,000, two and a half times the value at which Pritchard originally appraised it."

This was not the only case of a fraudulent deal. According to the FBI Art Theft Program, "Major General George C. Meade commanded the victorious Union forces at the Battle of Gettysburg during the Civil War and repelled the invasion of the North by the Army of Northern Virginia under General Robert E. Lee. After the Battle of Gettysburg, Major General Meade received a presentation pistol. The firearm had been in the Meade family since the Major General's death.

"In August 1997, Pritchard reached out to [the Meade family] and represented himself as an expert in the field of Civil War artifacts. He offered to appraise the mahogany-cased, .44-caliber Rem-

ington presentation pistol with engraved ivory grips, silver-plated frame, and gold-washed cylinder and hammer. Pritchard appraised the Meade firearm at between $180,000 and $200,000 and falsely stated that he was acquiring the firearm for the National Civil War Museum in Harrisburg, Pennsylvania, for permanent display.

"In October 1997, a private collector paid Pritchard $385,000 for the firearm; in return, Pritchard paid a Meade descendant just $184,000. Then, Pritchard faxed a letter to the mayor of Harrisburg, stating falsely that the Meade family was not interested in selling the firearm for inclusion in the city's National Civil War Museum."

There was evidence of other similar incidents, and George Juno and Russ Pritchard III eventually were indicted. In 2001, Juno pled guilty to the theft of the Wilson sword. According to the FBI, "On July 11, 2002, Russell Pritchard III was sentenced to one year in prison and was ordered to repay $830,000 for staging phony appraisals and defrauding Civil War militaria collectors. Pritchard III, 39, also pleaded guilty to making false TV appraisals."

"When we learned of all this starting in the fall of 1999, we were very disappointed," Cook said. "As things began to unravel, we felt that they may have done this sort of thing on other occasions on our show. It was an uncertain time for us: Chris Jussel had decided to leave the show to take another job at Sotheby's, Aida Moreno was leaving, and change was in the air.

"The watermelon sword and other incidents really just started out as allegations, and our first instincts were to defend our guys. We felt that they were innocent until they were proven guilty in a court of law, and it took us a while to

> **THE WATERMELON SWORD** AND OTHER INCIDENTS REALLY JUST **STARTED OUT AS ALLEGATIONS,** AND OUR FIRST INSTINCTS WERE **TO DEFEND OUR GUYS.**

CODE OF CONDUCT

There is now a stringent, written code of conduct for the appraisers, and it is contained in the Appraiser's Handbook and the "appraisal event participation agreement." What follows was taken from the handbook for Season 13:

Under "Solicitation" in the *Appraiser's Handbook*:

✳ "...Under no circumstances may any appraiser solicit business from the public at any *Antiques Roadshow* event.

✳ "You may not offer to buy any item or ask a guest if they are interested in selling or try in any way to convince any attendee to consign an item to you or a colleague. Any inquiry about any kind of business transaction must be initiated by the owner of the item and may not be discussed until *Antiques Roadshow* has ended its stay in the participating city.

✳ "Under no circumstances may you ask for an address or phone number, hand out (or have someone else hand out) your card or promotional materials, or try to schedule a meeting."

Every year, the appraisers sign an "appraisal event participation agreement" and the section on solicitation outlined above is included. But following that there is a section titled "Objectivity," which reads:

✳ "You agree that all items which you appraise will be appraised objectively and independent of an outside influence. You will not cause, solicit, or otherwise arrange for an item to be brought to an event for appraisal by you."

Additionally, every guest who is taped signs an agreement called Antiques Roadshow/WGBH/Combination Appearance/Materials Permission and Release, that includes:

✳ "In addition, I [the guest] represent that the information I have given or will give with respect to the origin, history or ownership of the Licensed Materials is true and correct to the best of my knowledge and belief. If I become aware of any error, omission or potential misrepresentation with respect to this information, I will inform representatives of *Antiques Roadshow* or WGBH immediately....

✳ "I [the guest] further represent that I am not an employee, or household member of an employee, of WGBH, another public television station, or an underwriter of *Antiques Roadshow*, and that I have no business or any other relationship with any of the appraisers appearing at this *Antiques Roadshow* location; or, to the best of my knowledge, with any other appraiser associated with *Antiques Roadshow*...."

All of these rules are strictly enforced!

find out that they had done wrong—and that they had actually done wrong to *Roadshow.*

"In the beginning, the allegations had nothing to do with what they had done in Seattle [the watermelon sword appraisal], and we were not completely disposed to sever our ties. We were reluctant to act until we finally had the goods on these guys [Pritchard and Juno], and because of this we were pilloried in the press. We took some serious hits for a few months.

"We took steps to see that it did not happen again. First of all, there is no evidence that this has happened since the first year, and there has been no allegation that this sort of thing was going on. And believe me, we were on the lookout for this sort of thing. We believed that when an appraisal opportunity seemed to be too good to be true, it probably was.

"We developed a well-defined policy: except for eight to ten pieces of furniture that are chosen to be brought in before the show, no appraiser is to know what is coming, and if for some reason he does, another appraiser will have to do the appraisal."

Peter McGhee, who you may recall is really the father of the American version of *Antiques Roadshow,* does not remember this incident in detail, but says, "Basically, this was a door left unguarded because we did not know any better. In hindsight, should we have been more alert? I suppose so, but at the time no one knew what a success the show would be or by extension how great might be the reward to someone who cheated, as Juno and Pritchard did.

"During the first year, we had an implicit code of conduct, but by the second year, we understood the pressures and the opportunities of our show, and we made the code of conduct mandatory. It was written down, but really, in the first year, no one knew that this show would make the appraisers nationally recognized experts."

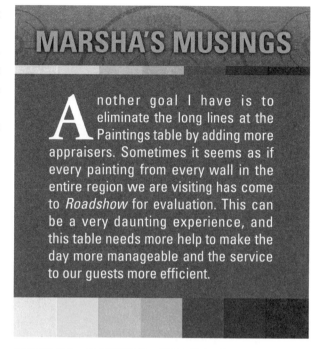

MARSHA'S MUSINGS

Another goal I have is to eliminate the long lines at the Paintings table by adding more appraisers. Sometimes it seems as if every painting from every wall in the entire region we are visiting has come to *Roadshow* for evaluation. This can be a very daunting experience, and this table needs more help to make the day more manageable and the service to our guests more efficient.

NEWER, BETTER, FRESHER

Every year, we strive to make *Roadshow* fresher, to add new elements to the show that either enliven the event or make it a more convenient and pleasant experience for our guests. In the beginning, as we have already mentioned, tickets were not pre-allotted, and those who wanted to attend *Antiques Roadshow* often slept outside the event arena in order to preserve their place in line so they could be one of the lucky few who got in to show their items to the appraisers and perhaps appear on national television.

In the fifth season, that all changed when we started to allot tickets beforehand. Now *Roadshow* receives more than 34,000 requests for tickets at some venues. Tickets have appointment time slots so guests don't have to spend all day in the crowd, unless they want to—and some do. Recently, we increased the number of time slots with the idea of making it even more convenient for the guests. (See the introduction for more information on obtaining tickets.)

MARSHA'S MUSINGS

This is a poem read with zest by Linda Townsend, a guest in the Feedback Booth at the San Antonio, Texas taping in 2007. It captures the fun of the *Roadshow* experience:

We waited for years as you can relate
*   for the* Roadshow *to come to our*
*   Lone Star State.*
We rushed to San Antonio with our
*   hopes so high,*
that our special antiques would
*   appraise sky-high.*
We waited in line, we watched all
*   the others,*
And about our antiques, it was well
*   worth the bother.*
The Roadshow *was wonderful, the*
*   appraisers were great,*
Eat your heart out, America, 'cause
*   we're here and you ain't!*

Over the years, a number of innovations have been tried—some worked, some did not. For Season 10, *Roadshow* wanted to celebrate the occasion by having a contest to choose people who would have the contents of their whole house appraised by *Roadshow* experts. It was called "House Calls," and it was a Big Idea that generated a lot of excitement among *Roadshow* staff.

Unfortunately, visiting individuals' homes does not result in exciting and intriguing television: Appraisals work best when thousands of owners bring their two treasures to us. There was just not that much to talk about, so "House Calls" became available as a Webcast only and was never put on the air.

Another innovation, "Feedback Booth," did work and has become a viewer favorite. Originally, this was just a camera and a mark on the floor that indicated where people should stand while they talked to the camera about their *Roadshow* experience or the item they had brought to be appraised. There was no actual camera operator. Guests just stood in front of the device with their object and said whatever was on their mind for a few minutes.

This became a big success! It not only allowed guests who hadn't been taped a second chance to be on camera, but it offered the hope that what they said might be shown at the end of a *Roadshow* broadcast. The Feedback Booth has evolved into a kind of confessional that has a raw, "We are sharing our experiences with you" feeling. Now a cameraperson is on duty and generates between six and eight hours of tape for each two-minute segment that concludes the three episodes taped in each city.

Changes happen at *Roadshow* every year. Some are very noticeable to the public, but others are less evident. Every year, we hold a "postmortem" after the summer tour is complete. We want to figure out what we can do better to serve our guests and help our appraisers do their job.

There are always a lot of discussions about things that only *Roadshow* personnel might know about, such as changing the microphones or replacing a banner that does not match the rest of the set's color scheme. Beyond this, we are always looking for ways to shorten the wait our guests must endure, and fielding ideas for how we might entertain them more effectively while they are in line.

At the end of a recent season, we realized that we were having problems with guests bringing in more than two items with each ticket. Obviously, this took appraiser time away from people who followed the two-item rule. In one city, a conscientious staff member pointed out a guest who had a large wagon, piled high with twenty-seven containers of items. Now, this could have been a collection of some sort, but it was excessive by almost any point of view.

In the season's postmortem, we discussed giving handouts to ticket holders saying that if they brought more than two items per ticket, they would have to return the overage to their cars before they could be allowed onto the floor for their appraisals. This was a little tough, but fair. Nonetheless, in the final analysis, we decided it would present a hardship for many, and instead we decided to control items coming into the set area.

Roadshow is now an ever-changing and evolving canvas. Every year is different from the last, and we are very excited to have generous commitments from our sponsors to continue for years into the future.

MARSHA'S MUSINGS

To me, at one time, one of the most important changes under consideration was eliminating the 5:00 PM appointment time on future tickets. At the end of each taping day, we wind up with huge—sometimes seemingly endless—lines of people waiting to see appraisers. If we slightly reduce the number of tickets being issued and make the last appointment time 4:00 PM, the day will shorten and the last few hours will be more endurable for everyone: crew, appraisers, and guests. Instead, we decided to give out fewer tickets and keep the 5:00 PM time. This allows for a more even distribution of guests throughout the day and keeps the length of the day reasonable.

Guests have their say in the Feedback Booth.

Heirloom diamond necklace appraised for $250,000

WHAT TO BRING TO ANTIQUES ROADSHOW?

When *Roadshow* announced it would be coming to Chattanooga, Tennessee, in 2008, a couple in faraway West Virginia obtained tickets. They drove seventeen hours straight just to let the appraisers evaluate a treasured diamond necklace, a family heirloom. It turned out to be worth a quarter of a million dollars!

Antiques Roadshow is nothing short of a cultural phenomenon. When dawn comes on the day of a *Roadshow* event, excitement runs high throughout the host city. Thousands of lucky ticket holders can hardly wait until it is their turn to be seen by of one of *Roadshow*'s appraisers. To many attendees, this is as thrilling as Christmas morning is to young ones who tumble joyously into the living room to see what Santa has brought during the night.

WKNO, the PBS station in Memphis, Tennessee, desperately wanted us to come to town for many years, but the city did not have a venue large enough or with the right configuration of space to hold the event (see chapter 3 for more information on site requirements). In 2005, we decided that the Cook Convention Center in downtown Memphis would work despite some minor problems (like insufficient parking and an unreliable elevator to get trucks up to the exhibit-area floor). Sally Stover, the special events coordinator for WKNO, remembers that when the announcement was made that *Antiques Roadshow* was finally coming, "The people of Memphis just went wild! They could not have been more excited if Elvis had come back from the dead and announced that he was once again taking up residence at Graceland!

"People were willing to connive and offer bribes just to have the opportunity to bring their items to the *Roadshow,*" she marveled. "Every time I looked up someone was approaching me trying to get the inside track to some tickets. I was stopped in the grocery store by people wanting tickets, and the phone at the station rang constantly. Most amazingly—at least to me as a fund-raising person—was that when tickets were offered in our television fund-raising auction, viewers donated hundreds of dollars for each one!"

TICKET, TICKET, WHO'S GOT THE TICKET?

Although 3,200 pairs may seem like a large number of tickets, it is never enough to meet the enormous demand. In Raleigh, North Carolina, in 2009, 34,192 requests for tickets were received for the 3,200 tickets available by a random drawing. That means less than 10 percent of those applications could be accommodated using the show's ticket process. This ticketing procedure, however, is much better than it was in the early days of *Roadshow* when tickets were not used.

In the introduction, I related an event where we needed to turn away 6,000 people. *Roadshow's* head of security, Sean Quinn, recalls another occasion in Salt Lake City in 1999. More people than could possibly be admitted showed up with their prized possessions to be evaluated,

and it was Quinn's duty to deal with the crowd.

He says that it was like being surrounded by a sea of humanity. Late in the day, he had to take his bullhorn and tell 2,000 restless people—many who had waited for hours—that they would not be able to come in to see an appraiser. He admits he felt a little like Custer facing the Sioux at Little Bighorn. Luckily, the day ended without serious incident.

DECISIONS, DECISIONS, DECISIONS

Those who are lucky enough to get one of *Roadshow's* precious tickets have a vital and sometimes difficult decision to make and must ask themselves the serious questions:

- What two items do I bring for the appraisers to evaluate?
- Do I bring something just because it is old?
- Do I choose something because it has a long family history?
- Do I pick an object simply because family and friends tell me it is valuable?
- Do I select something because it is beautiful?
- Do I elect to bring an object because it is unusual?

One of the best choices might be an object that has an intriguing family history. In Wichita, Kansas, in 2008, a beautiful piece of furniture—an intricately inlaid Continental European secretary—came onto the floor. The appraisers were not really interested in appraising it for television because they felt it would be difficult to evaluate it in the approximately three minutes that are normally allotted for each piece. In fact, the appraisers all but ignored it.

Then the charming owner came in and told her story of the "lucky secretary" (lat-

Leslie Keno examines the "Lucky Secretary." Inset: The original owner.

er identified as a walnut Baroque desk and bookcase) and everyone's attitude changed instantly. It seems that the current owner's mother had booked passage in 1912 to come to America. In preparation for the journey she had decided to sell the secretary and had found a buyer.

Unfortunately, the buyer was killed in an accident while coming to pick up his purchase and the present owner's mother had to make arrangements to deal with the bulky piece of furniture. She decided to keep it and have it shipped to America, but she also had to cancel her transatlantic reservations—and the *RMS Titanic* sailed into tragedy and maritime history without her. And this is how this object became "the lucky secretary." The story made

this otherwise pleasant and attractive desk and bookcase into a star, and it was enthusiastically taped for television by Leslie Keno and appraised for $15,000 to $25,000.

Other good choices of pieces to bring to *Roadshow* are **items that the guest knows little or nothing about.** A guest's desire to know more about the history and significance of the object can make for very compelling television. In fact, on *Roadshow* we often say, "It is all about discovery!"

THE LEGENDARY HONUS WAGNER COMES UP TO BAT—AND STRIKES OUT

Paradoxically, one of the most disappointing experiences for an appraiser is when a guest knows *too* much about an item! In Baltimore in 2007, a guest brought in a Honus Wagner baseball card that was not in the best of condition, but to a layman it was not "bad looking." This was extremely exciting to our sports memorabilia and collectibles appraisers, because this is practically the Holy Grail of baseball cards.

It was issued in 1909 and distributed by the American Tobacco Company in packages of cigarettes. Wagner objected to this—some say because he was a nonsmoker, others because Wagner thought American Tobacco was not paying him enough—and the card had a very limited run. It is thought that fewer than 100 of these cards are in existence and not even ten of these are in superb condition.

Currently, the record price for a Honus Wagner baseball card is $2.8 million, with other examples in less perfect condition selling for significantly over one million dollars. It is reported that even an example in extremely poor condition would sell in the neighborhood of $150,000. At the time, the appraiser thought that this particular Honus Wagner card would probably be worth in the range of

The 1909 Honus Wagner baseball card: One of the most valuable finds (that audiences never saw).

$500,000 to one million dollars because of its less than pristine condition.

This card might very well have been the most valuable thing ever brought into *Roadshow*, but during an in-depth discussion, we discovered that the guest knew everything there was to know about his card. The card had been professionally appraised. All he really wanted was to go on television and have a *Roadshow* appraiser put the "*Roadshow* seal of approval" on his incredibly valuable possession—and we simply will not do that.

We would rather televise people finding out about their items—their joy, surprise, and vali-

Appraiser Nicholas Lowry hard at work at the Prints & Posters table.

dation. The bottom line is that we are about education and not about promotion of an item for personal profit.

In addition, the guest had gotten his ticket through one of our appraisers, whose expertise was in a related field. According to Sam Farrell, supervising producer, who did The Pick for this particular item, "This is a red flag to us, and we were more than a bit uncomfortable taping it. We want no hint of impropriety, and a connection between an appraiser and a guest is a problem."

THE APPRAISERS SPEAK—THEIR VIEWS ON WHAT *NOT* TO BRING TO *ROADSHOW*

The appraisers are the people in the *Road-*

show trenches, courageously dealing with wave after wave of guests coming at them for ten to twelve hours, all bearing their treasures. Most of these objects will be worth very little money and will not have a great deal of interest for anyone other than the owner. Still, each object—despite its lack of monetary value or general interest to the public—is cherished by those who went to all the trouble to bring it to *Roadshow*.

Nicholas Lowry

Nicholas Lowry, president of Swann Auction Galleries in New York City, remembers his first experience as an appraiser at *Antiques Roadshow*, which was in Richmond, Virginia, in 1999. "This was before we gave out timed tickets," he said, "and the first person through the door came running up to the table bringing a turn-of-the-century postcard that was not in great shape. She had been waiting in line for perhaps twelve hours, and when she was told that her item was worth about five dollars, she was still thrilled just to have had the experience of being with us.

"There must have been a store in Richmond at one time that sold copies of Leonardo da Vinci's *Mona Lisa*," Lowry continued, "because we saw a number of them that day. I was new to the show and did not feel comfortable appraising them so a veteran, Christopher Lane of the Philadelphia Print Shop, talked to the lady. He went through the whole thing of how the original was painted by da Vinci and was currently in the Louvre Museum in Paris—and if she had the original, it would be worth more money than either of them could possibly imagine.

"He valued the print at $25 and the lady was happy. A bit later, another woman came in with the same print, and I was still feeling that there was no way I was going to do this, and Chris once again went into his spiel and covered the same ground he had with the first lady. This one, however, had a quite different reaction. She fixed Chris with a steely stare and complained bitterly, 'You mean I waited in line seven hours for you to tell me this?!'

"Unperturbed, Chris coolly replied, 'When you woke up this morning, you did not know what you had. Now you know and that is something worthwhile.' This mollified the woman a bit, and she did leave the table in a less an-

gry mood." The point of this is that coming to *Roadshow* requires an investment of time and energy, and it is very important to choose wisely what is brought in for evaluation.

Kathleen Guzman

When I ask collectibles specialist Kathleen Guzman what people should bring to *Antiques Roadshow*, she quickly responds, "Don't you mean what they should *not* bring to *Roadshow*? That seems more easily answered and perhaps more to the point."

Guzman, who is an independent appraiser in New York City, recalls with a laugh, "People bring in the strangest things to *Antiques Roadshow*. There was a man

Watch out for those Winkie Swords! Kathleen Guzman appraised these *Wizard of Oz* spears for $30,000.

MARSHA'S MUSINGS

Those sweet Hummel figurines are collected by so many people. In a *New York Times* article in January 2009, *Roadshow* appraiser Rudy Franchi remarked, "There must be billions of these little collectibles out there and billions of people collecting them....It's like they breed at night—the figurines, that is."

who brought in a potato he had grown in his backyard, and when he dug it up, he decided that it looked a lot like the face of Richard Nixon."

Rather ruefully, she continues, "He dressed the potato in a red, white and blue suit, and brought it into one of the tapings of *Roadshow*. It actually did look a lot like Nixon, and the owner thought that it would be worth a great deal of money because the original Mr. Potato Head in its box is valuable—so, why not this homegrown version? It was funny, of course, but I had to tell him that his curiously shaped potato had no monetary value, except maybe in a grocery store.

"We also have local artists bringing in their artwork, hoping to get on television and [enhance] the value of their pieces. In one instance, an Asian gentleman brought in some watercolors on rice paper. They had been painted the day before and since they were new and he was not an artist of repute, they were virtually worthless in an antiques and collectibles sense."

Making a short list of what should *not* be brought in to *Roadshow*, Guzman ticked off a few items in her area of expertise (Collectibles). Heading the list was **Franklin Mint, Department 56, Hummel figures, and things that are mass-produced in general**. When questioned about the Hummels, she said, "Yes, there is one valuable Hummel, and we had it come into the *Roadshow*, but unless you have an early 1940s figure of a little boy with an airplane you are kind of out of luck."

Adding to her list, Guzman suggests that **paintings on black velvet** should be left at home as well as **most religious items**, unless of course they are many hundreds of years old. "Most of the religious items we see," Guzman said, "are twentieth century and not worth talking about." Continuing, Guzman also feels that **Boy and Girl Scout memorabilia** should be left at home, as a general rule.

When she was working at Christie's, she recalls Robert Baden-Powell's personal Scouting handbook coming in to be sold. Lord Baden-Powell (1857–1941) was the founder of the Scouting movement and has been called "chief Scout of the world." At first thought, it would seem that his personal Scouting handbook would be something of an icon and perhaps worth a great deal of money.

"It sold for only eleven-hundred dollars," Guzman says. "So you see, if Baden-Powell's handbook brought this little, just think how modest the value of all the cloth sashes filled with merit badges of some long-forgotten Scout must be. We see a number of these at every taping of *Roadshow*," she concludes, "and the market for these Scouting items is just not there."

Among the more inexplicable items Guzman remembers being brought to *Antiques Roadshow* was a pheasant that had been stuffed by a taxidermist and placed under a glass dome. "The bird was in bad condition—in fact, it was molting," Guzman remembers with distaste. "Before I could tell the lady who brought it in that the piece had no monetary value, she said that it had been killed in an interesting way.

"At *Roadshow* the story can be all-important, and I was intrigued. She then told me that the bird had been killed when it was hit by a car driven by her father-in-law. He was very proud that he had somehow managed to run down such a beautiful bird and had it stuffed like a trophy and placed under a glass dome. It had eventually come to her husband, who thought it was valuable. He kept it displayed conspicuously on the mantel in their home for years and would not let it be moved.

"At this point," Guzman continues, "I had to tell her the news that despite the story, her piece was virtually worthless. Much to my surprise, she practically lunged across the table and kissed me, saying that she was so grateful because now she could tell her husband that the awful thing was not worth anything, and they could put it in the basement where it had belonged years before."

Jim Baggett: Fiddling Around

Most of *Roadshow*'s cast of appraisers are reluctant to suggest what guests should and should not bring. Jim Baggett of Mass Street Music in Lawrence, Kansas, speaks for almost everyone when he says, "I really hesitate to address the question of what not to bring to *Roadshow* because I do not want to discourage our guests. Being in the retail business, I have always felt that the customer is right, and at *Roadshow* the people who bring in their items are our customers, in a sense, and we are there to supply information, positive or negative."

However, after being pressed, Baggett does come up with one group of items that should be left at home: **violins with Stradivarius labels**. In Wichita, Kansas, the people at the Musical Instruments table were asked how many violins with these Stradivarius labels they had seen that day. An appraiser looked up with a weary glance and said, "a hundred and fifty." Then, he glanced back at his next guest who was opening a violin case and said, "No, make that a hundred and fifty-one." Violins with

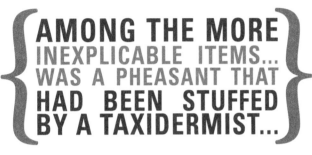

{ AMONG THE MORE INEXPLICABLE ITEMS... WAS A PHEASANT THAT HAD BEEN STUFFED BY A TAXIDERMIST... }

Stradivarius labels were made in vast quantities at the turn of the twentieth century, and they are really Stradivarius model violins that were sold as student violins. They were widely used in America's parlors and elsewhere for entertainment before the advent of radio and television. There are also German copies of violins that have the labels of other famous Italian violin makers, such as Amanti, and these too are just inexpensive reproductions.

The life history or "provenance" of nearly all genuine Stradivarius violins is well-known to experts and the chance of a private individual owning a real Stradivarius is indeed very slim to absolutely none. However, Baggett issues a strong warning about rushing to a hasty judgment about the contents of a violin case. He cautions, "There is sometimes a bow in the case along with a fake Stradivarius violin, and **the bow can be worth several hundred to several thousand dollars**. This should not be overlooked or ignored."

PLEASE LEAVE HOME WITHOUT THESE ITEMS

- Folk art appraiser Allan Katz of Allan Katz Americana in Woodbridge, Connecticut, says to bring anything you are curious about, but keep in mind that we see 100 to 150 **twentieth-century quilts** at every *Roadshow* taping, and they are seldom worth very much money. These quilts are primarily family pieces made by mothers, grandmothers, and favorite aunts who were often

{ I THINK IT'S A SHAME... TO SEE PEOPLE WAITING IN LINE FOR HOURS WHILE HEFTING A 40-POUND BIBLE THAT IS WORTH VERY LITTLE... }

following patterns they found in magazines and newspapers. The value of these quilts is not so much monetary as it is sentimental. This is true of the thousands of twentieth-century quilts in patterns such as "double wedding ring," "sunbonnet girl," "Dresden plate," "flower garden," and the like, but there are a very few patterns, such as those with pictorial elements, which would be highly desirable if a collector should ever find one.

- Andrew Brunk of Brunk Auctions in Asheville, North Carolina, also feels that it is tricky giving people this type of advice, but admits **pieces of furniture signed with little metal tags** are often a waste of everyone's time. "This eliminates a lot of the office furniture and items that were mass-produced in Grand Rapids, Michigan, and elsewhere during the late nineteenth and early twenti-

eth centuries." As a general rule, these are of limited interest to collectors.

- From the perspective of the Books & Manuscripts table, nineteenth-century Bibles are at the top of the list of things not to bring to the event. Christopher Coover, senior vice president and senior specialist, rare books and manuscripts for Christie's in New York City, feels strongly that, "**Family Bibles with birth and death records** are valuable for their genealogical information, but they have very little commercial value, and I think it is a shame to see little old ladies waiting in line for hours while hefting a forty-pound Bible that is worth very little monetarily." Also to be avoided are **old school textbooks** because, "Even the early ones have only a slight value. I know that sometimes these schoolbooks are the oldest things that people have in their homes, but they are worth very little—and if they have been crayoned in, they are even less valuable."

- Another big no-no from the Books & Manuscripts table are **documents such as the Declaration of Independence, the Gettysburg Address, the Bill of Rights, and the Constitution**. These often look very old because they are on fake parchment that has a crinkly, fragile-feeling texture and brown color like it has been soaked in tea. These documents are almost always later reproductions, originally purchased at various historical sites around the country.

- **Most old letters** should be left at home. **Collections from Revolutionary or Civil War soldiers with insights into these conflicts are an exception as are letters from famous people** such as Benny Goodman, Georgia O'Keeffe, Helen Keller, Mark Twain, George Gordon Lord Byron, and letters from U.S. presidents, to name just a few. What are *not* valuable are letters from governors and mayors, even famous mayors such as Fiorello La Guardia. An exception to this might be governors or mayors who later became presidents of the United States.

- **Most old cameos and bar pins** should not be brought in because, according to Joyce Jonas, "We see hundreds of them at each taping, and they do not make it onto television because they are all the same and not particularly interesting or valuable."

- Try to avoid bringing **objects with significant damage**. A tiny nick on a rare and expensive piece of glass or pottery might be acceptable, but big missing chunks or serious cracks can make the piece almost worthless.

- Caroline Ashleigh of Caroline Ashleigh Associates, Inc. of Birmingham, Michigan notes that the appraisers at the Rugs & Textiles table see far too many **twentieth-century machine-made tapestries**. "These were made in Belgium, France, and Italy and they are pictorial, usually with scenes depicting such things as courting couples, exotic Middle Eastern harem scenes, scenes reminiscent of the court of Louis the fourteenth, and so on. They were manufactured in various sizes, and they came to this country in vast numbers with military personnel or with tourists returning home. They are very decorative and people used them as table toppings, piano scarves, and wall hangings. Unfortunately, they are always worth less than a hundred dollars."

EN ROUTE TO ST PAUL, MINN.,

April 13th 1911.

Dear Mr Minister:

Cannot you and Mrs Egan spend a night with us at Oyster Bay ? Perhaps I shall find when I reach home that you have made some arrangement with Mrs Roosevelt to do so. I must see you and have a chat with you.

Faithfully yours,

T. Roosevelt

This 1911 Teddy Roosevelt letter is a piece of history valued between $8,000 and $12,000.

CARNIVAL GLASS
ITEMS WE DREAM ABOUT SEEING AND ONES WE SEE OFTEN

Carnival Glass is a mass-produced product that was first manufactured in 1907 and thereafter copied by many manufacturers in the United States and abroad. It came in a vast variety of shapes, patterns, and colors. When it was made, it was inexpensive, but today there are many extremely valuable pieces. The good news is that the majority of Carnival Glass patterns are still affordable, and it is a beautiful and popular item to collect.

Carnival Glass is a mainstay at our Glass table and keeps our appraisers busy. Appraiser Kathleen Bailey says, "Although some people complain about Carnival Glass, I say bring it on! I know Carnival Glass collectors would not want to be discouraged from bringing any piece about which they have questions. Also, Carnival Glass in a specific pattern may have one or more major colors in a specific shape that we haven't seen before. Not all Carnival Glass has been discovered to date, and many rare patterns and shapes show up every few years."

So what are some of the pieces that Bailey would like to see walk through the door? And what are some patterns she sees at almost every show?

KATHELEEN BAILEY'S DREAM ITEMS:

- Millersburg "big fish" pattern, especially the Rosebowl in Carnival Vaseline. It is worth more than $15,000 (prices listed are auction estimates).
- U.S. Glass Company's "frolicking bears," the pitcher in olive green with a single tumbler would be worth between $40,000 and $50,000.
- Northwood's "acorn burrs" pattern can be very inexpensive, but if you have the punch bowl and base in aqua opalescent, it is worth between $30,000 and $40,000.
- Millersburg's "mitered ovals" vase in marigold is worth $7,000.
- Northwood's "grape and cable" pattern can be very inexpensive, but if you have an amethyst spittoon in this pattern, it is worth between $6,000 and $8,000.

PATTERNS SEEN AT ALMOST EVERY SHOW:

There are many patterns of Carnival Glass that guests typically bring to *Roadshow*. A few of these include Imperial's "acanthus," Fenton's "acorn," Northwood's "apple and pear intaglio," Fenton's "April showers" except for a red vase, Dugan's "beauty buds," Millersburg's "fleur-de-lis" except for bowl in Vaseline or green compote, Higbee's "Hawaiian lei," Westmoreland's "interior rays," Fenton's "peacock and dahlia" except if ice-green opalescent (as this one is yet to be discovered), Imperial's "windmill," and many more.

- **Tourist etchings brought back from Europe during the 1920s and 1930s** can make up to 90 percent of the items brought to the Prints & Posters table at each *Roadshow* taping. According to New York City appraiser Nicholas Lowry, whom we met earlier in the chapter, these are lovely, but they are "a dime

A should-bring piece of Carnival Glass: Northwood's "Grape and Cable" pattern.

a dozen and worth only one hundred dollars to one hundred and fifty dollars each at most. I sometimes think to myself that the present owner's ancestors went to England, and all they brought back was this etching?" Also to be avoided are **nineteenth-century prints of Jesus or Mary and any print of The Last Supper**. "These images were widely reproduced and bought by devout people for display in their homes, but they are not valuable," Lowry concludes.

BRING IT ON DOWN

Longtime appraiser, J. Michael Flanigan of J. M. Flanigan Antiques in Baltimore, Maryland, echoes Allan Katz, the folk art dealer we met ear-

lier, and says, "*Roadshow* is a once-in-a-lifetime chance to use a panel of top-notch experts to your advantage. To get the most out of [your] experience, bring the items that you want to learn about the most." He goes on to express the firmly held belief among many *Roadshow* appraisers that money is the least important part of the *Roadshow* process, because it is the information gained that is the most significant aspect of the experience. Flanigan stresses that it is a waste of time for someone to bring an object that he or she already knows about, because *Roadshow* is all about the unraveling of mysteries and making startling and illuminating revelations.

Joyce Jonas of Joyce Jonas & Associates in New York City advises people to bring something that has a good story. "I remember a lady once brought in a diamond ring that she had found while cleaning off her roof. It was in a bird's nest, and the lady who found it speculated that the bird must have been attracted to the shiny stone, snatched it up with its beak, and just dropped it into its nest. The ring turned out not to be worth a great deal of money, but it was more than she had before it was found in the bird's nest on her roof!" Jonas also urges guests to "**Bring in things that will challenge us**. If you are thinking, 'Bet this is something that will stump them!' bring it in and try to baffle the experts. It will be fun and a challenge for all of us."

And then there are:

- **Twentieth-century first-edition books**. Since every book has a first edition, these should be important books by important authors, and first editions of first books by authors who would later become significant literary figures. Small details in this cate-

> { **THE ASSUMPTION IS THAT OLD THINGS ARE ALWAYS VALUABLE, AND THIS IS SIMPLY NOT THE CASE.** }

gory can make big differences in value. For example, most twentieth-century first editions need to have their dust jackets, and they need to be in very good condition. The first edition of *The Great Gatsby* by F. Scott Fitzgerald without its dust jacket is worth maybe $1,500 (depending on condition), but one with the dust jacket may be worth as much as $140,000!

- **Early maps (printed before 1815)**— especially world maps and maps of America. Maps of obscure places such as little-known provinces of Silesia or Russia are of little interest to most collectors in this country.

- **Wallace Nutting photographs.** These photos are generally not very valuable, but there are rare images such as "On the Way to Bethany," "Children of the Sea," "The Sand Mirror," "By the Cottage Door," and "A Gloucester Peter" that are candidates to be brought to the *Roadshow*. One caveat, however: These rare Wallace Nutting items must be in excellent condition, in their original frames, and with their original matting that includes the title and Nutting signature.

- **Handblown art glass.** Look for a "pontil" (this is where the glass blower breaks off from the punty rod). Is it smooth? Usually a smooth pontil will suggest a better piece of glass, but not always. Names such as Tif-

fany and Steuben are always good to find on a piece of glass. However, a signature doesn't always mean the piece is valuable— and fake signatures and marks abound. And do remember, some of the best glass is completely unsigned. Loetz, Webb, and Durand are just a sample of companies that did not sign all their glass. Comparing signed, known copies with unsigned pieces can help authenticate. Also, it is not just late-nineteenth- and early twentieth-century art glass that is valuable. Signed pieces by artists from the 1950s and later can have significant value, including pieces by Venini, Seguso, Charles Lotton, Dale Chihuly, and Harvey Littleton.

- **Ordinary items that are valuable by association.** Such things as Abraham Lincoln's Bible (yes, this is a Bible that will have monetary value), Jefferson Davis's shaving kit, Charles Lindbergh's hat, Andrew Jackson's walking stick, Elvis's belt, and so forth. In other words, items that in and of themselves are rather ordinary but have a provable association with a person of almost iconic importance.

- **Items of American coin silver made before the middle of the eighteenth century**. Particularly significant pieces of holloware (bowls, cups, teapots) made by famous makers such as Paul Revere (both father and son), Jeremiah Dummer, Nathaniel Hurd, John Coney, John Hull and Robert Sanderson, to name just a few. Specifically, important pieces by the top makers in such cities as Boston, Philadelphia, New York, and Charleston tend to be the most sought after.

- **Early needlework**, especially samplers and needlework pictures with elaborate pictorial content. Pieces need to be in good condition, and in the case of needlework pictures, the watercolored elements should be well-done. Samplers stitched with just the alphabet, numbers, and maybe a Bible verse are of little interest or value to most serious collectors.

- **Handmade American furniture from the eighteenth and early nineteenth century**, especially those pieces with paper labels or stenciled signatures by people like Thomas Seymour and William Savery. Pluses would include pieces with unusual forms, items with their original finish or examples with particularly beautiful (and intact) painted finishes.

AGE IS THE THING—EXCEPT WHEN IT ISN'T

Many people decide what to bring to *Roadshow* based on whether or not they think an object is "old." The assumption is that old things are always valuable, and this is simply not the case. According to Andrew Brunk, "My fellow appraisers at *Antiques Roadshow* have a saying that might bear repeating: 'Things that are old are not necessarily valuable, but things that are valuable are not necessarily old.'"

At this point, Brunk chuckles and mentions that he had a sideboard in his family's auction gallery in Asheville, North Carolina that had been made during the mid-twentieth century by Philip and Kelvin Laverne and would not be technically "antique" for another half century. Brunk felt that despite its relatively recent date of manufacture, it would probably sell for more than $10,000 and was worth considerably more for insurance replacement purposes. "It does not have great age," he commented, "but it does have a significant dollar value, and many of today's collectors are eager to have it. The first question when valuing an object

All that's old doesn't glitter: Even though this ceramic jug dates back only to the 1950s, it was valued at $5,000.

is not 'how old is it?' but rather 'who wants it?' Demand in the marketplace is what determines value."

MAKING IT ALL ADD UP

In addition, Brunk said, "People need to be careful with their math when they are trying to figure out how old an object is." You cannot determine the age of a piece by reasoning that the item originally belonged to your great-grandmother, who lived to be ninety-two; then was passed to her daughter, who lived to be eighty-seven; then to her daughter, who passed away at ninety-three; and finally, to you—and you have had it for twenty-five years. Some people take all these numbers, add them all up and conclude that the object has to be at least two

THE 25 APPRAISAL STATIONS OR TABLES

As can be seen in the diagram, the apprasial stations are arranged in a circle around a center section where the cameras are actually located. Spaced around this center area are three interview areas where the appraisals that are being taped are done. The 25 appraisal tables are:

* Antiquities
* Arms & Militaria
* Asian Arts
* Books & Manuscripts
* Clocks & Watches
* Collectibles
* Decorative Arts
* Dolls
* Folk Art
* Furniture
* Glass
* Jewelry
* Metalwork & Sculpture
* Musical Instruments
* Paintings & Drawings
* Photographs
* Pottery & Porcelain
* Prints & Posters
* Rugs & Textiles
* Science & Technology
* Silver
* Sports Memorabilia
* Tools & Implements
* Toys & Games
* Tribal Arts

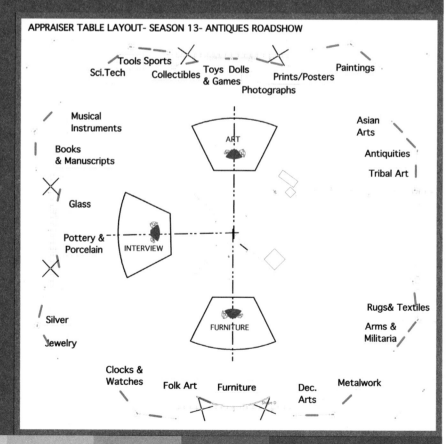

Floor diagram for the *Roadshow* set.

hundred and ninety-seven years old—and this cannot be the case.

"Most of these people lived concurrently, and the great-grandmother may have owned the piece for just a few years before her death. This means that the object is much younger than the family might suppose. You also have to be very careful with family history," Brunk advises. "It often gets embellished along the way and becomes less and less accurate. A real determination of an item's age needs to be based on intrinsic factors such as style, construction methods, and materials used."

VENTURING TO THE APPRAISAL TABLES

Near each appraisal table or station is a volunteer with a walkie-talkie. If an appraiser is excited about an object or its story, they get the attention of the volunteer, who calls the producers to notify them that an appraiser wants to make a pitch.

The people who choose items to be taped for broadcast are called the "Pickers." They rush to the various appraisers as quickly as possible because by this time, guests are weary of waiting in line, and sometimes it's hard to get them to wait much longer. At this point, the appraiser has not been allowed to tell the guest anything whatsoever about the object.

Such discussions must wait until after the producers decide whether or not to appraise the item on camera. The idea is to preserve the element of surprise, so it can be captured as a truly genuine moment.

So the guest, who is usually very excited at this point, is typically ushered behind the walls of the set behind the appraiser's table. There, they take a seat while they wait for a producer to arrive. Usually, the producer appears with two volunteers, one whose job it is to look after the guest if the item is picked to be taped.

GREEN WITH ENVY

Now the excitement builds! If the producer chooses the guest and her item for taping, she

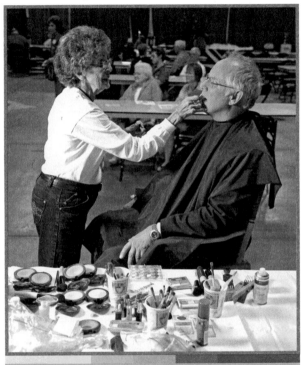

In the Green Room, Louise Miller applies makeup to appraiser Ken Farmer while guests and their families wait for their item to be taped for television.

is guided by the volunteer to the Green Room, a curtained-off area—a kind of sanctum sanctorum—with tables, chairs, television sets (showing the appraisals as they are being taped), tables with water and food, and two professional makeup artists.

Here, the guest is skillfully primped, and waits to be taken to the set to have his or her segment taped. The appraiser taping the appraisal also arrives for makeup. The wait in the

Green Room can be as short as fifteen to thirty minutes or as long as two hours, especially during the busiest part of the day.

No one is allowed in the Green Room except *Roadshow* staff, the guest, and the appraiser. The rule is: No talking about the item to be appraised until it is time to do the taping. When the guest and appraiser have been escorted onto

Record manager Judy Cronenberg adds Marsha's Pick to the Record Order in Honolulu.

the set and are ready for the taping, her family and friends who have been waiting with her typically huddle around the television monitors waiting anxiously to hear the appraisal.

I love hearing the conversations that go on! "Grandma would get up from her grave if she knew that!" "Aunt Gertrude gave that to me, and I'm sure not giving it back!" As

the appraisal builds toward revealing the item's worth, the people in the Green Room quiet down, sometimes gasp and sometimes cheer. There's lots of backslapping, hugging and kissing too!

MAKING THE PICKS

Doing The Picks is not as easy as it appears. In the early morning, they might go fairly leisurely, but as the day progresses, the list of those waiting to be seen by a producer lengthens and the pace picks up considerably.

The reality is: Eighty to ninety items must be selected for taping at each appraisal event. This amount may not seem like much, especially when compared with the 10,000 to 12,000 items brought in total by all the guests. But the amount can be daunting if interesting items do not turn up in significant numbers. The truth is the vast majority of items do not have significant monetary value or a compelling story; they are interesting to—and cherished by—no one except their owners.

So those eighty to ninety items can become the proverbial "needle in a haystack," and it is difficult winnowing out all the relatively routine items to find things with just the right pizzazz. Here's what that means:

- The item is in a category that has not been featured on *Roadshow* recently, and it needs to be an object from which something can be learned. For example, if the piece being considered for taping is a Tiffany lamp—a wonderful, beautiful, and expensive item that almost anyone would be proud to own—the critical consideration is, can we learn something new from this particular example in order to make it worthwhile to television viewers? We have seen dozens of these lamps in the past. If we cannot offer something new and educational, the item probably will be passed over. Joyce Jonas of Joyce Jonas & Associates of New York City is still a little upset that a hair jewelry broach with intertwined brown and blond hair that once belonged to Confederate General Jeb Stuart and his wife was not taped. The subject of hair jewelry had been covered on the show recently and in depth, and nothing new could be presented.

- Both the appraiser and the guest must be enthusiastic about sharing the item with *Roadshow's* audience. The excitement must be genuine, and if either the guest or the appraiser is missing the zest to show it on television, the piece will not be chosen for taping.

- The appraiser must be able to "sell" the item to the producer. He has to explain why this particular object is so unique, what the story is, and how it can be presented on television to the best effect. The appraiser must demonstrate that he is well-informed about the item, excited to see it, and able to suggest a price.

- The guest can communicate fairly well on tape without appearing too nervous. Can she tell the story of the item clearly and concisely? After all, each segment lasts for only a few minutes and long stories that ramble won't work well. The producer speaks informally with each potential, on-air guest to determine his or her television presence.

- The guest knows little or nothing about the object. During this informal conversation, the producer discerns what the guest does and doesn't know. (See the section "Talk to Me" on next page for more details.)

- The item must be the only one in the family considered for taping. We have a hard-and-fast rule: Only one item per family can be chosen for television. This is because families with more than one household can acquire multiple pairs of tickets. If all of the items in the family happen to be chosen, this one family would monopolize camera time from other guests with interesting objects and stories. To prevent this, the producer talks to the guest whose item is being considered for taping to learn whether other family members have been chosen too. Many times we find that while we are considering an item brought by Dad, Grandmother is in the Green Room being made-up for taping, and Daughter-in-Law is getting interviewed by another of The Pickers. When this happens we examine all the objects being considered and choose the one we want the most. Regretfully, we disallow the rest.

FABULOUS FAKES (A LESSON)

Not every Pick is a treasure, of course. Many times, viewers can learn as much from a fake as from the genuine item. Unfortunately, as the value of antiques has risen, so has the number of fakes made to deceive. There is a sea of fake Gallé and Tiffany glass, and no shortage of fake early-American furniture.

In Tampa, Florida, in 2005 appraiser J. Michael Flanigan encountered what appeared to be an early nineteenth-century American Federal card table that looked quite impressive. In fact, this table looked so good that it had been previously appraised in 2004 for a respectable $10,000.

The guest thought that the piece might have originated in either Maryland or Virginia. But right from the start, Flanigan identified it as typical of the style associated with Boston—and more specifically, the North Shore of Boston. To tell the complete tale of this piece, it had to be turned over, and the details of its construction had to be examined thoroughly.

Underneath, it was crudely made. That was the first red flag. Eighteenth or early-nineteenth-century cabinetmakers were trained to be meticulous in their work. Sloppy craftsmanship would never have been tolerated in establishments that created this type of card table. This is an important point—some people associate crude with old, and this is not the case in many instances.

The next problem was a machine-made metal screw where there should have been a wooden pin. To be sure, the screw may have been a later replacement, but it did appear that the screw was the original. Finding metal screws in furniture that was supposedly made in the eighteenth or early nineteenth-century is always a problem

that needs to be investigated.

Still another warning sign was the yellow pine from which the piece was made. While it is not entirely impossible that yellow pine could have been used in Boston, this wood is more commonly associated with southern furniture. In Boston, white pine would have been more typical.

Lastly, Flanigan inspected the mahogany boards that comprised the top and found two boards when there should have been only one. In the late eighteenth and early nineteenth century, mahogany boards, as much as thirty-six inches wide, were easy to find, and a craftsman would have used only one board for the top. In the late first or early second quarter of the twentieth century when this piece was actually made,

Early nineteenth-century American Federal card table—looks good, but is it real?

these wide boards were not available and two had to be used instead.

Case closed. The card table was an out-and-out fake worth maybe one-tenth of the price for which it had earlier been appraised.

TALK TO ME

As mentioned earlier, The Picking Process is informal but purposeful. The producer might open the conversation by asking the guest, "Has the piece ever been appraised before?" This is a loaded question, and certain answers can cause a piece to be disallowed, especially if the owner seems too well-informed.

Of course, if the guest answers, "Yes, the piece was appraised ten years ago for one thousand dollars," and the producer knows (because we've already talked with the appraiser) that this is a very low or very high number, the guest's item may be chosen if the appraiser can impart good information and a monetary surprise—pleasant or not.

The producers can get rather nosy. They want to know:

- How did the guest acquire the item?
- Was it a gift from someone? Was it inherited?
- Was it purchased, and if so when, where, and under what circumstances?
- If it was purchased, how much did you pay? If the answer suggests a lot of money, we want to know why. "What prompted you to spend so much for this particular item, and why did you think it might be worth more today?"
- Did you find it in the trash? When and where?

Sometimes, however, guests stretch the truth just to get on television. Over the years,

The Pickers have become very adept at ferreting out these fabrications. The questioning of the guests is very friendly and somewhat lighthearted, but somewhere buried in the judgment of the producer is a district attorney cross-examining the witness, looking for the telltale discrepancy.

THE ESSENCE OF GREAT TELEVISION

Many viewers may find this hard to believe, but The Pickers (Jill Giles, Sam, and me) are not really looking for the "gee-whiz" factor while searching for things to put on

{ SOMETIMES, HOWEVER, GUESTS STRETCH THE TRUTH JUST TO GET ON TELEVISION. }

tape. "That is worth what?!" is not the prime reaction being sought. Oh, yes, it is nice sometimes, but it is not great television, in and of itself.

What *is* great television is the conversation generated by the object's proud owner, talking with an engaging appraiser who presents the details surrounding the item with scholarship and passion. The producers are really looking for the history and the narrative, and to paraphrase Shakespeare (rather loosely)—the story is the thing to catch the imagination of the audience, which is king.

NOT EVERYTHING MAKES THE CUT

What happens when an object is rejected for taping? First, we never tell the guest why the item is declined because we do not want to get into a debate. The producer's decision is final. We graciously thank the guest for coming to *Roadshow*, and then allow the appraiser, who initially proposed the item, to give the appraisal. At that time—and only at that time—the guest finally learns their treasure's history and value.

Interestingly and not completely intentionally, the time of day can make a difference in what gets taped and what gets passed over for one reason or another. Early in the day, we are more selective and may pass on items that do not fill our exact requirements. After all, the day is young, and the possibilities—with 10,000 to 12,000 objects coming through the doors—are endless. By midday, it becomes clear what we must do in order to fulfill our requirement of taping eighty to ninety items. If a large number of objects have been taped in the morning, the teams can be a little more discriminating in the afternoon. But if The Pickings have been slim, the pressure increases. This means that items passed over earlier are now more interesting. The Pickers try to keep items rolling into the Green Room at a steady pace in order to keep the taping stations full and busy all day long.

YOU'VE BEEN TAPED, NOW WHAT?

Guests are ushered from the Green Room to one of three taping stations located in the center of the appraisal floor. Not every item we tape makes it to television—and we never promise a guest that his piece will be included in a future show. When we return to Boston from an appraisal event, we typically have between eighty and ninety recorded appraisals. Of these, fifty-five or so are what you imagine when you think of *Roadshow*: an appraiser and a guest sitting at a table. These are shot in the center of the set with four cameras, which we call the "formal" appraisals. We shoot about another thirty segments with just one camera known as the "informals"; these segments are not recorded in the middle but instead at the appraisal stations on the edges of the set in with the crowd. Of the fifty-five formals, ten get cut right from the start. We know we can get what we need to make the three episodes we produce from each event with the informals or with the alternates/cut list from the formals.

We cut the weakest appraisals. Generally, the problems have to do with performance issues. While all of our appraisers have talent and bring something different to the show, some of our appraisers are dynamite; others are not. Some appraisers can appear nervous and that is really communicated to the camera. In a way, the appraisers are competing with each other to see who can deliver the most informative, most comfortable performance with the most interesting guest.

There are a 101 reasons why an item might not be used on television. The most important one is verification of facts, which we do intensively. (See chapter 4 for more on this.) The following is one compelling example.

WILL THE REAL WYATT EARP PLEASE STAND UP

Wyatt Earp strode into Las Vegas, Nevada and made quite an impression. No, not Wyatt Berry Stapp Earp (1848–1929), who became famous at the O.K. Corral, but another Wyatt Earp, who claimed to be the famous lawman's grandson. Incidentally, the Wyatt Earp who came into *Roadshow* in Las Vegas in 2007 claimed that the O.K. Corral was a myth and never actually happened.

Our present-day Wyatt Earp brought in an album of photographs that he claimed were of the Earp family and friends, and a pair of blue-tinted glasses that he said had originally belonged to another legendary Western figure, Doc Holliday. The album was full of tintype and *carte de visite* photographs that supposedly included images of such people as Josie Earp and Big Nose Kate.

Josie Earp, incidentally, was the original Wyatt Earp's "wife," although there is no official record of their marriage. Born Josephine Sarah Marcus and variously nicknamed Josie and Sadie, she was born about 1861 in New York State and died in 1944. Josie's family moved to San Francisco when she was young. Eventually she became an actress, a reputed prostitute, and spent much of her life with Wyatt traveling around the West and gambling. Later in life she authored a book about her marriage to Wyatt. Only one photograph of her is known, and the one in the album taken into *Roadshow* was from a different angle than the known example by C.S. Fly.

Big Nose Kate, on the other hand, was born Mary Katherine Horony in 1850 and died in 1940. She had a string of aliases, including Kate Fisher and Kate Elder, and once again, she is said to have been married to the infamous Doc Holliday, but there is no proof the wedding was official. In any event, she was attractive, hot-tempered, and worked as a "sporting woman"—or less euphemistically—a prostitute. At one point, she was also the madam of a house of ill repute.

I was called in to make The Pick, and had a fascinating talk with Mr. Earp, who produced a valid driver's license and other paperwork to prove that his name was indeed "Wyatt Earp." He said that his father was the illegitimate son of Wyatt Earp, and he himself had been born on an Indian reservation in Alaska where no birth records were kept.

The original Wyatt Earp in a photo taken in June 1883.

This was a potentially exciting find with historic implications, and there was no way that we would not tape it. The appraiser, who was David McCarron of McCarron and Associates in Bloomfield, Michigan, discussed these treasures with the modern-day Wyatt Earp and they had a fascinating exploration of the Old West with talk of such notables as Frank James and Johnny Ringo, as well as the original Earp's trip to Australia to prospect for opals.

At the end, McCarron told his guest that if the items he owned could be authenticated, they were conservatively worth $15,000 to $20,000 at auction for Doc Holliday's glasses and $30,000 for the album. This was very exciting news for the present-day Earp, especially when it was explained that his collection might actually bring more with solid authentication.

However, when we got back to Boston and started our laborious fact-checking process we immediately had serious doubts. First of all, the experts agree that Wyatt Earp had no children, which would mean that our Wyatt Earp could not, therefore, be his grandson.

Secondly, in a newspaper article that appeared in the *Las Vegas Review-Journal* on September 8, 2002 with the byline of Martin Griffith, we discovered the headline, Historians: MAN CLAIMING EARP RELATION A FRAUD. There was no picture with the article so we can't be sure that the Wyatt Earp we met in Las Vegas was the Wyatt Earp discussed in the newspaper article.

That Wyatt Earp had disappeared from the Goldfield, Nevada 100th anniversary celebration on August 23, 2002, after being accused of being an imposter. Most disquieting was the fact that the stories the two men told were very similar in that the accused imposter in Goldfield

claimed that "...his father, Nicholas Porter Earp, was born on an Indian reservation near Nome, Alaska, in 1919."

Everyone we asked said this story could not be true, and when we sent pictures of Josie Earp's tintype to our photo expert, she could not confirm that it was indeed Mrs. Earp, and our Old West specialist said that it absolutely was not. This left us with some very big question marks and the realization that we could not air this piece without conclusive proof, which the modern Wyatt Earp did not (or could not) supply.

If his story can be proven, it would stand accepted American history on its proverbial ear and be a very big story indeed. Maybe someday we will be given the substantiation we need— but for right now, there it is no possible way we could air this appraisal.

NOW YOU KNOW—SORT OF

Even with the information presented here, what to bring to *Antiques Roadshow* is still a tricky decision when you're inspecting your belongings, but it is central to the whole *Roadshow* experience. Your choice can determine whether or not you get on television. But perhaps much more importantly, it can clear up generations of uncertainty about what a family heirloom happens to be, its historical importance (if any), and its monetary value.

I'll end with what appraiser Rafael Eledge of Shiloh Civil War Relics in Savannah, Tennessee quipped when asked for advice on what to bring to *Antiques Roadshow*: "Few people have this problem. They usually bring items that, if the house were on fire, these are the things they would save—after their loved ones, of course." Whatever you bring, I guarantee you'll enjoy the experience!

At dawn, the *Roadshow* truck prepares to leave under police escort from the Honolulu, Hawaii, docks where it arrived by cargo ship from California.

ON THE ROAD WITH *ROADSHOW*

Taping day is what 10 million people see each week on *Antiques Roadshow*, but there's so much more! In this chapter, we journey through the never-previously-told happenings leading up to and on the day *Roadshow* comes to town.

SELECTING THE CITIES

We begin by selecting the cities we intend to visit during the summer taping season. Associate producer Jill Giles and event producer Amy Santamaria are in charge of presenting viable options, and are responsible for working several seasons ahead of the rest of the staff.

"We are often courted by convention centers, visitors bureaus, and some proactive PBS stations to visit a particular town or city. Some groups contact us more than once a month, and some even visit us when we are on the road to see what they can learn in order to make a visit to their town more practical and possible," Giles says.

Giles says that occasionally these organizations send little gifts—generally fun things with a

BACK TO THE PAST IN BISMARCK

We made some compromises to go to Bismarck, North Dakota, because we had never been there before. It turned out to be one of our most pleasant visits. "The excitement began with the site evaluation," Giles says. "It was February and cold and snowy. We were met at the airport and taken to Fort Lincoln, which is normally closed in the winter. When we got there, a car pulled up and out stepped a historical reenactor, who was dressed in full soldier's uniform. His opening line was, 'Shall I tell Mrs. Custer you will be here for dinner?' and that began a delightful two-hour experience that took us back to nineteenth-century North Dakota and concluded with *Antiques Roadshow* visiting in July 2005."

local flavor, such as food baskets during the holidays or a book that tells us more about the town.

When Giles was asked what the crew's favorite city was, she answered without hesitation, "Hot Springs, Arkansas!" She recalls, "They really rolled out the red carpet for us. A woman who owned a mansion out on a lake extended her hospitality and her home to the staff, crew, and appraisers in a dramatic way. There were fireworks, boat rides, Jet Skis, and a private chef. Everyone had a great time."

According to Giles, "City selection begins about eighteen months out, and we use a database that we have created called CityTracker that lists all the convention centers around the country that we have researched.

"Marsha's office has a large map of the United States plastered with sticky notes that shows us all the cities we have visited. If we were in Baltimore one year, we would not want to visit Washington, D.C. the next." Although recently there have been two or more repeat cities per tour, Giles and Amy Santamaria ("Just like the ship, only one word") focus on where *Roadshow* has *not* been and work hard to go to these cities even though they may not quite fit our exacting criteria (see box on page 54 for more on this).

We roughly divide the country into regions: Northeast, Southeast, Midwest, South, Southwest, and West. Of course, some of these regions overlap, but we try to put two cities from each region on our short list — six primary cities and six backup cities. Our goal is to cover the map. We do not want to go just to large cities; we try to include the smaller places as well. We are convinced that our efforts to cover the whole country will result in discovering more hidden treasures as well as give us a true picture of American life.

WORKING OUR WAY BACK HOME

"Ideally, we want to start on the West Coast and work our way back east," Giles says. This way, the *Roadshow* truck that carries the set and equipment can start out by going directly to the West and then over time work its way toward home base in Boston.

In 2008, the season started in Palm Springs, California; moved on to Dallas, Texas; then Wichita, Kansas; from there to Chattanooga, Tennessee; then Grand Rapids, Michigan; and finally to Hartford, Connecticut—which isn't far from our headquarters. Scheduling isn't always easy as some convention centers often book up years in advance, and so we often have to change the tour route to accommodate a facility that is hard to book. In 2009 we reversed our route in order to go somewhere we have never been—San Jose, California. Their convention center was only available in August, so *Roadshow* started in the east at Atlantic City, New Jersey; then moved south to Raleigh, North Carolina; then west to Madison, Wisconsin; Denver, Colorado; Phoenix, Arizona; and then finally ended up on the West Coast in San Jose.

ONE SIZE DOES NOT FIT ALL

"We do make a serious effort to work with facilities in cities we would like to visit, even if the space is not ideal." Giles continues, "For ex-

MARSHA'S MUSINGS

Many cities are very anxious to have *Roadshow* come to their town and there are some factors that will help their chances. Of course, as I mentioned, it helps if a city is in an area that has not been visited before. We also believe that we can't return to a taping location without at least five years between our visits. If we go back too soon, we can almost feel a slight lack of enthusiasm at the taping event.

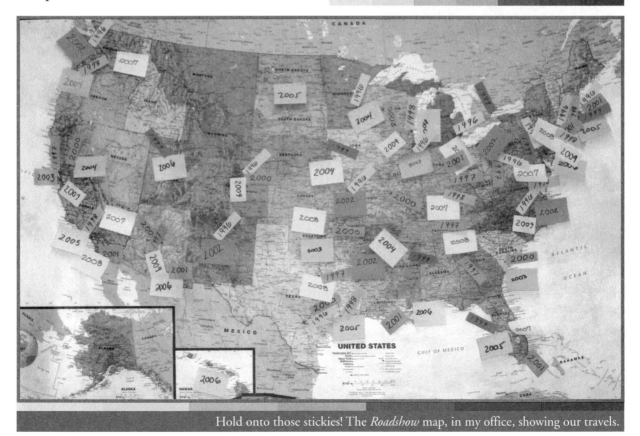

Hold onto those stickies! The *Roadshow* map, in my office, showing our travels.

* A facility must have at least 80,000 square feet of usable space in order to accommodate 5,000 to 6,000 visitors and allow for good crowd control. It must have wheelchair accessibility and adequate parking facilities for people with physical disabilities.

* It must have a permanent divider or an airwall, which is a temporary floor-to-ceiling partition made up of panels that are 4-to 5-feet wide, which physically divides a larger space into two smaller spaces and dampens the sound between both rooms. On one side of this wall we erect our set and television production area, on the other we place the mobile truck, the Green Room (see chapter 2), and house the crowd as they wait to be admitted. The wall is necessary because the crowd waiting to see the appraisers makes a lot of noise and this din, otherwise known as ambient sound or "ambo," must not be too loud in the area where the taping is actually being done, since it would make the recorded sound unintelligible. (Ambient sound is the natural sound an environment produces.)

* If a facility has columns, they must be at least 90 feet apart, otherwise this could very easily interfere with *Roadshow*'s lighting setup, which has a carefully crafted and standard configuration.

ample, in 2008 the convention center in Wichita was not perfect for our purposes (our truck could not be placed inside the convention center as we normally prefer), but we wanted to do an event in Kansas so we made some allowances and decided to be a little creative.

"The convention centers we are considering working with send us a CAD (computer-aided design), which is an electronic architectural drawing of the floor plan of their facility. We import the file and add graphic symbols of our set into the plan to see if it works logistically. If it looks like it will work on paper, either Amy or I will travel out with an engineer and inspect the site for other considerations such as noise levels, lighting, and power. Of course, there are other important aspects such as convention center rates and fees, parking availability, and exclusive convention center vendor requirements."

THE SECURITY BLANKET COVERS EVERYTHING

Once the cities have been selected, the process is still fairly complicated. "Our project funding must be in place so we have the resources to execute our plan. And contracts have to be signed," Giles explains. After the cities are selected, but well before *Roadshow* arrives, security director Sean Quinn visits each of the towns where the events are going to be held, "in order to make recommendations regarding our security plan." The responsibility is a big one for Quinn, who is obliged to keep about 6,000 people—guests, appraisers, and crew—safe.

Initially, he surveys the facility to see if there are any glaring problems that need to be addressed. "We hire security guards, arrange for local police representation, and make sure that we have direct access to all arms of law enforcement. We never divulge how many actual security personnel there are at any one taping, but we have officers both in uniform and plainclothes. We arrange to have paramedics present on Friday, the day before taping, in case there is an accident or emergency during setup and again on Saturday in case we have medical problems. Security preparations are intense but all is handled well before the first crew member leaves Boston."

MEET OUR HOST: MARK L. WALBERG

✳ Mark Lewis Walberg was born on August 31, 1962, in Savannah, Georgia and raised in Florence, South Carolina. Married in 1987 to actress Robbi Morgan Walberg (they met when Robbi came to the restaurant where Mark worked as a singing and dancing waiter), they have two children.

✳ Mark's first job in television was with Dick Clark Productions. He remembers, "I started as a runner—a gofer really—working show-to-show, one day at a time. One day the warm-up man did not show, and Dick had me go on in his place, giving out T-shirts, asking trivia questions, and trying to make the audience laugh before the show began. I just did my thing."

✳ In the early years, Mark did a little bit of everything. He recalls, "I was on a ladder hanging some lights for a television show when I heard that a dancer had dropped out. I came down the ladder and told the production people that I could do the dance.

They put me in a tux. I did the dance, took off the tux, and went back up the ladder to finish the lights."

✳ One of Mark's early shows was *Shop 'til You Drop* where he served as Pat Finn's sidekick and announcer from 1991 to 1994. The first time Mark appeared on television was in *USA's Gonzo Games* (1991).

✳ He hosted a sports-magazine show on ESPN where the late television executive, Brandon Tartikoff, noticed his work. Tartikoff helped Walberg get his own self-titled nationally syndicated talk show in 1995.

✳ Over the years, Mark hosted such popular television shows as *The Mark Walberg Show* (1995), *The Big Date* (1996), *Temptation Island* (2001—2003), *House Rules* (2003), *Anything for Love* (2003), *Russian Roulette* (2003), and his most recent, *Moment of Truth* (2008).

✳ Mark became the host of *Antiques Roadshow* in 2005.

SUMMERTIME—AND THE LIVING IS NOT ALWAYS EASY

June, July, and August find *Roadshow* moving swiftly to the six cities where the tapings take place that year. Some *Roadshow* crew and staff leave Boston on Wednesday because their work begins early Thursday morning. Most of the crew and staff head out early on Thursday in order to make an afternoon meet and greet with the convention center staff.

On Thursdays, the *Roadshow* crew that works with host Mark L. Walberg gathers to create a "field piece" that will be featured in one of the three shows from that city. These segments, tied to collecting, reveal local flavor and places of interest. Let's look at a 2008 segment taping on Coleman lanterns in Wichita, Kansas to experience one *Roadshow* field trip.

A DAY IN THE LIFE OF A *ROADSHOW* FIELD TRIP IN WICHITA

7:00 *am*

At dawn, two large vans and a load of camera and audio equipment wait under the porte

Louise Miller makes up *Roadshow* host, Mark Walberg, before shooting a segment in Cheney State Park in Kansas.

SETTING UP THE OUTDOOR SET

8:00 am

The team arrives at their campsite. The location is a pristine wooded area near a lake, very beautiful and very quiet. No one is around except the *Roadshow* crew and one helpful member of the park staff. The backs of the vans open and equipment gets pulled out. It's obvious these people have done this many times before in just this way.

8:30 am

cochere of the downtown hotel where the staff is staying. Segment producer Sarah Elliott, associate producer Adam Monahan, cameraman Bob Birkett, sound engineer Charlie Collias, and makeup artist Louise Daniels Miller, are ready for pickup. Host Mark Walberg emerges from the hotel brimming with good cheer: "This is going to be the best day ever!"

The destination is Cheney State Park, about twenty-four miles from the hotel. It's an appropriate setting for an informative segment about vintage camping equipment.

Despite having directions, finding the ranger's office is not easy, and Mark announces that this is the "*Into the Wild* edition of *Antiques Roadshow*." Seated in the front, he sings his own version of Johnny Cash's "Ring of Fire." "Down, down, down …the burning ring of fire," then announces, "Today we sing camping songs: 'Happy Wanderer,' 'Camptown Races,' 'Rocky Mountain High,' and 'Happy Trails.'"

Collector Jim Nichols and his wife Jan pull up in a pickup truck full of Coleman camping equipment, including the vintage Coleman lanterns. Nichols, Walberg, and several members of the crew pitch a tent that will be used as a backdrop. The group gathers to discuss setup, including the camera. We're still two hours away from shooting.

9:00 am

Makeup artist Louise Miller sets up her station on a picnic table and begins applying makeup to Mark and Gary Piattoni of Gary Piattoni Decorative Arts, in Evanston, Illinois, the appraiser working with Mark on the Coleman segment. When she's done, a crew member spreads out apples, bananas, cheese and crackers, candy, gum, and little cans of potato chips on the same table, along with Mark's favorite "health food"—strawberry toaster pastries. And, of course, there's bug repellant too.

As preparations continue, Elliott, Piattoni,

and Jim Nichols discuss the important talking points and the items to shoot. Meanwhile, Mark is like the proverbial kid in a candy store. He eyes the pieces displayed, picks up a rare Coleman lantern from the early twentieth century and exclaims, "Look at this bad boy!" Everyone seems to be having fun, and Mark quips, "We are going to have to work at some point—right?"

9:45 am

The campsite is up, the camera is ready to go, and those who are going to be on camera are "miked" (fitted with a wireless microphone).

PRACTICE MAKES PERFECT

Mark and Gary Piattoni sit at a picnic table, ready to rehearse. The script on Sarah Elliott's clipboard—which is more outline than line-by-line script—covers all the important points and facts that Mark and Gary will discuss. Everyone is reminded to turn off cell phones—more than once a ringing phone has ruined a take.

10:00 am

Taping begins. Unfortunately, the weather does not cooperate. The wind starts blowing and soon rain falls. The crew jumps into action to store the camera and cover the picnic table with the display of vintage Coleman products. The cast and crew take cover in the vans or tent pitched as part of the set.

11: 00 am

It's a good time for lunch.

After this the rain stops, but now some of the preparations must be repeated: Makeup gets refreshed, camera and items to tape get restaged, and Mark and Gary rehearse once more.

12:30 pm

Finally, the crew can get back to taping the Coleman collectibles discussion, and then get cutaways (close-up shots of the featured items). Some Coleman tidbits of information:

- In 1914 the Coleman Arc Lantern put the company on the map. Since its founding in 1901, more than 60 million Coleman lanterns have been sold.
- During World War I the American government declared portable Coleman lanterns essential for the wartime effort.
- Many collectors of vintage Coleman products buy, sell, trade, and share their information through the International Coleman Collectors Club (www.colemancollectorsclub.com).
- The Coleman Company is based in Wichita, Kansas.

Mark Walberg and appraiser Gary Piattoni discuss Coleman lanterns while Sarah Elliott directs.

MARSHA'S MUSINGS

**HERE'S A LIST OF WHAT'S ON THE
ROADSHOW TRUCK:**
* Props: gun displays, easels, jewelry
  displays, pedestals
* Ott lights: daylight color tempera-
  ture task lights
* Monitors
* Security equipment: including metal
  detectors, surveillance equipment,
  and gun locks
* Road boxes on wheels
* *Roadshow* library
* Release binders
* Green Room supplies
* Scanners and other Web supplies
* Pop-up screens
* Welcome banners
* Projectors and twenty-foot screens
  for the waiting area
* Camera pedestals and tripods
  (carried in mobile unit)
* Jimmy Jib (a small camera crane)
* Custom drapery walls
* Custom stretch fabric walls and frames
* Custom specialty banners
* Work/tool road boxes for lighting
  and scenic departments
* Feedback Booth equipment

3:00 pm

After waiting out yet another rain delay, the cast and crew complete the segment. Everyone helps to break down the set and methodically store the camera and sound equipment back into the van. The vintage lanterns and camping equipment are packed carefully for their ride home.

58

3:30 pm

The vehicles and the team leave Cheney Reservoir to return to the hotel in Wichita. It has been a long day!

On Friday, the crew and cast travel to the Kansas Aviation Museum to shoot a second segment on vintage air travel posters. On Saturday, while *Roadshow* hosts thousands of guests in the Wichita Convention Center, they go out a third and final time to the Wichita Art Museum to tape a piece on Steuben glass. This last segment takes only a few hours since Mark has taping to do on the convention floor during showtime.

ALMOST SHOWTIME: GETTING READY FOR APPRAISAL DAY

Of course, the field pieces are a unique but small part of *Roadshow*. The main event occurs at the convention center, beginning on Friday, the day before the crowds arrive.

Walking into the hall just before 7:00 AM, the only thing one sees is a cavernous space that echoes with footsteps. A rolling cart arrives with iced beverages, and coffee and doughnuts can be found at the end of the vast room. There are about two dozen people here, ranging from *Roadshow* crew and supervising personnel to representatives of the convention facility and local workers hired just for this event. Everything is relaxed and low-key.

THE BIG UNLOAD

A supervisor announces that the eighteen-wheeler *Roadshow* truck is ready to be unloaded and suddenly road boxes and parts of the set start coming into the cavernous space like the wagons in a circus parade. A scissor lift leads the way, followed closely by a forklift. The scissor lift has a mechanism that allows it to raise its operator to the ceiling of the convention hall. Almost immediately, the lift scissors up and the operator begins walking on the catwalk above the floor, disconnecting lights that would otherwise interfere with the set's own lighting that will soon be installed below.

Meanwhile, stanchions—which are properly called "crank-up lifts"—get set up around the floor, and numbered boxes and bins roll out of the truck, one after another. Locally hired crews work alongside *Roadshow* staff carrying large ladder-like pieces of equipment, with triangular sections and metal grids up all three sides. Once assembled, these pieces form an X-shaped, ground-supported lighting truss. The truck on the loading dock quickly disgorges its load, and even half-full, the inside of the vehicle looks as

Workers unload a section of the lighting grid in the early morning.

organized as an operating room.

Things do go wrong, of course. In one city, the forklift driver arrived late, slowing down the whole process. Yet the setup timetable allows for minor hiccups and the problem was made up for by mid-morning.

The lighting grid is assembled with the crank-up lifts.

MARSHA'S MUSINGS

To give you a good understanding of our lighting design, I asked lighting director Chas Norton for a little help. "The lighting design is based on the use of professional daylight color temperature fluorescents. By using them, we emulate daylight and we are efficient in our use of power and in our generation of heat. With this design scheme, we are able to have a consistent look from convention center to convention center. Windows are covered, in-house lighting is turned off directly over our production set, and by the time we are set up, we could be in any city.

"Stagehands or local lighting techs accustomed to working in our venues can easily assist us in the setup of what can be called a 'rock-and-roll style truss.' By bringing our own ground-supported lighting truss, we save time and money by not rigging lights to the ceiling. Rigging can often quadruple the price and time of the lighting setup. We do, however, hang safety chains from the ceiling when we are on the West Coast in case of an earthquake."

REPETITION IS GOOD

Amy Santamaria, the event producer, breezes across the floor looking well in charge of the situation. She comments, "We use a mix of help to get this done: WGBH and *Roadshow* employees, plus local crew. The truck has a diagram of how it is packed, and we have done this so many times that we can do it with remarkable efficiency.

"Summer can be very stressful for the crew," Santamaria says. "They leave one city for home on Sunday, and sometimes have to reverse and go to a new city on the following Wednesday. What changes about *Roadshow* is the guests and the items they bring; everything else happens virtually the same way, week after week after week."

Also hurrying around the set is Kristine Holmes, the set decorator. She is opening bins, cleaning items, and rolling out a long piece of plastic on which she places a variety of equipment.

Holmes and her assistant start assembling the iconic lightweight pieces of scenery that are so familiar to *Roadshow* viewers. In just a few minutes the desk and chairs used by the appraisers for the taped interviews are ready to go; drapery is slid onto pipe frames.

Besides her setup duties, Holmes oversees the set displays during the tapings. She is responsible for showcasing the items that may appear on TV—a baseball, a piece of jewelry, a poster, a quilt, a painting, some oddly shaped whatsit—so they are camera-friendly. If you see a collection of diverse items—say, badges, a photo, and a handwritten letter—displayed skillfully on a covered board for the cameras, you can probably thank Holmes for that.

THE GENESIS OF THE SET

Most of the items coming onto the floor are relatively light and can be moved about by just one person—part of the original concept by the set designers. According to the first *Roadshow* executive producer, Aida Moreno, "The initial rule when designing the set was, 'If Aida cannot carry it by herself, it has to go back to the drawing board and be redesigned.'"

Lighting director Chas Norton says, "This early rule is not true now. I like to see two people on the crank-up lifts rather than one, and there are some truss sections that need more than one person to handle them."

The atmosphere of the hall is punctuated with the *beep-beep-beep* of forklifts raising truss sections, and it looks a bit like we're building a bridge with a giant erector set. When the trusses are on top of the stanchions, the whole thing is about five to six feet tall. After the truss sections are on top of the crank-up lifts, lights are attached to the trusses. It is hard work, but the crew makes the operation look remarkably simple and straightforward.

The lights may look a little strange to some because many of them are fluorescent and are reminiscent of those in a tanning bed. "We had to decide what kind of lighting to use for the set and our choices came down to either tungsten (the normal lights used for television) or fluorescent (Kino Flo lights). Even all those years ago, we went green and decided on fluorescent because it used less power and cut our costs, which has always been very important."

It is now around 8:00 AM and the truck is completely unloaded. The loading dock doors of the convention center close at 10:00 AM and finally the air-conditioning is turned on. Only an hour has passed, but in that time the convention center went from empty hall to a bustling staging area with strange metal objects growing rapidly in its middle.

MID-MORNING AND THINGS ARE TAKING SHAPE

A little later, familiar set designs begin to take shape. The large sailcloth structure, decorated with silhouettes of various stylized antiques that forms the backdrop for the furniture area, is set up. Except for a small card table, there are no tables for the appraisers to sit at; furniture appraisals are done while participants and apprais-

This unassuming spot is the "nerve center" of *Roadshow* on the road.

ers stand in front of this backdrop.

The crew assembles easels in preparation for displaying paintings and continues to hang the lights on the lighting truss in great profusion. The floor is an anthill of activity, quiet yet purposeful. In a part of the hall that will become the temporary production office, post production supervisor Brian Beenders is setting out six suitcase-type bags that are dark blue with a distinctive pink tape, and are very identifiable. Each of the cases has the name of a *Roadshow* staff member on it and into them will go the tapes that will be shot the next day. The blank show tapes are shipped to each city but these bags will be used to transport the recorded tapes back to Boston. The staff

FURNITURE TRANSPORTATION RULES

To be considered for the selection process and potential free transport, the piece has to be:

* Large furniture (not simply a heavy object)
* Located within fifty miles of the convention center
* Easily accessed by a moving truck. (Once we disallowed a piece because it was located at the end of a long dirt road. We feared that the moving truck would not be able to reach the owner's home and get out again without serious difficulty.)

members who carry them become responsible for their irreplaceable contents. Beenders explains, "These tapes are priceless. We never check them as baggage onto an airplane out of fear of losing them. They stay with us at all times." Beenders is working in one of the nerve centers of the show: the production office that houses the library and computers used by the appraisers for research. Meanwhile, the cameras are mounted on pedestals. It's 10:30 AM and it's beginning to look like the very recognizable *Antiques Roadshow* set.

THE BIG FURNITURE MAKES ITS APPEARANCE

Large pieces of furniture swathed like ancient mummies in modern packing materials (wrapped in plastic instead of linen) come rolling off a moving truck and are placed in front of the furniture backdrop. This furniture was selected weeks earlier by *Roadshow* staff and appraisers and shipped from the owners' homes by *Roadshow*'s specialized art movers. Months before the event, the local PBS station runs promos, asking viewers to submit an application to have their large furniture pieces—items they might not be able to get to the convention center—chosen and transported at *Roadshow*'s expense.

The number of furniture requests we receive varies from city to city and in proportion to the number of times the local PBS station airs the taped request for the furniture submissions and—more importantly—in relation to the population of a city. In Palm Springs, California, for example, only 414 requests were received, but for *Roadshow*'s latest trip to Dallas,

"I could get excited about this!" said Leigh Keno when he pitched this French provincial armoire the day before Saturday's *Roadshow* event in Wichita. It is shown here on taping day with its happy owner. Keno valued the armoire between $11,000 and $12,000.

Texas, 596 requests were received by postcard and 1,308 by e-mail. In each city only nine or ten pieces are chosen.

BEING CHOOSY

According to former production secretary Kristin Hocevar, "These large furniture pieces are the only things we prescreen on *Roadshow*. When we make our request for furniture submissions, some people send photos of non-furniture items, which of course are not selected. Some people send in multiple pieces while others send in pictures of just about everything in their house."

Once all the pictures are in for all the cities in a season, two of our appraisers review the photos three cities at a time. The appraisers choose their top twenty pieces and then the senior production staff whittles that number down to just nine or ten and an alternate selection. Then the owners of the final contenders are contacted and asked the following questions:

- Can you make it to the show?
- Do you own the item?
- How easily can it fit through a doorway?
- Is it sturdy?
- How much does the item weigh?
- What are its dimensions?
- Does it come apart? What kind of assembly does it require?
- Is there any damage to the item already?
- Can a moving truck or tractor trailer (forty-five feet long) come down your street? Can it turn around?

"On occasion," Hocevar says, "the owner changes his or her mind, or there is some reason why the piece cannot be picked up, and we have to use an alternate selection."

Once packing materials have been removed, the pieces of furniture are set up so that they

MARSHA'S MUSINGS

It may be hard to imagine, but a piece of furniture can be offensive to television audiences. I remember one spectacular piece: A large, probably late nineteenth-century, mahogany coffer decorated with carved images of dragons, mythological beasts, and griffins. It was an exuberant piece, but it had one very serious problem—the base was composed of two mythological beasts with huge humanlike—but hairy—bare breasts. It was a real "yikes!" piece, and again, could not be used on television for fear of offending viewers or incurring the wrath of the FCC (Federal Communications Commission).

can be viewed later in the day by the furniture appraisers and the production staff.

THE SETUP CONTINUES

It is now about 11:00 AM and the floor still buzzes with activity. Electricians drop power at various locations. Internet connections are set up in the production office and on the set. Decorators drop sandbags for the bases of the pipe and drape backdrops. There will be no chance these fabric "walls" will topple over on someone or be accidentally pushed out of place.

Suddenly, the light on the lighting truss is turned on, and workers begin to crank up the lighting truss to its proper overhead height of fourteen feet. In a very short while, the lighting grid is in place. Before noon, things begin to quiet down, the set is beginning to look very familiar, and the crew can head to lunch.

Finally, around 3:30 PM the lighting is checked, the appraisal tables are assembled, the camera positions are set, and the desks where the appraisers will talk with guests and do the various tapings are in place.

THE FURNITURE APPRAISERS MAKE THEIR FIRST PITCHES

Also at 3:30 PM, the furniture appraisers meet on the set to examine the furniture the art movers brought in that morning and pitch their selections. The idea is to pick two items to start the next morning's taping as early as possible. On Saturday, every minute counts.

This grouping of furniture can be something of a mixed bag. This particular day, there was a strange piece of furniture that was referred to as a "mid-boy" as opposed to a highboy or lowboy. The term was completely foreign to the appraisers and it left them bemused and scratching their collective heads. It did not take long to figure out that this was a drastically altered piece of furniture. It was certainly a curious modification—but since none of the appraisers found it of interest, it was not even pitched.

There was also a fascinating folk art "box" commemorating events in the Spanish-American War; the outside showed shallow, carved images

Appraiser Ken Farmer appraises a Russian Mennonite dower chest from the late 1860s. The original owner painted the watercolor pictures inside the lid.

of a U.S. soldier chasing a mostly unclothed Filipino woman. As interesting and unusual as this was, it could not be used on television because the imagery was just too violent, insulting, and xenophobic in tone.

The process of making the furniture pitches actually reveals a great deal about an appraiser's interests. The first pitch of the afternoon was for a lovely table designed by famed mid–twentieth-century designer Robsjohn-Gibbings, and made by the John Widdicomb Company of Grand Rapids, Michigan. The piece caught the appraiser's attention because it was in his field of specialization. It was turned down for taping because the owner already knew all there was to know about the piece. There would be no sense of discovery.

Appraiser Ken Farmer takes a chest apart and scatters the drawers around the floor as he goes into a long explanation about what is wrong with this piece ("See, there are too many boards in the top") and how the chest is newer than it purports to be. It too was rejected for taping.

Leigh Keno pitched an eighteenth-century French provincial armoire. He examined the back of the large piece and proclaimed, "See, the back is almost as beautiful as the front." Keno strongly pitches the piece for television. He explains how he can tell the story of French provincial furniture, and while he is talking, he is down on his hands and knees examining the construction underneath the armoire.

The guest's letter says the interior door bears the date 1776 with a cross, and Keno exclaims, "I could get excited about this!" Keno concludes that the armoire is from the 1770s and worth $11,000 to $12,000. I chose the piece to be taped.

After that, Farmer enthusiastically pitches a dower chest with prints and watercolor pictures pasted inside the lid. It turns out to be a Russian Mennonite dower chest probably made in southern Russia in the late 1860s. The watercolors on the lid were done by the original owner, and Farmer puts the value in the neighborhood of $3,000.

The chest might have been more valuable if it had been made at an earlier date—late 18th century or even early 19th century—and was American in origin rather than Russian, but since it is a rather unusual piece, it is selected for taping.

THE DIRECTORS' MEETING

At 3:30, the directors' meeting takes place in the center of the set. The directors, John Boyle and Bill Francis, prep both the *Roadshow* crew and local crew to make sure that we are technically up to speed. The directors explain the production schedule, technical parameters, and the individual roles the local crew has in the recording of our unique live-to-tape, unscripted show. Since we are often telling our camera operators to "follow the ball," we find that the local hires with live sports backgrounds work well with our team. As with live sports, we need people who can think on their feet and always be ready for the occasional curve.

This meeting is also a chance for the directors, camera operators, stage managers, lighting crew, audio, video and videotape technicians to go through a practice run before the big day. John Boyle adds, "This is our only opportunity to explain our approach to the production, both technically and aesthetically. We need to make sure that all new technicians are on the same page and know the overriding guidelines to follow in order to produce a consistent, high-quality program under tight time constraints." During the practice run, the crew performs their various functions. We'll often rehearse with fake props and give some of the newer appraisers an opportunity to practice. Not only is this a great opportunity for appraisers to get acclimated to presenting on set and ask specific questions related to on-camera best practices, but it gives the technical crew the chance to rehearse and test all equipment. Any technical glitches can be dealt with now while we have a minute to address it. On Saturday, a few minutes spent dealing with a technical issue means one less appraisal in the can.

THE VOLUNTEERS' ORIENTATION

Around 4:00 PM members of *Road show* production staff meet with the 110 to 120 volunteers who will be working the next day. Event producer Amy Santamaria tells them at least twice, "You are the face of *Antiques Roadshow*. There are lots of different jobs to be done, all are equally important, and they need to be accomplished with patience, courtesy, and kindness."

Security director Sean Quinn talks to the volunteers about specific procedures. "Guests bringing in guns must have them checked by a policeman who will affix a large white tag to the firearm. If you see a gun without a tag, call a supervisor and *Antiques Roadshow* security immediately!"

He informs them that two paramedics will be on duty, and cautions volunteers, "Please do not help people struggling with an antique. We do not want the piece damaged by one of our volunteers, and please do not appraise any items yourself." That comment always makes the volunteers giggle. The meeting ends as they follow the *Roadshow* staff to learn the details of their specific jobs.

Most, if not all, of the volunteers are there because they love *Antiques Roadshow* and

relish the opportunity to be in the thick of things. To actually be at "ground zero" and meet the appraisers and see all the fascinating items coming in is very exciting. For their services, the volunteers get a *Roadshow* polo shirt and the right to bring two small items to be appraised.

THE APPRAISERS' MEETING

At 5:00 PM we hold the appraisers' meeting. Here, new news is announced (sponsorship updates, new programs, etc.) and old business is discussed (such as complaints and compliments received by e-mail since the last taping). Every e-mail gets forwarded to the appropriate person, and I encourage everyone to take comments seriously and constructively.

Then we review some basic dos and don'ts of taping, such as:
- Be a generous interviewer
- Allow your guest to talk
- Don't interrupt a guest
- Give values in context (is it a retail, auction or insurance price?)
- Make sure you give the as-is price first
- Be certain that the price is not the first thing guests hear
- Do not tell a guest why their piece was turned down for taping
- Do not tell people we are out of time
- Do correct yourself if you realize you've made an error
- Do not have dirty fingernails
- Do allow the guest to react and don't "step" on the guest's reaction

After each taping, transcripts are made and e-mailed to each appraiser as soon as possible, so the appraisal is fresh in their minds. I remind appraisers to check the transcripts from the previous taping sessions for accuracy, and we all leave the meeting feeling excited about what we might discover on the following day.

RAH-RAH *ROADSHOW*

A "rah-rah" is my affectionate term (derived from "rah-rah *Roadshow*") for an evening soirée hosted—usually by the local PBS station or one of *Roadshow*'s sponsors—the Thursday or Friday night before the event. A kind of pep rally and fund-raiser for those who support *Roadshow*, the event includes *Roadshow* executive staff and publicists, Mark Walberg, six to twelve appraisers, the press, local dignitaries, and donors to the hometown PBS station.

One of the more elegant and memorable of our rah-rahs was held in 2008 in the home of United States Senator Bob Corker, a conservative Republican from Tennessee. Irrepressible and charismatic appraiser Nicholas ("Nicho") Lowry, president of Swann Galleries in New York City, arrived at the senator's home wearing buttons on the lapels of his saffron-colored sport coat that very visibly supported the national Democratic Party: two were for Barack Obama and one for Hillary Clinton. Fearing that they might offend the evening's host, we asked him to ditch the buttons. Instead, Nicho assured us that the senator would be amused—and as it turns out, he was absolutely correct. According to Nicho, "The senator was a most gracious man. But one of his angry constituents said that I should at least be wearing a Corker button. I said, 'of course' and asked the senator if he had one. He admitted he did not but

would bring me one at the event the next day. How accommodating is that!"

Invariably, some guests bring small objects for the experts to appraise. We try to discourage this, of course, but if the guest is not coming to the convention center the next day, we try to pull aside an appraiser who feels comfortable about offering an offhand opinion. Rah-rahs tend to end fairly early because the next morning is our big day.

"ROADSHOW!" the staff and crew yell in unison. It's time to allow the guests onto the floor.

SATURDAY: IT'S SHOWTIME!

It is 7:00 AM and relatively tranquil inside the convention center. Outside, the crowds have been gathering for an hour or more and the first of the crew have already been at work since 5:45 AM.

About 300 people—volunteers, *Roadshow* staff, and appraisers—gather for a buffet breakfast in a meeting room or ballroom. The mood is upbeat and expectant. Whereas the volunteers know little about what lies ahead, the seasoned appraisers ready themselves for the controlled chaos to come, with they themselves at the epicenter. Most of them wonder: Will we see any missing masterpieces today? Will it all be junk? Will our knowledge and expertise be tested? Or will it be our patience?

THE GUESTS GATHER

Whatever the weather, guests wait outside, usually perched on collapsible chairs, sitting canes, and anything else they brought in anticipation of a long wait in line. The first tickets are for 8:00 AM, and while we ask that attendees not arrive more than thirty minutes prior to the time on their tickets, people inevitably do come earlier.

With them is everything that can be imagined. Many have paintings or prints, some have old washing machines, some have boxes and boxes of who-knows-what, and others are carrying swords and guns. According to event producer Amy Santamaria, "There have been small cannons, twelve-foot-long Asian screens, airplane propellers, surfboards, and numerous bear traps."

Most of the guests waiting in line are casually and comfortably attired, but a few are dressed as some sort of character. In Memphis, "Elvis" entered the building, and it is not uncommon in certain parts of the country to find someone outfitted head-to-toe like a cowboy or frontiersman carrying a big firearm of some sort. Santamaria also remembers the person who showed up in Grand Rapids, Michigan, as Johnny Depp's character in *Pirates of the Caribbean*. "And oh, it was a 'she' dressed as Captain Jack Sparrow.

"There are all kinds of people on line wearing T-shirts that say 'I'm here at *Antiques Roadshow*, and it is my birthday.' One woman even created a small sandwich-board advertisement announcing her fortieth birthday and wore it during the entire event."

RUNNING THE TRIAGE GAUNTLET

When the guests finally enter the building a little after 7:00 AM, the first *Roadshow* appraiser they encounter is a generalist who inspects their items so they can direct the guests to a specific appraisal table. Ramona Hillier-O'Hara is the head of *Roadshow* Triage, as we call this process, and has been doing this since the second season. "It can be an overwhelming twelve-hour day," she says. "We begin early, taking a cart of tickets down the line around 7:15 AM. This way, we are ready to start the minute the appraisers are in their places.

> { **THERE ARE ALL KINDS** OF PEOPLE ON LINE WEARING T-SHIRTS THAT SAY "I'M HERE AT *ANTIQUES ROADSHOW*, **AND IT IS MY BIRTHDAY."** }

"In the beginning," Hillier-O'Hara continues, "we chose appraisers' spouses or traveling companions to work Triage, but now we prefer appraisers with knowledge and experience in the business. Otherwise, the guest's item may go to the wrong place. I really hate it when guests have to go from table to table looking for the proper person to appraise their item. It's inefficient and frustrating to everyone, guests and appraisers alike.

"We have a Triage meeting the afternoon before the event begins to discuss issues we may encounter during the day. For instance, if we have a guest with a Russian or Greek icon (a very traditional and specific type of painting on wood made for religious purposes in Eastern Orthodox Christian traditions), we usually need to send the guest to the Jewelry table, not to the Paintings or Decorative Arts table as some might suppose. If

Items are examined at one of the Triage tables before being assigned to one of the appraisal stations.

we happen to get American Indian jewelry, we send it to the Tribal Arts table, again, usually not to Jewelry, and if we get entertainment and popular culture autographs, they go to Collectibles, while autographs of literary and historical figures go to Books & Manuscripts."

People manning the Triage area see about 6,000 people carrying 10,000 to 12,000 items. This is quite challenging for first-timers and seasoned appraisers alike, but it is excellent training for appraisers new to the show who aspire to have the opportunity to appraise on air. All those men, women, and children coming at you hour after hour is good preparation for working with guests at the appraisal tables, where an appraiser's composure and expertise go on trial.

You never know what might turn up at Triage. Hillier-O'Hara remembers a shrunken monkey head and a hair collection—no, not hair jewelry, which turns up fairly regularly, but plain old hair in tiny, little gold frames supposedly from the heads of Napoleon Bonaparte and John Lennon, among others.

"Once," she muses, "someone brought in life-size figures of Neanderthals. They had been exhibits in a museum and had been discarded and subsequently sold in a thrift store where the guest bought them. They just rolled them in and we had to decide where the heck to send them.

"We do have problems with people bringing in more items than they are allowed. It seems everyone brings in a few items 'just in case.' It is true that *Roadshow* allows people to bring entire collections, but often guests tote disassociated items and just call them a 'collection.' Just because all the items belonged to Grandma or were bought in a box lot at an auction does not make them a collection."

MEANWHILE, BACK ON THE SET

On the appraisal floor, it is somewhere between 7:30 and 7:45 AM. The volunteers, crew, and production staff gather in the center, get a pep talk, form a circle, put their hands together, and yell in unison, *"Roadshow!"* This is the signal to admit the guests onto the floor. The appraisals begin!

I can't say it enough…this is the real fun of spending the day at *Roadshow*. In the early morning, trips to the appraisers are quick, but as the day progresses the waits get longer and longer. For some popular areas, such as Furniture, Paintings, and Collectibles, the lines can leave the area of the set, pass through the backdrop, and then snake around the convention center like a giant anaconda.

Luckily, most people have come prepared and make themselves as comfortable as possible. As they wait, their treasured possessions are littered around them. Some bring them in wagons or shopping carts, on jerry-rigged sets of wheels, on dollies and hand trucks. Others just drag them any way they can. If the event was 150 years earlier, we would experience a scene that looked a bit like a wagon train of emigrants, marshalling their prized possessions, heading west.

DEALING WITH REJECTION

One by one, the guests approach their designated appraisal table. Most learn that their objects are not of great value, others learn about the historical importance of their items, and a few are chosen for television in the process that has been previously discussed. Guests with objects the appraisers want a producer to see wait expectantly behind the set. They do not yet know the appraiser's thoughts. They have lots of hope, of course: That they possess the treasure of the ages, or an item so important and valuable that they can retire comfortably.

When the producer arrives, their tale is told again and they answer a battery of questions. After this, some are chosen for taping and are escorted to the Green Room to be prepared for television; others are referred back to the appraiser to get their evaluation. For one reason or another, there will be no television for this group, but we hope they are satisfied knowing that their item was interesting enough to catch the appraiser's attention. Still, rejection—even a gentle, polite rejection—can be difficult.

David Lackey of David Lackey Antiques in Houston, Texas, says that most people whose items are rejected take it very well. "I always tell them right up front that there is a chance they will not be picked. So, when it happens they are a little disappointed, but not overly surprised. I also want to say that The Pickers do a great job of letting people down gently and politely. They are never dismissive and manage to convey how pleased they are that the guest brought this particular piece to *Roadshow*."

After the piece has been turned down, the appraiser does the appraisal. Lackey explains, "I propose items for television that I really like, and if the item is rejected for some reason, I give the guest a hundred-dollar appraisal, meaning I sit down with them and spend more time than I could if we were out at the table."

Lackey went on to say that he is sometimes rather saddened by the items that are rejected because he believes in them. He recalls a woman who brought in a pair of German figures that were made in a factory owned by the Nazi Party. "After they were rejected for taping, the lady and I spent some time talking. She told me about her family owning a restaurant in France during the war and about hiding Jews in the basement while Nazi soldiers ate upstairs."

EVERYBODY NEEDS A LITTLE FEEDBACK

Of the approximately 6,000 people who come to each taping of *Roadshow*, less than 2 percent will be lucky enough to have their item taped for potential use in an upcoming show. Most will not make it in front of the cameras on the set, but all will have the opportunity to share their items and their stories at our Feedback Booth, if they so desire.

As mentioned in chapter 1, this is a chance to face a camera and tell the story of the object or maybe just comment on the show and the experiences had on the occasion. The Feedback

state their first name and where they are from, and then tell what they brought to *Roadshow*, how they had a great time, how excited they were just to be there, how they always watch the show, how they thought the item they brought was going to be worth thousands, but ended up being worth only $20, and on rare occasions a complaint. *Roadshow* intern Vanessa Peleggi says, "A lot of people also express their 'love' for the Keno brothers; they seem to be a crowd favorite."

PARTY LIKE AN APPRAISAL STAR— THE END OF THE SEASON

The last guest is seen, all the appraisals have been taped, the Feedback Booth is shut down. Another *Antiques Roadshow* event has come to an end. Staff and the production crew break

> { **OUT WALKED NOEL BARRETT OF** NOEL BARRETT ANTIQUES AND AUCTIONS. **HE HAD HIS LONG HAIR DOWN AND HE WAS** WEARING A BEIGE MINISKIRT. }

Booth is an opportunity for guests to have a few minutes of fame—and maybe, just maybe, if the tape is interesting enough, it might be used in one of the end segments on an episode of *Antiques Roadshow*.

The Feedback Booth usually yields six to eight hours of tape for each city visited, which translates into about 300 separate guest spots. Back in Boston, *Roadshow* interns view the tapes and try to select seventy-five that catch their interest. These go to series editor Jeff Cronenberg and editor Kelsey Bresnahan, who then select the most entertaining and suitable guest spots to be included in a *Roadshow* episode. Of the 300 that were shot, about twenty make it to the air.

A parade of people come up to the camera,

down the set and pack the truck while a fair-sized group of staffers and appraisers meet in the hotel bar to exchange "war stories." For others, the twelve-plus-hour day ends with a good dinner, maybe a glass of wine, and an early retirement in preparation for leaving town early the next day.

However, one of the highlights each season is the summer's *Roadshow* family poker party—even if you don't play. The brainchild of Mark Walberg and David Rago, of Rago Arts & Auction Center of Lambertville, New Jersey, it all began in Bismarck, North Dakota, in 2005. "There was not all that much to do in Bismarck on that particular Saturday night—it's a lovely city, but it is in the middle of a prairie." Now poker night is always held in the city that is second to last on

It's a wrap... party: appraisers Todd Weyman, Berj Zavian, Arlie Sulka, and Noel Barrett celebrate the season's end.

the summer tour. And many people come.

"We play tournament-style with a fixed number of chips. The game starts right about 9:00 PM, and it is generally over by 3:00 AM. It's a great bonding experience; as people get knocked out of the tournament, they stick around until the wee hours of the morning."

Of course, the players have nicknames. As appraiser David Rago explains, "I am called 'Don Rago' in a reference to Don Vito Corleone of *The Godfather*," while Berj Zavian is "Diamond Berj"; Arlie Sulka is the "Black Widow" because she played a mean game that first year; and Nicho Lowry has become "Boss Tweed" because of the tweed suits he wears. Rafael Eledge says that he has never really heard a nickname for himself ex-

cept maybe "*Roadshow* Hillbilly," and when Rago was asked what my nickname was, he quickly replied "Mrs. Bemko" or "the Boss!"

In 2008, another competition took place in Wichita. Mark Walberg and associate producer Adam Monahan proposed a bowling tournament that many of us hope will become an annual tradition.

IT'S A WRAP!

Perhaps more purposeful—but still great fun—is the wrap party held on Saturday night in the last city of the summer tour. It's time to toast the accomplishments of the season's tapings, and say good-bye to good friends; many of us will not see each other again for eight months. We feel like a family, and emotions and team spirit run high on this last night of the season.

It is such a team effort to get *Antiques Roadshow* out the door we relish the opportunity to unwind together. We also celebrate the joy and sadness we shared with tens of thousands of people across America.

The party is very informal, and Mark, an appraiser, and I usually have something to say to all gathered. One year, in Indianapolis, Indiana at the end of Season 6 (summer 2001), some of the appraisers put on a skit. Actually, they roasted staff members, including me!

Out walked Noel Barrett of Noel Barrett Antiques and Auctions in Carversville, Pennsylvania, who is one of our most popular appraisers. He had his long hair down, which is the one and only time he has ever been seen this way, and he was wearing a beige miniskirt, a version of the skirts I sometimes wore at the time. What unfolded was very funny, but I was so embarrassed that I couldn't watch. I remember my face getting very red and burying my head into the shoulder of the person standing next to me. Needless to say, I don't recall the details.

Dredging up memories from the participants, it seems that Nick Dawes, an independent appraiser and auctioneer from New York City, who cowrote the script with John Buxton, played a biblical figure bringing the holy grail to *Roadshow* to be appraised. Why the holy grail? Because appraisers and staff often joke that this legendary object is the "ultimate *Roadshow* treasure." Others grumble, "Even if we had the holy grail, we couldn't get on television!"

Barrett remembers that Leigh Keno played the appraiser pitching the grail to "Marsha" and trying to get it selected to go on TV. Of course, Noel Barrett in a miniskirt mimicking me must have been hilarious, but truthfully, Barrett said, "I don't remember much of my routine, but you were a great sport."

When the wrap party ends, the appraisers scatter to their homes, and the crew and staff return to Boston. What has been accomplished during the tour seems overwhelming, but it is really only the beginning of a lot of arduous work that takes a team of skilled professionals to turn the raw material into a finished product. You'll read more about this in the next chapter.

Marsha, appraiser Noel Barrett (dressed as Marsha), and appraiser Richard Wright after the wrap party roast.

The *Roadshow* crew captures the emotions of a guest in Savannah, Georgia, as appraiser David Rago values this Newcomb College chocolate set at $50,000–60,000.

THE HARD WORK BEGINS

Though some fans love *Roadshow* because it is "part history lesson, part adventure story, and part treasure hunt," others point to the fact that the show is just so darn entertaining to watch. That doesn't happen easily. The production comes together thanks to a talented, discriminating and dedicated staff of fifteen men and women who carefully craft twenty episodes (eighteen weekly shows plus two specials) that are exactly fifty-six minutes and forty-six seconds long.

NO REST FOR THE WEARY

The process is continuous through each taping season's exhausting summer tour and into the fall. After each city's appraisal event, videotape operator Steve Barasci prepares a special set of DVDs for me to view on the airplane as I travel back to Boston (you may recall from chapter 3 that the actual tapes are placed in dark blue suitcases and sent home with designated staff members). Out of the ten or eleven hours of recordings made that Saturday, Steve makes a stack of DVDs and hands them to me late that evening.

MAKING THE GRADE

As I watch the DVDs, here's what I do: I focus on all the appraisals from that city, making notes and grading every appraisal the same way a schoolteacher grades homework papers and tests. The perfect A consists of good performances by both the appraiser and the guest, and an interesting object too. But truthfully, I don't give out many As; there are just a handful for each city that *Roadshow* visits.

Likewise, Fs are truly rare, but there are a few Ds. Most are graded with Bs and Cs. Some appraisals that I initially award a B can be edited to elevate them to an A. This is because the editing process takes out the weak spots and makes the appraisal stronger and more compelling. You'll read more about this later.

Before organizing the shows, I look at the list of those that received a C or less. From that I cut out the weakest appraisals, then I tentatively organize the remaining ones into three hour-long episodes. I make certain that every show has a furniture appraisal and a porcelain appraisal, and I attempt to cover as many categories of objects as possible. About seventy appraisers attend each event, and each show needs to have a relatively even mix of appraisers from the large auction houses as well as independent appraisers. And every show needs to start with an A appraisal. I strive for a perfect balance—much like a chef creating the perfect meal—and at this point I start to imagine how each show is going to "feel."

Many appraisals do not make the show, but I also create a list of alternate appraisals if, say, an appraisal fails its fact-checking or is removed from a show for another reason. Sometimes, the

MARSHA'S MUSINGS

I bought a portable DVD player some years ago when I got stuck on a Sunday night in a week when I had to fly to the next city on a Wednesday. Now I always have it with me when we're shooting. As I fly home, the DVD player is plugged into the airplane seat, and I watch the appraisals that were taped at the event. It generally takes me twelve to fourteen hours to get through the footage. On a cross-country flight, I can see about four hours, and this makes Monday, when I finish watching the "formal" appraisals, a little more manageable. Once home in Boston, I make sure I view everything by Monday night.

alternate list contains as few as six appraisals, and to me, that's cutting the number close for second-choice possibilities.

Once I have my list of appraisals and alternates, I hand both to Jeff Cronenberg, our series editor.

THE EDITING PROCESS

According to Jeff, "The work of editing the show begins as soon as we arrive back in Boston. While Marsha is choosing the appraisals to be included in the final shows and making her notes, an assistant editor begins capturing the raw footage into our editing computer. There are four camera angles being simultaneously

MARSHA'S MUSINGS
MAKING THE CUTS

Deciding which appraisals to cut is one of the hardest things I do. It's hard not to feel emotion or sentiment toward either the guest or the appraiser. Many of the experts we work with have become my friends; I can't let that influence my decision-making. I've learned to watch the rushes (raw footage) with objectivity. I need to remain unbiased when it comes to my feelings for the guests. In the introduction I told you about our Grand Rapids guest who holds the distinction of being the only guest to ever bring me to tears while doing The Picks. The gentleman had brought us an 1885 print in honor of his wife who had died after receiving her event tickets but before the event. I did tape that item but, frankly, it wasn't strong enough to compete with the other footage and it did, as they say, land on the cutting room floor. And yes, as you might imagine, that was a tough decision. Nonetheless, it was the right one.

recorded during the entire event, plus an overall reference tape. When you add in the footage from the EFP [electronic field production] units shooting the field trips and the informal appraisals, we are left with about sixty hours of raw footage per city, and from those sixty hours will come three one-hour episodes.

"I start with a prescreening to get familiar with the footage," Cronenberg continues,

"then Marsha sends me her list of preferred appraisals. Editor Kelsey Bresnahan will begin by roughing in the appraisals, which are usually about ten minutes long, editing them down to four or five minutes each. Eventually I will cut them down even further, so that each appraisal runs about three minutes.

"A big part of the editing has to do with seeing to it that the story is told clearly, concisely, and accurately. To help with that, along the way I will take out many of the verbal distractions: the aah's, the um's, the you-knows. There's even the occasional 'nasty' word sprinkled in, but sometimes we just bleep those, because they can be entertaining. We do tend to err on the side of politeness and good taste. After all, this is a family show."

During the editing process, music is added. "I try to select something that is appropriate and fits the mood of the segment that Mark Walberg does for each show. For example, we taped a piece with marionettes, and I chose music that sounded like the tunes used on children's television shows from the 1950s, such as *Howdy Doody*.

"Editing is incredibly precise work and it is not quick. It takes time to make the end product look believable and seamless. People think that what they see on television is a real-time event—that it happened just the way they are seeing it. Of course that's not true. However, if editor Kelsey Bresnahan and I have done our jobs well, no one will ever know that we were there, smoothing out the rough edges.

"Sometimes, editing does involve a bit of smoke and mirrors. On occasion, for example, after a piece has been shot and the raw footage is in the can, we discover something that needs to be addressed or removed because further research has proven that what we believed to be true at the time of the shoot may not be entirely accurate.

"One example is a shoot that was done at

Geppi's Entertainment Museum in Baltimore. We had set up three examples of classic Sunday comics (or so we thought) only to learn after the fact that one of those examples was actually a reproduction. Not only that, but the repro was placed smack-dab in the middle of our setup. We couldn't go back and reshoot, so by using the editing tools available and some creative thinking, we were able to crop out the offending piece and at the same time create a look that fit the feel of comics and the funny papers. Lemonade from lemons, if you will.

Original setup of classic Sunday comics showing the Dick Tracy reproduction smack in the middle.

"I want to stress that even though we have the technical ability to make anybody say practically anything we want, we are careful to preserve the journalistic integrity of the segment. In other words, in the end we want to tell the truth accurately, but in a concise manner.

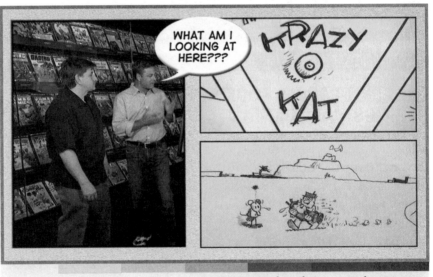

Creativity plus editing saves the segment.

"For the appraisal segments, we have four cameras shooting tape, and if there is a spot that needs to be covered, we can draw on the images taken from one of the four cameras. If someone misspeaks, we can sometimes take out the word and cover it with a shot so there is no jump in the video. Also when we are doing pickups (shots taken after the appraisal is over to get close-ups of objects discussed or clarify something that was said) we get people to tell their story again, and this gives us footage that might help us smooth things out during the editing process."

Cronenberg concludes by saying, "Editing is part storytelling, part technical adventure, and it's a joy to be able to use the tools available to help bring peoples' stories to the viewers."

Series editor Jeff Cronenberg at work.

THE FIRST PASS: A LOOK AT PALM SPRINGS, CALIFORNIA

After editing, Cronenberg creates a tape for the first screening, called the first pass. Screening day is intense. The room used is full of couches, chairs, tables, and a large flat-screen, high-definition television. We begin first thing in the morning: By 9:00 AM the coffee is brewing, and on occasion someone brings in home-baked cookies or supplies the requisite box of doughnut holes: twenty jelly, twenty glazed, and ten chocolate (yes, the same inventory appears every time).

Associate producer Jill Giles explains, "In the morning before the first pass, we carbo-load and prepare to have our opinions heard. It is a long day, but it is also fun and exciting. We try to be polite to one another and respect each other's opinion, but sometimes we respect our own opinion more."

In attendance are me, the executive producer and master of ceremonies for the screening, along with all of our producers, business manager, staff, the editor who cut the show, and often *Roadshow*'s publicists. When everybody attends there are fifteen people, and usually fifteen opinions, on everything. Everyone settles in and I announce, "Let's watch TV"—and the "battle" begins.

THE CRITIQUE

The *Roadshow* episode the group is about to see is from Palm Springs, California, in 2008 and took Jeff Cronenberg about a month to create. It is much longer than the final version. This is part of the process: For first pass, the appraisals are left lengthy on purpose (also called "fat") so the group can work together trimming them, requesting fact-checks, and maximizing their entertainment value until the segments begin to approach their proper length.

The group critiques the entire show from the opening "tease" to the closing Feed-back Booth. The first appraisal features a Victorian Herter Brothers (New York City) table that was part of the Mills estate in Oakland, California. The original owner was Darius Ogden Mills, who was a Forty-Niner and his residence was charmingly dubbed "Happy House."

On the piece of furniture there is a burned-in Herter Brothers signature (the owner offers, "Just thought it was a burn mark") plus a somewhat hard-to-see pencil inscription that reads *Mills.* The story is told how the Herter Brothers decorated Happy House twice, and the piece is valued at $40,000 to $45,000. It all sounds rather straightforward, but when the tape is turned off, the questions and criticism begin:

Michael Flanigan and the Herter Brothers' table from the Mills estate valued at $40,000–$45,000.

- "Will everyone know what a Forty-Niner is? Will they think it refers to the football team or will they know it is a reference to the prospectors who came to California during the 1849 Gold Rush?"
- "This is a great story, but it is a tad long. And the advice the appraiser gives to the collector may seem a bit patronizing."
- "It was said this was a 'local piece.' Well, Oakland is not 'local' to Palm Springs where we were doing the taping."
- "Much of the time the camera was focused on Michael Flanigan [the appraiser] and I would have liked a longer look at the table."
- "Can we highlight the signature so that we can better see the *Mills* written on the piece?"
- "I think some of the information was ambiguous."

Finally, the group scrutinizes the "lower third," the terms used for the bottom portion of the screen where price information is revealed. "Can we add 'Mills estate' in the space allowed on the lower third?" someone asks.

WHAT A DOLL

After about ten minutes of back-and-forth dialogue, the group moves onto the next appraisal, which concerns a French Jumeau bébé doll. Jumeau is the best known of the French manufacturers of dolls. The doll was appraised at $10,000 to $12,000 by Andy Ourant of Village Doll and Toy Shop, Adamstown, Pennsylvania. Immediately, associate producer Adam Monahan is asked to do some thorough fact-checking to make sure that all the information is correct.

Then, the comments begin to fly:

- "Does the piece have to start where it does now?"
- "I did not understand the doll was a bébé—do we need to include accents in that word if we print it on the screen?" (A *bébé* is a French child doll with a "dolly face.")
- "The appraiser says a couple of things incorrectly. In reference to the wig, he says 'goat skin' when he means 'goat hair.' I think I understand how to fix it."
- "Does the audio make him sound like he was underwater?"

Finally, there is a discussion on the proper pronunciation of the phrase *Médaille d'Or*, which is stamped on the torso of most Jumeau dolls after 1878.

THE KING'S BELT AND THE ROOSTER CROWS

The next item is a large collection of Elvis Presley memorabilia, appraised by Gary Sohmers of Allcollectors.com. The main piece in the collection is a macramé belt worn by Elvis during a performance. Everyone thinks this collection is surrounded by a great story (the guest had been collecting memorabilia since 1969, saw Elvis perform in concert seventy-six times, and met him at a party when she was sixteen years old), but the group discusses cuts to

Jumeau doll; note the wig which became a subject of some debate.

Collection of Elvis Presley memorabilia; the guest met Elvis at a party when she was 16 years old and saw him in concert 76 times!

make the appraisal shorter. At one point, some-one suggests editing out everything but the belt because, "The rest of the appraisal exists just to get an 'Oh, really!' response from the guest, and it is just not very entertaining." The group disagrees strongly and the appraisal of the full collection, which is appraised for $10,000 to $15,000 and includes an autographed scarf, photographs, buttons, ephemeral items, and of course the belt, remains intact. So does the guest's reaction: "This is just the tip of the iceberg. I have tons more at home."

When the tape starts again, Jody Wilkie, vice president and international specialist head, European ceramics and glass,

Christie's, New York, is appraising two Italian majolica brackets made by Ulisse Cantagalli, one of which the owner thinks is a fake. It turns out that both pieces were made from the same

Pair of Cantagalli shelf brackets

WHEN THE ROOSTER CROWS

Ulisse Cantagalli took over the family faience (tin-glazed earthenware) factory in Florence, Italy in 1878 and began making highly decorated wares in the Renaissance style. He adopted the crowing cockerel as his mark, and his wares were very popular in the United States and England. The factory traded as "Figli di Giuseppe Cantagalli," and made imitations of early Italian majolica made by master potters in Urbino, Faenze, Gubbio, Deruta, and the Florentine, Della Robbia workshop. The factory also imitated wares in the Turkish Isnik style and in the Persian manner.

The most admired Cantagalli work is their Art Nouveau wares with elongated plant motifs and the pieces designed by William De Morgan, who was one of England's most talented pottery and tile designers of the late nineteenth and early twentieth centuries.

Cantagalli died in 1901 but his wife and daughter continued to operate the factory, using the crowing cockerel mark. In 1934, they sold the trademark to Amerigo Menegatti, the factory's former artistic director. Economic conditions forced Menegatti to supplement the artistic wares with more utilitarian products, but all bore the cockerel mark. Cantagalli closed in 1985, but the Menegatti family still owns the trademark.

mold and are contemporary with one another. Then, there is a flurry of fact-checking to-dos: "Make sure *Cantagalli* is spelled correctly, and find out if the name of the company really means 'Singing Rooster.' Research the statement about majolica and sixteenth-century techniques."

Once again, the group considers several cuts to make the piece more cohesive, and someone suggests, "We can cut out the lengthy history of the manufacturer and lose the whole exposition on Renaissance style."

JUST THE FACTS, ADAM, JUST THE FACTS

"During the screenings of each show, close attention is paid to the specific details an appraiser conveys about dates, manufacturing processes, names, and other facts," Adam explains. "Marsha keeps a list and expresses to me the issues and information she would like to have double-checked.

"Each fact-checking always begins with a computer search. I browse around different sites to try and confirm information in multiple locations. A Google search might, for example, lead to Wikipedia, but due to the nature of Wikipedia, with its unconfirmed information supplied by a variety of Web users, I do not use it as a source to determine the validity of a fact, but I will use it as a resource that may lead me to more dependable information.

"Many times, my Google search returns results from books.google.com, which has scans from actual reference books that are published online. When biographical information about artists is necessary, I utilize askart.com or in some cases artfact.com. Both of these are pay sites, but the public can generally access them for a modest daily fee.

"With specific fields of expertise, I will often contact independent sources and ask for assistance. For instance, we had a slot machine from the Palm Springs, California, appraisal event where there was a question regarding the production dates of the machine.

"Since it was difficult to determine from online sources, and none of our appraisers are specifically slot machine experts, I contacted the president of the Coin Operated Collectors Association [coinopclub.org], who was nice enough to get back to us with the information we needed. This happens quite frequently, and usually members of collector organizations, representatives of museums, and educational institutions, to name a few, are always happy to help out.

"A Web site that I visit about once a year is curtispublishing.com/list/magazineimagegallery.htm. This is an archive of every *Saturday Evening Post* cover from 1923 to 1975. In my tenure as *Roadshow* fact-checker, we have had the art for two original *Saturday Evening Post* covers. One of them turned out to be an illustration for a story within the publication, rather than a cover. We had to edit out any reference the appraiser made about the piece being the cover art for an old *Saturday Evening Post*."

7TH INNING STRETCH

With this said, everyone stands up for the traditional "lunch and stretch." It's a good time to check messages, take a quick walk or share a few personal stories. About one hour later, everyone reconvenes, refreshed and ready to go to work.

A BRIEF BREAK FOR GOOD NEWS

The next item is a porcelain vase that requires a lot of fact-checking, but toward the end of the group's discussion, the phone in the room rings. Usually, these meetings are not interrupted by telephone calls, but this one turns out to be very important. We learn that a major sponsor has just committed to underwrite the show

for three more years, and the room erupts with applause and congratulations (and high spirits that our plans and budgets are on track). And then it is right back to work. Celebrations will have to wait.

RECORD PRICES OR THE PRICE OF RECORDS

The remaining appraisals (seventeen in all) are handled much the same way. The group debates whether or not a statement spoken by a guest actually affects the value of the item being evaluated. The item is an autographed Beatles album jacket. When talking about the record inside the jacket, the owner admitted, "I wore it out playing it." Was this a figure of speech or was the record literally worn out? And if it was, did that affect the $130,000 to $150,000 value that the appraiser assigned to the album jacket? We decided that the owner's words simply expressed how much he enjoyed the recordings and nothing more.

STICKLEY BUSINESS

For the first time in thirteen years of *Roadshow*, a pair of Gustav Stickley iron andirons comes up on the screen. We are so excited! It was appraised by Eric Silver, director of Lillian Nassau, New York. Since we never before had this information presented, we have to start from the beginning. This realization brings a storm of discussion and a flurry of fact-checking to-dos: "Did Stickley make iron andirons or were they copper like so many of the other objects he made? Wouldn't copper andirons melt in the intense heat of the fire?" Also in the appraisal, a reference is made to Stickley's other economic activities, in particular a Stickley restaurant. This too needs verification. Finally, we

MARSHA'S MUSINGS

A subsequent check of the 1910 Stickley catalogue reveals that the only andirons offered were wrought iron. They were 28 inches high and had a depth of 26 inches. Their original cost was $24. Eric Silver appraised these particular rusty examples for $10,000 to $15,000 in today's market, and the Stickley andirons did stay in the show.

agree we must carefully check the details, and until we do, as far as the first pass is concerned, this piece may have to come out.

CUT TO THE QUICK

We did cut the next item appraised by Kathleen Guzman, an independent appraiser from New York City. The subject was "trade stimulators" (a type of early vending machine). This particular vending machine, circa 1930, was made to sell cigarettes and depicted the cartoon character the Yellow Kid. Although Guzman did a good job of explaining the vending machine, her appraisal didn't properly explain the complicated origins of the term *yellow journalism*, which was derived from the *Yellow Kid* comic strip and so we could not show the appraisal.

During the first pass, we spend a great deal of time suggesting ways to make the show shorter (with both big and little cuts here and there) and requiring fact-checking every possible detail. In one appraisal near

For the first time in thirteen years of *Roadshow*, Gustav Stickley andirons make an appearance. These were appraised by Eric Silver.

Oh really? That's what our guest said when she learned the value of this Clyfford Still painting. As of this writing, it remains the second highest appraised item ever to come to *Roadshow.*

the end of the episode, Ken Gloss of Brattle Book Shop in Boston discusses an archive of Secret Service–related documents and memorabilia. We argue whether or not the current owner has the right to possess these particular government documents, and we eventually conclude that the circumstances surrounding the acquisition of these pieces suggests he does. *Roadshow* must carefully ascertain the proper ownership of an item before it's selected to go on air.

BE STILL, MY FOOLISH HEART

The last item we review happens to be the most exciting: It is one of the most valuable items ever brought into *Roadshow*! And, as I mentioned in the introduction, it *was* the most valuable ever featured on our television

series until our Raleigh, North Carolina event on June 27, 2009 (See box "A New Record in 2009" on page 88 for details). It is a 1937 painting by Clyfford Still, featuring an image of the Grand Coulee Dam under construction, and it was appraised by Alasdair Nichol, vice chairman of Freeman's Auctioneers in Philadelphia.

At the time of the appraisal, the record price for a Clyfford Still painting was over $21 million, but it was a somewhat later piece and was painted in Still's mature and highly desirable Abstract Expressionist style and therefore, much more valuable (monetarily) than this figurative example from 1937. For insurance replacement purposes Nichol appraised this piece at $500,000.

Later, Nichol recalls that another professional art appraiser thought that this $500,000 fig-

CLYFFORD STILL

Still was an important American artist born on November 30, 1904, in Grandin, North Dakota, but he spent his childhood in Spokane, Washington and Bow Island, Alberta, Canada. He is credited with being one of the founders of Abstract Expressionism and was a leader of the first generation of that art form.

As an adult, Still held several teaching positions on the West Coast, and at that time, his work was representational. His more highly regarded abstract work came later. The painting evaluated by appraiser Alasdair Nichol was from Still's early period, but it did show some leaning toward Abstract Expressionism in its coloration and his expressive figurative style.

Still started moving toward the style for which he is best known in the late 1930s, but it was not until he was teaching at the California School of Fine Arts in San Francisco (now known as the San Francisco Art Institute) that he made his breakthrough into Abstract Expressionism.

Still is also called a color-field painter because his mature and most desirable work juxtaposed areas of different color—most commonly seen are irregular flashes of color against a contrasting background. The artist died in 1980, and in 2004 the city of Denver, Colorado, was chosen to receive the art from Still's estate. It is estimated that this collection contains 94 percent of all the pieces Still ever created, which makes pieces in private hands uncommon, to say the very least.

ure might be a little high because this painting was so utterly different from Still's mature style. Months later, and after due reflection and examination of the transcript of the appraisal, Nichol adamantly feels it was the right figure for this particular piece, and expressed the necessity to be conservative when doing appraisals.

During the first pass, several passages were slated for removal from this appraisal. These included a reference to the name of a moving company because it bordered on being promotional, and another reference to this painting having been the subject of a doctoral thesis. This latter fact was something that Nichol thought enhanced the value, but it was cut nonetheless.

The meeting breaks up after seeing the first pass of the first (of three) Palm Springs shows.

The notes taken at this meeting are typed and series editor Jeff Cronenberg prepares to make the cuts and changes that will be viewed at the second pass, which in this case happens just two days later. Cronenberg admits that getting ready for the second pass is actually relatively easy. "The first pass takes weeks to prepare; the second pass happens quickly."

HEAD THEM OFF AT THE SECOND PASS

The viewing of the second pass takes place on the second morning after the first past, meaning there is only one full day between the first and second pass. Such speed is necessary: The delivery deadline for the first *Roadshow* episode of the new season is mid-November and nineteen other shows must go through the same process on schedule.

It is amazing how much smoother the second pass is compared to the first pass. The tape is shorter; it contains sixteen rather than seventeen appraisal segments, and each one has been carefully edited to move the total show time closer to the final specifications of 56 minutes, 46 seconds.

Cronenberg has accomplished a remarkable amount of work in a short time. Old hands at this process might not find this all that surprising, but many of us agree it is almost like magic. We particularly note the word-error correction in the Jumeau doll segment; the context is now accurate, very smooth, and makes perfect sense.

For this pass, we don't start and stop the tape. The session is more low-key and fluid. To be sure, there are glitches, but as long as the facts check out and the editors successfully smoothed over the rough spots, all goes well.

Still, we do discuss ways to tighten up this spot and that phrase with the goal of getting a show that has the right feel and runs the exact length of time it is allotted. However, at this point, we do not yet finalize the order of placement of all the appraisals.

During our meeting, the appraisal of the Elvis belt undergoes a great deal of scrutiny and we debate how it can be extensively cut. Then, someone remembers that an Elvis Presley belt had been previously appraised on the show. Our next step is to check that appraisal to make sure this belt was appraised at the same or comparable value. Our fact-checker Adam Monahan quickly points out that this had been done, the two pieces had been similarly appraised, and all is well.

After this meeting, the second pass tape goes back to Cronenberg for further refinement.

MARSHA'S MUSINGS

Behind closed doors with all telephone calls on hold, I watch the tape from beginning to end in order to get a sense of what it is going to be like when the program is eventually aired.

There is always something that needs to be changed, always something that I have not noticed or heard before. For instance, I try to remove all the extraneous spots that are not moving the show forward, and I pull out unnecessary phrases in order to tighten up the dialogue just a bit. At this point, all the hard cutting is done, and I will make suggestions to Jeff Cronenberg; he'll implement all those that are possible and those things that can't change are part of what gives *Roadshow* that live-to-tape feeling. I do the final fine-tuning—well, almost the final fine-tuning. The show now needs to be mastered—meaning high resolution video—and audio mixed.

THE THIRD PASS IS THE CHARM

After the corrections are made, the third pass is ready for viewing. This is not a committee effort; it is my responsibility alone.

After I find the last remaining glitches, we then "lock" the show, known as the "picture lock." Once we lock picture, we create the master tape, the one that will be broadcast. One person other than me watches this version as a final review. Usually it's Sarah Elliott, segment producer or Jill Giles, associate

A NEW RECORD IN 2009: THE $1.07 MILLION APPRAISAL

The "Great White Whale" of 2009:
Ch'ien-Lung Dynasty jade.

For thirteen years, we hoped to feature a million-dollar appraisal on *Antiques Roadshow*; it was our "Great White Whale." We finally captured this elusive trophy at our Raleigh, North Carolina, event on Saturday, June 27, 2009. Asian arts appraiser James Callahan of Skinner, Inc. gave four pieces of Chinese carved jade and celadon from the Ch'ien-Lung Dynasty (1736–1795), including a large bowl crafted for the Emperor, a conservative auction estimate of as much as $1.07 million. The owner inherited the collection from her father, who bought the objects in the 1930s and 1940s while stationed in China as a military liaison. Callahan noted the fine quality of the pieces, evidence that they were not made simply for the tourist trade, and he found a mark on the bottom of the jade bowl that translates as "by Imperial order."

The Jade collection now tops our list of high value appraisals. It moves to second place the 1937 painting by American Abstract Expressionist artist Clyfford Still, found in Palm Springs, California in 2008.

producer. This person makes sure there are no typos in the wording that appears in the prices or descriptions on the bottom of the screen or any other errors that might have slipped everyone's notice.

TAKE 2!

But sometimes changes are necessary, especially with all the visual and factual material that comprises *Roadshow*'s weekly programs. Such tweaks are almost inevitable. You've seen how hard *Roadshow* staffers work, but occasion-

ally there is a slip between the appraisers' lips and the finished tape, or some other reason to revisit a completed episode.

In 2002, there was such an incident in an episode taped in Seattle. The item being appraised was a rare, highly desirable, and very valuable photograph of Marilyn Monroe. But this was not just any photograph. In it, the actress was completely nude.

After the segment aired, we heard from both stations and viewers about their extreme unhappiness at seeing all that movie-star flesh at 8:00 on a Monday evening.

A vocal minority vowed never to watch our program again and/or to withdraw their support from their local PBS station altogether. Not long after that the FCC abruptly changed how it defined indecent programming when Bono used the F-word at the 2003 Golden Globe Awards. The FCC's position was amplified a year later with its reaction to Janet Jackson's breast-exposing dance during the Super Bowl halftime show.

With the FCC crackdown, we decided to re-edit the Marilyn segment before the episode aired again. We judiciously displayed the "naughty bits" (as one of our guests said in the Feedback Booth) to make it more PG-audience friendly. Today, we would edit such an appraisal very carefully before the first broadcast. This is because the FCC could fine stations carrying the show, even if those fines might be overturned in court, and since a segment can't be removed from an episode, some stations would be reluctant to air that hour. Their tentativeness is a direct result of the caution all broadcasters feel since the Broadcast Decency Enforcement Act was signed in 2006. In all candor, this limit on expression is not only troubling to me but to most every other television producer in the nation.

YES, MASTERING

So how does *Roadshow* go from the picture lock to the high-definition master tape?

According to Cronenberg, "In the finishing process, we go back to the computer and replace every frame with high-definition images. During this process, the computer will tell us, 'I need tape three or I need tape eight' and we put in tape three or tape eight and the computer then does most of the work. This is also when Kelsey will do a final color correction and quality control pass."

When the tape is done, it is ready for broadcast into millions of homes. The process is laborious, and the steps are the same for all twenty shows that we produce each year. During and after the summer taping tour, the editing process at WGBH goes on practically twenty-four hours a day, with two or three shifts of editors.

Cronenberg sums it all up when he says, "In this chapter, you may have learned something about television production, but rest assured, editing *Antiques Roadshow* has certainly taught me a thing or two, and it's absolutely changed the way I approach a yard sale!"

Original Marilyn Monroe photograph.

"Go ahead and put it on!" Marsha wearing the Elvis jacket at the Memphis *Roadshow.*

ANTIQUES ACROSS AMERICA

Over the years, as I have crisscrossed America with

Antiques Roadshow, a number of objects have captured my imagination and become my personal favorites. In Memphis in 2004, I spotted a sparkly black suit completely studded with rhinestones; it turned out that it once belonged to Elvis Presley. As I examined it closely, I must have had a look of longing in my eyes. Watching me, our guest insisted, "Oh, go ahead and put it on." She must have read my mind!

The suit was appraised by Beth Szescila of Szescila Appraisal Service, and she was just as taken with it as I was. Beth said that if the guest could prove that Elvis wore it on his Comeback Tour in 1968, it might be worth as much as $100,000. If he wore it onstage during his Las Vegas years, the value is closer to $30,000, and if he owned it but never wore it, the value declined to around $15,000. We still hope that a photograph will turn up that shows Elvis in this black, rhinestone-studded suit onstage at a particular time and place.

FROM SEA TO SHINING SEA

We are a country of diverse national origins and ethnic groups and almost any type of object can and will turn up at an *Antiques Roadshow* event.

The bulk of what we see is American and European in origin. But objects from all continents—and many island nations as well—are likely to make an appearance. In some cases, it is clear why an object is found in a certain location, but in other instances, its presence in that particular place is almost inexplicable.

Let us share some extraordinary finds with you. We consider these to be the best, the most interesting, and the most historically important items uncovered during the last thirteen years. We'll journey in the same direction we prefer to travel across the country: starting in the far west and working our way eastward toward our home in Boston. And we'll contrast obvious regional items with an item discovered at the same place that seems totally out of place in light of where it turned up. The big takeaway point here is that with the constant migration of Americans, *anything* might be found *anywhere,* or as Colleene Fesko of Boston has said, "Stuff has feet."

MARSHA'S MUSINGS

Marilyn Monroe's dress from the iconic movie *Some Like it Hot*.

Another of my favorite items also was appraised by Beth Szescila, this time in Palm Springs in 2008. It was a black *peau de soie* (a soft silk fabric of satin weave with a dull finish) fringed dress worn by Marilyn Monroe in the 1959 movie *Some Like It Hot*. Orry-Kelly, the Oscar-winning costume designer, created the dress specifically for her. At auction, it would sell for $150,000 to $250,000.

I can visualize Marilyn in this dress, strumming the ukulele and singing "Running Wild" while Jack Lemmon and Tony Curtis, dressed as women, played sax and bass in the background. I was amazed how small Marilyn was and surprised to learn that she was sewn into her dresses to give her that signature, curvaceous shape. Although this time, I didn't try it on (it looked like a size 2!), I connected with this dress, and I am touched by the person who wore it fifty years ago—her incredible talent and her tragic life.

HONOLULU, HAWAII

We ventured off the road and far from home when we visited Honolulu, the capitol of Hawaii, in 2006. The Hawaii Convention Center brimmed with objects showing local heritage, history, and culture, but as Amy Santamaria observed, "The crowd was more diverse than anywhere we had ever been." The same can be said of the items we encountered.

OH, POI!

In Honolulu, an important ancient Hawaiian *Umeke 'ai* or poi calabash came in to be appraised. Although it looked like nothing more than a big wooden bowl, *Roadshow* appraiser Irving Jenkins knew this piece was an incredible artifact of Hawaiian culture.

The term *calabash* is usually given to a bowl made from the calabash gourd. Although this

The very distinctive shape of Hawaiian poi pounders.

bowl was made from native Hawaiian wood, the name is applied because it resembles a calabash gourd.

According to the guest, this piece had been in the family since the 1880s. It rested on her husband's grandmother's living room floor for seventy years. The children in the family would sit in the bowl and spin around until they became dizzy, or as the years went by, too big to play.

This bowl had been repaired, and although you might assume this would reduce its monetary value, in this case it does not. Appraisers expect to see a certain amount of damage in items that were used every day. In fact, the repairs add to their charm and historical interest.

This particular bowl was crafted sometime in ancient Hawaii from wood taken from the crotch of a tree, which gave the material a swirling effect, and from three cores where branches intersected with the main body. These cores have end grain that tends to rot over time. In the 1880s a German repairman named Herrick repaired this piece.

Herrick's trademark is the combining of three or more different patches, and this particular example has a large wooden patch, some small pegs, and a butterfly-shaped patch also with pegs. Jenkins says, "Each repair becomes a little picture." This bowl might be considered to be a Hawaiian national treasure, and it was valued between $20,000 and $30,000.

BRITISH ART HAWAIIAN-STYLE

Of course we expect to see an item like a Hawaiian poi calabash in Honolulu. This is no surprise. But many objects brought to *Roadshow* are far removed from their places of origin. At that same appraisal event, a grouping of documents, letters, and photographs relating to the founding

FROM SEA TO SHINING SEA

Poi is one of the traditional staple foods of Polynesian people. It is a paste made from the corm or underground stem of the *kalo* plant, which is widely called *taro*. A corm is similar to a bulb, but it has no scales. Hawaiian poi should not be confused with Samoan poi, which is mashed bananas and coconut cream.

According to legend, the *kalo* plant is the elder brother of humans. Kalo was the first child of Wakea, "Sky Father," and his daughter Ho'ohokukalani. The "child" was named "Haloanakalaukapalili." He was stillborn and his parents buried him in the soil, and from this grave sprang the first taro plant.

of the Tate Gallery in London happened to turn up. How did this important historical archive get halfway around the world to Hawaii?

A Hawaiian resident brought the collection to *Roadshow*. It had been given to her by her aunt, the second wife of Sir Henry Tate, who founded the Tate Gallery, now known simply as Tate. This archive was a time capsule that illuminated the founding of one of the world's most famous museums and provided a rare look into the process of establishing an art collection.

Catherine Williamson, director, fine books and manuscripts at Bonhams & Butterfields in Los Angeles, valued the collection at $10,000 to $15,000, and said she could, "think of many people who might like to have this archive for their library."

ALL ABOUT TATE

Originally, Tate was called the National Gallery of British Art, and was located on the site of the old Milbank Penitentiary in London. The idea for an institution focused solely on British art germinated in the 1820s, and over the years many art collections were donated.

In the 1880s, Sir Henry Tate, who had risen from grocery apprentice to sugar magnate and baronet, proposed to provide the funds for the building, and gave the new institution his extensive collection of contemporary British art. Specifically, he donated 80,000 pounds—a huge amount of money at the time—and sixty-five paintings and two sculptures.

The Tate Gallery opened on July 21, 1897. It began expanding beyond the confines of British art in 1917 when it acquired the collection of European modern art bequeathed by Sir Hugh Lane, the collector who established the first known public art gallery of modern art in the world. By the mid–twentieth century, the Tate had begun showing the history of British art along with international modern art.

LOS ANGELES, CALIFORNIA

We visited Los Angeles twice, once in 1998 and again in 2005. The City of Angels is the largest city in California and the second largest city in the United States, and not surprisingly we found a wonderful assortment of treasures in this rich and varied area.

GLOBAL FINDS IN A GLOBAL CITY

With its inhabitants hailing from all over the world, we knew that anything could turn up at *Roadshow* LA. Our 2005 event produced some truly exotic and unexpected items from India and Russia to the Philippines and Massachusetts:

Rare Goanese cage doll circa 1750, appraised between $30,000 and $35,000.

- Ivory and wood Goanese "cage doll," circa 1750. Goa is located on the west coast of India, and it was a Portuguese colony from 1510 to 1961, when India took it over. This doll has an ivory head and ivory hands and a wooden cage body covered with an elaborate silk costume that is of the period and decorated with sequins and metallic thread. It was not a plaything; it was a religious object—a depiction of a female saint. Actually, this piece may not have been made in Goa, but could have originated in a Portuguese or Spanish colony in Southeast Asia. Appraiser Stuart Whitehurst thought this saintly Californian immigrant was worth between $30,000 and $35,000.

- Russian imperial charger made by the Popov Porcelain Factory (established early in the nineteenth century). This beautiful charger—which is a plate with a large diameter—was decorated with the seal of the ruling Romanov family, and the outer edge was surrounded with a ring of glorious floral painting. Appraiser Peter Schaffer of A La Vieille Russie valued this nineteenth-century piece of Russian imperial porcelain at $65,000.

- Fernando Amorsolo painting, signed oil on canvas (full name: Fernando Amorsolo y Cueto 1892–1972) and dated 1948. This painting made its way to the western United States from the Philippines, and is a rural scene depicting women working and resting under a tree. Amorsolo is considered to be one of the most important of all Philippine artists and his work is gaining in monetary value. Frank Castle of Castle Fine Arts appraised this work at $25,000 to $35,000, but it should be noted that one of Amorsolo's paintings entitled *The Marketplace* sold in 1996 for $174,000.

- Massachusetts shelf clock made by Aaron Willard. This piece is a "case-on-case" clock and has a balloon top with a kidney dial resting on top of a roughly rectangular base that has wonderful brass cured feet. It was made in the late eighteenth century from mahogany and has its original finish with no paint loss to the dial. Sean Delaney of Delaney's Antique Clocks appraised the piece for $125,000 to $150,000 and said that any museum or serious collector would be glad to own it.

LOS ANGELES: THINGS THAT STAYED CLOSE TO HOME

* We came across a schoolbook originally worth perhaps 15 cents, but it had been inscribed by the Japanese-American internees at the Santa Anita Assembly Center. With these writings, the book is a poignant piece of American history with a value of $700 to $900.

* This very unusual and very rare desk lamp (see the photograph below) was made by artist Elizabeth Burton around 1910. She worked in her Santa Barbara, California, workshop until around 1920 and then had a shop in Los Angeles. She was a little-known artist in the American Arts and Crafts movement, and this lamp was valued at $5,000 to $7,000.

Elvis Presley memorabilia is associated both with his home in Memphis, Tennessee and in Las Vegas, his entertainment home in his later years. While in Las Vegas, the great entertainer gave an autographed record album and a macramé belt (different from the one mentioned in chapter 4) to a guest who brought it to *Roadshow*. These items were given an auction estimate by Philip Weiss of Philip Weiss Auctions for $7,500 to $10,000.

LAS VEGAS, NEVADA

In 2007 *Roadshow* visited the largest American city founded in the twentieth century, the city of bright lights and twenty-four-hour diversions—Las Vegas. Of course we saw items relating to gambling and entertainment, but we also encountered objects that challenged our expectations.

MAY I HAVE YOUR AUTOGRAPH?

The Nevada flag has a slogan, *Battle Born*, which relates to the fact that Nevada became a Union state during the Civil War in 1864. Yet the state was far removed from the war itself, and so it was a bit unusual that an outstanding autograph book from this war turned up at the appraisal event.

Highlights of this book included a number of

Civil War era autograph book appraised at $75,000–$100,000. The signatures of Union generals Grant and Sherman are in this book along with Jefferson Davis, President of the Confederacy.

important figures from both sides of the Civil War: General Grant, General Sherman (along with his photograph), Jefferson Davis, Robert E. Lee, and John Hunt Morgan, who had actually captured the man who compiled this autograph album during the Civil War. In addition, there were autographs of Frederick Douglass and Booker T. Washington. The book had been prepared like a piece of folk art, and appraiser Rafael Eledge of Shiloh War Relics appraised it at $75,000 to $100,000.

IN VEGAS, BUT OUT OF PLACE

- Many people associate the word *Belleek* with a town in Ireland and a very special type of Irish porcelain. However, some Belleek was made in the United States—but *all* of it was manufactured far away from Las Vegas. A guest brought a spectacular Belleek vase that he had purchased in a Las Vegas antiques shop, but this particular piece had been manufactured in Trenton, New Jersey by the Ott and Brewer Company. The vase had stylized dolphin handles and was decorated with flying cranes in the Japanese manner with a water scene behind. Appraiser David Lackey of David Lackey Antiques appraised it at $15,000 to $20,000.

- There are many places in Las Vegas where clocks are not allowed, but *Roadshow* is not one of them. Somehow, one designed by renowned Boston clock maker Aaron Willard made its way across the country and found a home in Las Vegas. It is a type of instrument known as a "tavern clock," which is a rather unusual

form. It has a mahogany case, and this example is still working. Unfortunately, says appraiser John Delaney of Delaney's Antique Clocks, the case of this piece had been refinished and the Aaron Willard signature on the dial had been touched up so that it was more visible. This hurt the value significantly, but the tavern clock was still worth the retail value of $15,000 to $18,000.

The owner of this nineteenth-century Belleek vase bought this Jersey gem in Las Vegas for only $65. When *Roadshow* appraiser David Lackey appraised it in 2007, its value had skyrocketed to $15,000–$20,000.

TUCSON: THINGS THAT STAYED CLOSE TO HOME

*C*harro is a term referring to a traditional horseman of Mexico. Mexican *charros* originated in the mid-1800s in Mexico City and Guadalajara. They were usually gentlemen ranchers with city homes. They would get together to have competitions of riding, roping, and other equestrian skills. The competitors were judged on style rather than by the clock as in U.S. rodeos. On Sundays they would ride in the park on their best horses wearing their finest clothing. In the late 1800s or early 1900s the National Charro Association was formed in Mexico and the activity was codified with rules and regulations for the competitions. Today rodeo show people provide high-quality entertainment and both men and women participate.

TUCSON, ARIZONA

An old Tucson aphorism asserts, "You get paid in sunshine." We would add heat: It was 104 degrees when we visited! Nature has not created many more spectacular settings for a city. It is spread across a desert basin defined by four mountain ranges, each lying in a cardinal direction from the city's midpoint and each exuding a different character. We found the same diversity in the objects we discovered at our appraisal event in 2006.

SADDLE UP!

While taping in Tucson, no one was shocked to see a Mexican *charro* saddle come in for appraisal. It was indeed a beautiful piece and it did have a few surprises.

San Antonio appraiser Bruce Shackelford told us that this saddle was beautifully embroidered—but not the kind of embroidery that was stitched using regular silk, cotton, or wool thread. Instead, this embroidery was done using fibers taken from the maguey cactus plant, also known as the *Agave Americana* or American aloe.

The silver on this saddle was produced in the town of Amozoc, which is known for its hand-chiseled or beaten silver on iron spurs, horse bits, buckles, and silver saddle trees. For more than 300 years at least one family in Amozoc has made spurs.

The saddle is from the 1930s or 1940s and was not new when it was given to the guest by her grandfather. There were burn marks on the saddle horn where the friction from a *charro*'s maguey rope had left its mark. Shackelford valued the saddle at $6,000 to $8,000, saying that if new, it would cost $10,000 to $12,000, and if

Charro saddle, embroidered with fibers taken from the maguey cactus.

you ordered one today you would have to wait a year or two to get it.

HARP AND SOUL

While we expected to see an item like the *charro* saddle around Tucson, an eighteenth-century harp from the French royal court certainly is not typical. While attending an estate sale, our guest—a professional harpist—was asked to look at this instrument to see if it was suitable as a practice instrument for a beginner.

Our guest concluded it was an antique and not appropriate for learning to play. She decided to buy it for herself, but the harp had already been sold to a local antiques dealer. The guest and the dealer were able to work out a deal, and the harp went home with the harpist for $2,400—not a steep price for the average harp, but this one was far from average.

It bears the mark of Jean-Henri Naderman (1735–1799), who was made harp-maker to Marie Antoinette in 1778. (Examples of his work are marked *Luthier Facteur de Harpe Ordinaire de Service de la Reine*, which translates as "harp maker in service of the queen.") Naderman was a prominent builder of single-action pedal harps and a publisher of chamber music, especially for the harp.

The soundboard on the harp brought into *Roadshow* was decorated with depictions of roses, and the appraiser, Andrew Dipper of Givens Violins, expressed the opinion that this dated the harp to the year 1776. In France, 1776 was the "year of the rose." Dipper explained that this designation can be traced to Rose Bertin

Eighteenth-century harp made by Jean-Henri Naderman for the French royal court.

(1747–1813), Marie-Antoinette's dressmaker and milliner, who set the fashion style at the time: roses.

Because of the historical significance of this harp, Dipper valued it at $60,000. Who would imagine that a harp that may have been played by Marie Antoinette would turn up in the southern Arizona desert?

NEBRASKA: NEVER LEFT HOME

* A Mennonite cabinet, with a sponge-painted faux finish, circa 1890, was probably made in Nebraska. The appraised value was $8,000.
* A group of ephemera from the Trans-Mississippi and International Exposition held in Omaha in 1898. The collection, which included a never-used poster and a photograph of the guest's great-great-grandfather dressed in the uniform of an English bobby to patrol the exposition ground, was valued at $2,955 to $3,165.
* Frank Lloyd Wright plans for a prairie-style house built in Nebraska. The grouping included letters and a drawing of the house. The lot was valued at $100,000 to $125,000.

OMAHA, NEBRASKA

Omaha was founded along the banks of the Missouri River in 1854 to outfit those traveling the Oregon and Mormon trails. Today, it is the largest city in Nebraska, home to a number of *Fortune* 500 companies, as well as to Warren Buffet, who is affectionately known as "the Oracle of Omaha."

Omaha's central location makes it one of the major crossroads in America, but when *Roadshow* visited in 2005, the city seemed like one of the great crossroads of the world. Take a look of some of the objects that turned up.

A BOWL OF GRATITUDE

One of the more intriguing pieces was a bowl that appraiser Lark Mason, president of iGavel, speculated was a gift from the Chinese Ch'ien-lung (Qianlong) Emperor (1736–1795), or a member of his court, to a Tibetan temple sometime in the late eighteenth century. The story of how this bowl got from China to Omaha is fascinating; it involves the Boxer Rebellion of 1900.

The bowl was a gift to the guest's great-grandmother when her great-grandfather was the secretary to the ambassador to China. For more than eight weeks her grandparents were caught in the Boxer legation siege in Beijing. After the harrowing experience was over, the bowl was given to them by grateful Chinese citizens.

This large blue and white bowl was decorated with the eight Buddhist emblems or the "auspicious eight": a conch shell, a lotus blossom, a wheel, a parasol or umbrella, an endless knot, a pair of golden fishes, a victory banner, and a treasure vase. Inside the bowl are other designs based on Tibetan Buddhist symbols, and on the bottom, the seal mark of Ch'ien-lung.

The appraiser, Lark Mason, valued this bowl at $40,000.

A WHALE OF A PIE

Omaha is a long way from the sea, and there is certainly no whale hunting in the Missouri River. But a pie crimper, carved from a whale's tooth (sometimes referred to as *whale ivory*) and embellished with abalone shell and baleen (the fringe that hangs from a baleen whale's upper jaw), ended up there anyway. This pie crimper was actually made from two different types of whales; the tooth was from a member of the Odontoceti family of toothed whales while the baleen was provided by a member of the Mysticeti or baleen whale family. To pass time on long whaling voyages, sailors carved items from whales' teeth and sometimes used other parts of their quarry to make keepsakes for loved ones back home. This pie crimper—with its mermaid handle—was probably intended for a wife or sweetheart, and was used to crimp the top and bottom crusts of a pie together before baking. Appraiser Ken Farmer of Ken Farmer Auctions was excited about this very rare piece and said that a pre-auction estimate would be $6,000 to $9,000.

THE CENTER OF ATTENTION TABLE

In Omaha, we discovered an exceptionally exquisite nineteenth-century table that a family would place in the center of its parlor for maximum attention. Its beautifully inlaid (marquetry) top contained images of birds picking nuts and

ROSEWOOD BY ANY OTHER NAME

Rosewood is derived from a variety of different trees that produce a brownish, richly veined wood that reportedly has a sweetish smell when sawn into lumber. There are at least two major varieties of rosewood:
* Dalbergia nigra or Brazilian rosewood, which is now on the endangered species list
* Dalbergia latifolia or East Indian Rosewood
* Only a few species of trees in the genus Dalbergia produce rosewood.

berries, all surrounded with a floral swag. The top was made in France and the base was crafted in New York City by a very skilled but anonymous cabinetmaker between 1865 and 1875. The wood is primarily rosewood, which does not come from a rosebush or a rose tree as many suppose.

This table had a long journey from France to New York to Omaha, and it suffered damage in its travels. The surface was split and there was loose molding, loose pieces, and minor breaks. Still, appraiser Brian Witherell of Whiterell's Americana Auctions believed that the piece was worth $10,000 in its current condition and $20,000 to $30,000 if properly restored.

Porcelain bowl made in China in the late eighteenth century and given to the guest's great-grandmother.

ST. PAUL, MINNESOTA

The citizens of Pig's Eye Landing decided that this was no name for a town, so in 1849 they renamed it St. Paul. Good thinking. Now known for its proximity to Minneapolis and its famous businesses such as 3M, St. Paul is an important Midwestern metropolis.

St. Paul and its twin city, Minneapolis (which we visited in 1996), have a diverse population, which was reflected in the objects brought to *Roadshow* in 2005.

DESERT VASES

We were amazed by a pair of vases that one would expect to find in the desert in the Southwest, particularly around Santa Fe and Albuquerque, New Mexico. They were the fairly early work of famed potter Maria Martinez (1887–1980), who primarily made black-on-

black pottery, working with her husband, Julian, when he was alive and then with her son, daughter-in-law, and grandson. A *true* pair of vases like the ones in St. Paul is very rare, and the appraiser, Bruce Shackelford, admitted they were the only matched pair he had ever seen. The decoration was of Avanyu, a Tewa deity who was the guardian of water. This pair of vases from the early 1920s was valued at $45,000 to $55,000.

A WATCH FULL OF SURPRISES

Who would have thought that the most valuable watch ever held by appraiser Paul Hartquist—an early-twentieth-century Patek Philippe pocket watch in an 18-karat gold case—would turn up in his own hometown at a *Roadshow* event? Patek Philippe is a manufacturer of fine timepieces in Geneva, Switzerland. This very complicated pocket watch

This rare pair of Maria Martinez Vases was valued at $45,000 to $55,000.

tells the time, of course, but it also has a split chronograph that allows the watch owner to time two events simultaneously, a minute register for the chronograph, and a minute repeater that chimes the time to the minute when a slide is activated. In addition, there is a moon-phase indicator and a perpetual calendar that adjusts for leap year. The watch comes complete with two extra mainsprings and an extra crystal. In 2005, Hartquist said that the Patek Philippe company was buying examples of fine watches such as this one at auction for its museum and would pay close to a quarter of a million dollars. This came as quite a surprise for the guest who had had it appraised fifteen years ago for a mere $6,000!

THE HARD LIFE TABLE

We may never know how a particular table, crafted and decorated in Baltimore, Maryland, got to St. Paul, Minnesota. But when Baltimore appraiser J. Michael Flanigan noticed it, he recalled, "They could have scooped me off the floor." This table had a very rough life; the paint had been stripped off its top and its legs had been shortened by about 6 inches. That would render most pieces of American furniture virtually worthless. But not this early nineteenth-century table. This is because the apron under the top of the table was still beautifully covered with

This 18-karat gold Patek Philippe pocket watch is worth close to a quarter of a million dollars.

original miniature American paintings. Flanigan reported that "Baltimoreans led every other city when it came to decorating their furniture with paint." Despite its alterations, this table was valued at $20,000 to $25,000.

THE LIFE AND TIMES OF GEORGE H. OHR (1857–1918)

* Born in 1857 in Biloxi, Mississippi, Ohr studied pottery under Joseph Meyer in New Orleans in 1879. Meyer taught Ohr how to make pottery.

* In 1882, Ohr returned to Biloxi and built his first workshop.

* In 1888, Ohr and Meyer became the potters for the New Orleans Art Pottery Company, which soon dissolved and became the New Orleans Art Pottery Club.

* Ohr and Meyer shared the philosophy that there would be no two pieces alike.

* In 1890, Ohr created the Biloxi Art and Novelty Pottery, but his facility burned in the 1894 fires that consumed most of Biloxi, destroying more than 10,000 of Ohr's pieces.

* In 1904 Ohr won a silver medal at the St. Louis World's Fair, but during his lifetime he sold relatively few works. In 1910, he closed his shop and turned it into the Ohr Boys Aut2 Repair Shop for his son.

* Ohr died in 1918.

One side note: Ohr packed a box of pottery for shipping and addressed it to the Smithsonian Institution, but the box was never sent. In 1973, when antiques dealer Jim Carpenter bought Ohr's stock (about 10,000 pieces), he saw the box and had it delivered to its intended recipient. Ohr would have been very pleased.

MOBILE, ALABAMA

We visited the state of Alabama twice, traveling to Birmingham in 1999 and Mobile in 2006. Mobile is a major seaport and is famed for its diverse architecture resulting from English, French, and Spanish rule.

DESK IN A BOX

The family of George and Martha Washington was represented in Mobile too. We encountered a box that opened into a small lady's writing desk (also known as a lap desk or traveling desk). It was initially given by the Marquis de Lafayette to Eliza Parke Custis, Martha Washington's granddaughter, who in turn gave it to her daughter Eliza Law in 1823.

The desk was obtained at the sale of the estate of Edmund Law Rogers Smith of Columbiana, Alabama (in Shelby County, near Birmingham), who was a descendant of Eliza Law.

Items at this sale, including this eighteenth-century writing desk, were known to have been at Mount Vernon while George and Martha Washington were alive. The desk is charming, with a place for paper, pens, and sealing wax, plus it had its original inkwell and sander. Such small eighteenth-century desks are certainly not unknown, but few have a significant monetary value. C. Wesley Cowan of Cowan's Auctions, Inc. of Cincinnati, Ohio, reports that this piece is much more valuable because of its ironclad provenance (its origin and ownership history) and its association with important American historical figures. In Cowan's opinion, if this piece were sold at auction, it would bring between $30,000 and $50,000.

THE MAD POTTER'S VASE

The renowned American ceramic artist George Ohr dubbed himself the "Mad Potter of Biloxi." Biloxi is a seacoast town located just about sixty-five miles southwest of Mobile, and finding an Ohr vase in Mobile was a pleasure, but frankly, not a surprise.

Suzanne Perrault of Rago Arts & Auction Center, calls Ohr "the greatest ceramic artist, living or dead, in this country." His work did not come to national attention until the 1970s, after Jim Carpenter bought Ohr's stock, which had been stored in the Aut2 Repair Shop. He began promoting Ohr's work and selling the pieces slowly. Soon the formerly obscure potter got the recognition he deserved.

A descendant of George Ohr through his son, Otto, brought the particular vase into *Roadshow.* It is a larger than normal piece for Ohr, who worked with pieces that were hand-sized. Anything larger is unusual.

The very attractive glaze on this vase, which is a mottled green and raspberry, also adds to its value. Many Ohr pieces tend to be black or brown and color that is this vibrant and alive is much appreciated by collectors.

The vase was appraised in the $10,000 to $15,000 range. The value was enhanced by the fact that the vase descended through the Ohr family.

This vase by Mississippi potter George Ohr was very valuable—especially because it descended in the Ohr family.

ORLANDO, FLORIDA

It is easy to associate Orlando, Florida, with sunshine, orange juice, massive conventions, and a plethora of amusement parks, but when *Roadshow* came to the central Florida city in the summer of 2007, we found so much more.

FAVORITE FINDS FROM FAR AWAY

• The weather was very hot in Orlando, so

appraising a painting of a snowcapped landscape seemed somewhat incongruous for both the time of year and the locale. This particular landscape was painted by Fern Isabel Coppedge (1883–1951), an American Impressionist who is best known for her snow-scene landscapes of the area near New Hope, Pennsylvania, and one of two significant women artists of the New Hope artist colony (often called the Colony). This is an unusually large and fine

Winter scene painted by Fern Isabel Coppedge.

example of her work, and Alasdair Nichol, vice chairman of Freeman's Auctioneers in Philadelphia, thought it was worth as much as $200,000. That is not bad for a painting that was given to the guest's grandfather, who was a surgeon, in order to settle a doctor bill!

- We examined an Egyptian stone sculpture that was a long way from home. According to the current owner, it was bought in Cairo by her grandfather from a man named Mr. Blanchard. Appraiser Anthony Slayter-Ralph of Anthony Slayter-Ralph Fine Arts commented that this particular dealer sold many genuine Egyptian artifacts to Western collectors and a number of these are now in museums. This piece was just a fragment of a female figure. Because it lacked part of its top and bottom, it was hard to determine with certainty who or what it represented. It might be the Queen of Pharaoh Psammuthes (Pharaoh of the 29th Dynasty, who lived circa 392 BC), or the image of a goddess. Slayter-Ralph felt this piece was worth $20,000 to $25,000 and maybe more if the hieroglyphs on the back could be deciphered to reveal that this was indeed a royal personage. Images of royalty, he says, bring more money.

- Who could imagine that four goblets brought into Orlando might be very rare? Certainly not our guest. They were beautiful with colors of green, ruby, yellow, and cobalt cut to clear. They were made in Bohemia, designed by Otto Prutscher and manufactured at the Bakalowits factory, circa 1907. Appraiser Arlie Sulka, who is managing director of Lillian Nassau, LLC in New York City, valued this set of four goblets in the range of $24,000 to $32,000.

ORLANDO: A GREAT OBJECT THAT STAYED CLOSE TO HOME

In Orlando, items that originated close to central Florida were few, but there was one object that stood out. It was a huge aerial photograph of the Disney property in Orlando that included notations about where the various facilities would be built. It was a monument, of sorts, to the revitalization of Orlando and was valued at $2,500.

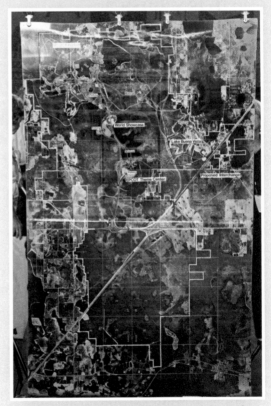

This aerial photograph of the Disney theme park property didn't stray far—its owner brought it to be appraised when *Roadshow* visited Orlando in 2007.

TAMPA, FLORIDA

On a 2006 visit to Tampa, Florida, we witnessed the way history comes in many forms and travels very far. A collection of circus photographs turned up, which is not hard to explain since the so-called "circus capital of the world" is located just a few miles south in Sarasota. But harder to explain was the appearance of the unexecuted 1805 marriage license that belonged to Davy Crockett. It came from the courthouse in Dandridge, Tennessee, which is almost seven hundred miles to the north of Tampa.

A PHOTO IS WORTH A THOUSAND WORDS

The circus photo collection featured an autographed picture of P.T. Barnum (Phineas Taylor Barnum 1810–1891), plus a number of prominent sideshow performers. In all, the guest assembled over 110 of these nineteenth-century photographs. Appraiser Daile Kaplan, vice president and director of photographs for Swann Galleries, appraised the lot for $10,000 to $15,000.

Among the collection, two images worth noting are:

- Millie-Christine, aka "the Two-Headed Nightingale": Millie and Christine were African-American conjoined twins joined at the spine. They were born in North Carolina in 1851, the slaves of blacksmith Jabez McKay, who had no idea what to do with them. He subsequently sold them to showman John Pervis, who exhibited them until he sold them to Smith and Brower.
- The Count and Countess Magri and the Lilliputian Opera Company: This is a two-pronged story. "Countess Magri" began life as Mercy Lavinia Warren Bump (1841–

This selection from an exceptional collection of circus-themed photographs depicts famous sideshow performers, the conjoined twins Millie and Christine.

1919). She became a schoolteacher around age fifteen, but left to work as a walking exhibit on a cousin's "floating palace of curiosities" on the Ohio and Mississippi Rivers. Lavinia Warren would later become associated with P.T. Barnum, through whom she met General Tom Thumb (born Charles Sherwood Stratton). They married on February 10, 1863, and Barnum sold tickets to their wedding reception for $75 each. Reportedly, Barnum received 15,000 requests for these tickets but only issued 5,000. Mr. and Mrs. General Tom Thumb made a fortune and lived a very lavish lifestyle.

"BORN ON A MOUNTAINTOP IN TENNESSEE"—WELL, NOT EXACTLY

We now insist on calling him "Davy Crockett," but the historic figure sometimes referred to as "the King of the Wild Frontier" preferred David, and exclusively referred to himself this way.

In 2005, a guest brought an unexecuted marriage license from October 21, 1805, to the appraisal event in Tampa, and its appearance there was something of a surprise. The hand-written marriage license was taken out in Dandridge, Tennessee (named after Martha Dandridge Washington, our nation's first, first lady), which was and still is in Jefferson County. The name of his bride-to-be was Margaret Elder, but she ran off with another man, supposedly breaking nineteen-year-old Crockett's heart. At the time, he decided he was, "only born for hardship, misery, and disappointment."

Davy Crockett's unexecuted marriage license that was almost tossed in the trash. It was valued for $20,000–$30,000.

DAVY CROCKETT IN A NUTSHELL

* The Crockett family originated in France. They were Huguenots, and when they were forced to flee France, their name Croquetagne became Crockett in the New World.

* Crockett married Polly Finley one day before his twentieth birthday, and they had two sons and one daughter. Polly Crockett died in 1812.

* In 1815, Crockett married Elizabeth Patton and they had three more children, a boy and two girls.

* In 1827, he was elected to the United States House of Representatives.

* In 1831, he opposed President Andrew Jackson and lost, but was elected to another seat in the House in 1833.

* When he ran for reelection, he was defeated and wrote to his constituents, "...you may all go to hell, and I will go to Texas."

Speaking to appraiser Francis Wahlgren, senior vice president and international department head of printed books and manuscripts for Christie's in New York City, our guest explained that this unexecuted marriage license was headed for the trash when the Dandridge courthouse was being cleaned out. The guest's uncle "grabbed it real quick" because he was a Crockett fan. Wahlgren valued this piece of very historical "rubbish" for $20,000 to $30,000 at auction, and $50,000 for insurance replacement value.

MARSHA'S MUSINGS

It was a bit hard to believe that these figures of Santa and the young Rudolph had really been the ones used to make the Rankin/Bass 1964 production of *Rudolph the Red-Nosed Reindeer*, but further research revealed the following:

* The figures were handmade by a skilled craftsman using wood, cloth, and plastic and were not mass-produced toys.

* Rankin/Bass gave their puppet creations to office staff through the years and considered the pieces to be souvenirs.

* Lipman suspects that several models of each puppet were made in case one was damaged, lost or destroyed, but these duplicates have not turned up for sale over the years.

Figures of Santa Claus and Rudolph the Red-Nosed Reindeer from the beloved television holiday special.

PROVIDENCE, RHODE ISLAND

Founded in 1636 by Roger Williams and one of the earliest cities established in the United States, Providence is the capital of Rhode Island. Closest to *Roadshow*'s home base in Boston, it is the final city we will visit on this chapter's *Roadshow* tour. Appropriately too—Providence has the largest number of working artists per capita in the country.

FROM THE RENAISSANCE TO RUDOLPH: WHAT IS IT DOING HERE?

* Some types of items do not come to *Roadshow* very often—for instance, old masters or genuine Italian Renaissance paintings. The few that do usually do not make it on television because the painting is unsigned and a meaningful attribution is difficult in the time frame available to the appraisers. In Providence, a guest brought in a roundel oil of a Madonna and child with an onlooker also in the painting. It was done in the Florentine manner and the artist was clearly influenced by the work of Raphael (Raffaello Sanzio 1483–1520). The guest told appraiser Alan Fausel, vice president and director of fine arts, Bonhams, that he thought the name of the artist was "Biggi." Fausel immediately informed the guest that this painting was no Biggi. Instead, the artist was probably named Franciabigio (1484–1525), who was a Florentine painter from the High Renaissance. This artist was known for his frescoes (paintings on plaster) and his portraits, and if this painting could be absolutely ascribed to him by specialists in the field, its value could reach $60,000 to $80,000. But if it is merely an attribution—meaning we are not absolutely sure who the artist was—that

value could be as little as $15,000. Still, not an inconsiderable sum.

- A vase evaluated by David Rago, of Rago Auctions & Art Center, looked a little drab with representations of flamingos that might have been pink, but instead were rendered in brown on a mottled brown background. It was made from stoneware, and at first glance it did not appear particularly valuable. Rago identified the piece as having been made by Boch Frères (Boch Brothers) in La Louvière, Belgium. The piece was also signed by artist Charles Catteau, a French designer who specialized in Art Deco designs. Rago said that this piece was dated from the period 1922–1930. It was a very special Art Deco piece by an important artist, and at auction could bring in $3,000 to $4,000. Take note: The current owner paid $25 for it at a flea market.

- We don't usually expect to find props used to make television shows in any locale. In Providence, a figure of Santa Claus and Rudolph the Red-Nosed Reindeer turned up. The guest said that the figures had been given to his aunt when she worked for Rankin/Bass Productions. Rankin/Bass was a famous stop-motion (frame-by-frame) production house best known for making holiday specials for Thanksgiving, Easter, Halloween, Christmas, and so forth. The guest claimed that they had been used to make the company's most famous animated special *Rudolph the Red-Nosed Reindeer* with Burl Ives as the narrator Sam the Snowman. This beloved program is an icon in American holiday TV fare and has been broadcast on television countless times since it originated in 1964. At the time, appraiser Simeon Lipman of Christie's felt that these figures were the real thing and should sell at auction for between $8,000 and $10,000.

PROVIDENCE: GREAT OBJECTS THAT STAYED CLOSE TO HOME

In Providence, a lot of items from New England turned up as might be expected.

✱ Rhode Island or eastern Connecticut curly maple highboy. Once the two sections were separated; now they are reunited. $24,000 to $26,000.

✱ The oval Nantucket basket made by Oliver Coffin on the South Shoal Lightship (a ship that worked as a lighthouse) circa 1870 that cost $1.25 when it was new and is now worth $6,000 to $7,000.

✱ Watercolor of a whaling scene done by Uncle Robert Joy of the ship the *Charles*. The image shows a fully rigged whaling ship and long boats in the water pursuing whales, and is a wonderful document of this occupation. $12,000 to $18,000.

✱ The incredible cute kitten in a can, an automaton by the Ives Manufacturing Company (established 1868) located in nearby Plymouth, Connecticut. When wound, the clockwork mechanism makes the kitten rise out of the can with the lid on its head and stick out its tongue. Valued at $8,000.

✱ A beautiful Whiting sterling-silver epergne made in Attleboro, Massachusetts. It is dated 1879 and has three-dimensional figures of bearded brewers on the base. $12,000 to $15,000.

FINAL THOUGHTS: APPRAISALS TO REMEMBER

As I think about my years with *Roadshow*, I am reminded of four appraisals that stand out in my memory. None of them is the most valuable or the most spectacular items that have been taped but each one has a special meaning to me.

The one and only time I saw an appraiser so overwhelmed by an object that he literally had tears in his eyes was in 2002 during a taping in Albuquerque, New Mexico. The appraiser was Lark Mason and the item was a carved marble lion from the Chinese T'ang Dynasty (618–907 AD). Lark declared it to be "among the finest examples of Chinese art that we have seen on the *Roadshow*." He called it masterful, truly magnificent, and from the "golden age of Chinese art." At the time, Lark valued the carving at $120,000 to $250,000.

My second favorite appraisal involved Allan Katz and a child's sled shaped like a swan that came into our Milwaukee, Wisconsin, event in 2006. It was so serendipitous. Allan was a last-minute replacement for an appraiser who had to withdraw because of a family tragedy. In came a beautiful, late–nineteenth-century sled shaped like a swan, which the guest bought for $35 at a rummage sale. Allan and his wife owned a larger, but similar version of this sled, and according to Allan, "What are the odds? I had lived with mine for twenty-five years and I knew every nail. Until that moment, I thought it was the only one in existence." The piece was carved from pine and was more than a mere child's sled; it was an important piece of American folk sculpture. Allan told us that he had been offered a substantial sum for the one he owned and accordingly valued this one at a conservative $20,000 to $30,000.

The third memorable appraisal involves the story of a German man who collected gold signet rings as a hedge against inflation. Dur-ing the terrible years of Nazi Germany, he had to bury them in his backyard. He survived and they survived, and eventually the man left Germany and moved to Las Vegas. He gave the rings to his daughter, who gave them to our guest who attended the Las Vegas *Roadshow* event and brought the rings in for appraisal. Remembering this story reminds me of the struggle some people face just to survive. Appraiser Barry Weber valued the collection at $19,000.

The last appraisal, also in Las Vegas, is about you and me—ordinary people collecting what they love without really knowing, or caring, what the pieces may be worth. The object was a piece of American brilliant period cut glass that was purchased for $25 in the 1960s. The family was not sure about its purpose, but thought it was a baptismal. The current owner cherished this piece and had actually been baptized with water from this vessel. It didn't matter that the baptismal turned out to be a punch bowl base that was missing its bowl! Appraiser Kathy Bailey felt it was worth $500 the way it was, but would have been worth much more if its bowl had survived. The guest was elated at finding out the story behind the object, and I just adore the look on her face as Kathy turns the piece right side up. The staff had the same reaction when we first saw the footage: Surprise along with a little laughter that we didn't recognize what Kathy immediately saw.

As *Roadshow* antiques its way across the country, we discover the incredible diversity of American material and historical culture. In many cases, as we go from city to city, region to region, we find what we expect to find— fine jewelry in New York; movie memorabilia in California; Native American artifacts in the Great Plains cities; and art pottery in Ohio— but then there are always surprises. The possibilities are endless.

A gathering of *Roadshow* appraisers for a segment on Jug Bands. From left to right Kerry Keane, Barry Weber, Gary Sohmers, Noel Barrett, Ken Farmer, Leigh Keno, Leslie Keno, Joyce Jonas, David Bonsey, Richard Wright, Andy Ourant

AN APPRAISER'S EDUCATION

"I have a piece and I saw one just like it on *Antiques Roadshow!*"

Roadshow appraiser Andrew Brunk confides, "Almost every appraiser has heard these words. But when the appraiser examines the object, he almost always finds it significantly different in some important details."

What details determine the difference between a table worth $1,000 and one worth $100,000?

There is no secret formula for acquiring the knowledge of an expert and there are no real shortcuts, as Brunk's more than twenty-five years in the field attests. For the most part, there is no school or class that will effectively teach the connoisseurship and savvy to understand the art and antiques marketplace. Acquiring that knowledge is invariably a process of osmosis: A gradual absorption of useful details gained by mingling and dealing with those who know.

MARSHA'S MUSINGS

What kind of person makes a good *Roadshow* appraiser?

✳ Our appraisers must be very friendly, knowledgeable, and yet never condescending, which is often a very fine line to walk. *Roadshow* appraisers share what they know with others in a generous and open manner.

✳ *Roadshow* appraisers must have the courage to say, "I don't know," when an object stumps them. But along with this admission should come a referral to someone the guest can contact who does know—and all of this offered with a smile. After all, people come to us with their hopes and dreams. We are touching more than their "stuff"—we are touching their hearts and emotions.

✳ *Roadshow* appraisers are comfortable on-camera and able to have a natural conversation with guests. They listen carefully to what the guest is saying, not concentrating on what they will say. (If the camera makes an appraiser nervous, practice will usually solve the problem.)

✳ *Roadshow* appraisers are good researchers on the fly. On taping days their cell phones are humming as they call on other experts to help solve a puzzle and provide special knowledge for a unique piece. Best of all, our appraisers know whom to call!

✳ A *Roadshow* appraiser is an enthusiast and good storyteller, and we rely on this dynamic to make our Picks.

DIFFERENT WAYS INTO THE MAZE

Many *Roadshow* appraisers started at a very early age, haunting antiques shops and flea markets and collecting the things they love. Others began their education in the world of art and antiques by soaking up all the knowledge they could from their parents or from any relative who was an antiques and collectibles enthusiast. Some studied fine arts, art history, history or even how to appraise in college classes or through fellowships and internships. Still others become entrepreneurs in the field of antiques, learning while honing their skills through the trial and error of buying and selling.

It is rare to hear our appraisers talk about themselves, so what follows is a unique look at their education, background, and experience, in their own words. They also offer thoughtful tips for aspiring collectors and appraisers.

EVERYONE IS KEEN FOR THE KENOS

Leigh Keno: Keno Auctions, New York City
Leslie Keno: Sotheby's, American Furniture and Decorative Arts Department, New York City

For the Keno twins, Leigh and Leslie, it all began as a treasure hunt. The two inquisitive young boys loved to explore their family farm in upstate New York where there were many outbuildings, each a world unto itself. There was a smokehouse, an early nineteenth-century homestead and other fascinating microcosms to explore—including an attic.

According to the twins, it was a *real* attic,

reminiscent of an old barn, with dusty, creaky floorboards and rickety stairs. "We went up there looking for things—always searching." In this attic was a box that might be credited with being the starting point of the Kenos' amazingly successful careers. The box was 3 feet by 4 feet and 1 ½- feet deep and was filled with all kinds of items that young boys might find fascinating.

There were parts of old things such as iron files, nails, nut and bolts, and even a spoon made out of coin silver. To the Kenos it was a treasure box and contained the essence of what appealed to them. They never permanently removed anything from the box, and it is still there today, filled with the items that were in there when they found it.

The next step in their careers was attending antiques shows with their parents. By the time they were twelve years old, "We had our own antiques booth—which helped us understand the business of buying and selling," remembers Leigh.

"We were blessed because we had parents who supported, nurtured, and encouraged us. We were convinced this was what we wanted to do in life. We had study hall at school on Friday and if there was an antiques show that weekend, our mother would call up and ask the principal if we could be released from school to go to the show because this would be our livelihood one day."

In their early years, the Kenos were aggressively buying and selling stoneware and they had their own checking account and business cards. Eventually, they would sell their extensive stoneware collection to help pay their college tuition.

Over the years, the Kenos learned important lessons from their collecting. One of their collections was of barn hinges and from these they learned to classify them as good, better, and best—in the same way that Albert Sack, the

Israel Sack is regarded as the preeminent specialist in antique American furniture and a model of ethical and aesthetic standards. A cabinetmaker who moved to Boston from Lithuania, he recognized the beauty of American craftsmanship and created his first collection in his small shop in 1905.

Israel Sack and his three sons—Albert, Robert, and Harold—became the "first family" among dealers in antique furniture, and helped form some of the country's most important private and museum collections. The firm's contributions include galleries in the American wing of the Metropolitan Museum of Art, the Art Institute of Chicago, the Hood Museum at Dartmouth, and New England College. Israel Sack, Inc. also played key roles in building collections of American antiques at Bayou Bend, now part of the Museum of Fine Arts, Houston, and the White House.

prominent New York American antiques dealer and a former *Antiques Roadshow* appraiser, had classified American furniture. "A collector sorts and evaluates a collection, otherwise we would all still be hunters and gatherers," according to the Kenos.

The twins went their separate ways when they attended college in 1975—Leslie went to Williams College in Williamstown, Massachusetts, Leigh to Hamilton College in Clinton, New York. They studied art, archeology, cul-

LEIGH KENO'S ADVICE FOR ASPIRING COLLECTORS & APPRAISERS

Follow your nose. "When examining an object, I believe in using all my senses—even my sense of smell. Not long ago, while smelling an Iroquois burl bowl (made from a knotlike growth on a tree), I detected a certain chemical odor that led me to the discovery that the piece had been repaired. What I smelled was the modern glue. I make it a practice to smell the inside of the drawers of eighteenth-century highboys, because they have wonderful scents like great wines, and the aroma helps put the pieces of the puzzle together."

tural and social studies, and even went on a few archeological digs at eighteenth-century sites.

LEIGH'S LEARNING TRAIL

After graduation, Leigh joined Doyle Galleries, the auction house in New York City, where within a few months he worked his way up to head of the Americana department.

"Bill Doyle became my mentor and gave me a checkbook for buying for the firm. I could write a check for up to sixty thousand dollars without his approval, but above that I had to call. Overnight, I was buying Tiffany lamps, Chinese porcelain and other big-ticket items, as well as entire estates. I was very uneasy about paying too little for something that I did not know enough about because I felt I had an obligation to pay a fair price. On the other hand, today as a dealer I am glad I have a basement, because it is now full of items for which

When they're together, it's easier to tell the Keno brothers apart—Leigh and Leslie—Twin Power!

I paid too much and am stuck with!"

After a stint at Christie's, Leigh realized, "I really wanted to be a dealer on my own, so with just six thousand dollars in the bank I started my own company, Leigh Keno American Antiques in New York City, dealing in eighteenth-century and early nineteenth-century objects. Recently I have decided to branch out to include more modern things because I love to be challenged and to learn. Today, when you walk into the office of my business, now called Keno Auctions, you might see an eighteenth-century Chippendale gaming table sitting next to a mid-century modern chair."

LESLIE'S LEARNING TRAIL

For his admission interview at Williams College, Leslie remembers walking into the waiting area and seeing parents and students sitting on period Windsor chairs from the Charles Davenport collection that had been donated to the college. There was also a Queen Anne highboy in the room, and Leslie could not resist removing the drawers and getting down on his knees and looking underneath the piece. He was fascinated by the highboy, and when he looked up from his rather single-minded examination, there stood the director of admissions. Despite—or perhaps *because* of—his unusual interest in the furniture, Leslie was admitted to Williams.

As a student, Leslie continued his fascination with the Davenport collection. There were about 160 pieces in all; furniture and some important paintings. In 1979, he prepared a small exhibition of thirty pieces in the Williams College Art Museum, where he hung up the Windsor chairs with fishing line so that visitors could see how they were made and appreciate the chairs as sculpture. The show was warmly

LESLIE KENO'S ADVICE FOR ASPIRING COLLECTORS & APPRAISERS

Leslie says that he is *still* learning at Sotheby's; not a day goes by that he doesn't learn something new. What's truly special about working in an auction house like Sotheby's is that there is such an amazing opportunity to see such a wide range of pieces in every medium and from every style and period. One week, there might be an exhibition of Greek antiquities, and the next week mid-century modern design. Unlike items seen in a museum, these pieces can be touched and handled—carefully!—and that is vital to the learning process.

received and earned an article on the cover of *Antiques and The Arts Weekly*, a prestigious collecting newspaper. "This was a great learning experience for me," Leslie said. "My brother and I had been dealing in a wide range of smaller objects such as early wrought iron, stoneware, weather vanes, toleware, British eighteenth- and nineteenth-century pottery, but now I was able to catalog and closely examine great examples of Pilgrim Century and Queen Anne furniture and it expanded my horizons. Also, as an art history major, I had a very special opportunity at Williams. Some of my professors were some of the greatest scholars in the world and that exposure, combined with the Clark Art Institute collection being within short walking distance of the campus, gave me a solid background that is essential to what I do now."

After graduating from Williams, Leslie entered Sotheby's training program, which involved rotating through a number of departments there. He was also expected to identify and value a very diverse range of items, from a French ormolu clock, to a Roman sculpture, and a piece of American furniture. Good mentors made the difference in learning how to do his job.

Leslie left the training program early to catalog furniture at PB84 (now Sotheby's Arcade). In 1983, he was made director of the furniture and decorative arts department at Sotheby's. He was 26 years old at the time.

NOTHING HEAVIER THAN A DIAMOND

Gloria Lieberman: Skinner's Fine Jewelry Department, Boston

Gloria Lieberman grew up in New York City and went to Queens College in 1966. She

After she wrenched her back, Gloria Lieberman followed her doctor's orders "not to pick up anything heavier than a diamond" and took a seminar on antique jewelry. The rest is history.

> ### GLORIA LIEBERMAN'S ADVICE FOR ASPIRING COLLECTORS & APPRAISERS
>
> Follow your passion and learn your field. Lieberman feels that most of her subsequent training has been learning on the job, although she continues to take courses in jewelry appraisal. Today, as a leading auctioneer and appraiser in the field of jewelry, she reflects happily on her "amazing cure" for a bad back.

started her career as an English literature teacher in the New York City school system, where she taught for five years, then moved to Washington, D.C., and then to Boston.

While she was raising her family, she ran a general antiques business that required her to do the heavy lifting and toting, which is routine in this very hands-on trade. She lifted one object too many and wrenched her back. The doctor told her something that turned out to be very prophetic—he advised her "not to pick up anything heavier than a diamond."

GLORIA'S LEARNING TRAIL

Taking the good doctor's orders, Gloria took a seminar on antique jewelry at the University of Maine, Orono (near Bangor) under Dr. Joseph Sataloff. "It was the only place that taught anything like it and it changed my life." Dr. Sataloff was a renowned physician who ran an annual conference on noise and hearing control for ear, nose, and throat specialists at the university. Medicine was his vocation, but antique jewelry was his passion and he ran a sort of "jewelry camp" at the university every summer.

Next, Lieberman worked with a jeweler in Boston for eight months, learning about gold, diamonds, and gems. She now knew that she wanted to specialize in this field and went to auction house owner Bob Skinner to tell him that she would like to start a fine jewelry department within his company—and he took her on.

ALL IN THE FAMILY

Nicholas Lowry: Swann Auction Galleries, New York City

A number of *Roadshow* appraisers come from families "in the trade," and they learn through their exposure to the things that interest their particular family group. According to Nicholas Lowry, president of Swann Auction Galleries in New York City, "I got my education through osmosis—no school, no classes, it was purely a learn-as-you-go approach.

Nicholas Lowry loves posters. And tweed.

NICHOLAS LOWRY'S ADVICE FOR ASPIRING COLLECTORS & APPRAISERS

Other than reading whatever is available on the subject, Lowry suggests that anyone interested in any field of antiques, art, and collectibles attend shows and auctions. It is an opportunity to experience the marketplace and how it works, as well as the chance to physically see and compare all sorts of items that might not otherwise be available.

But, Lowry says, "If you are not able to attend poster auctions or sales in larger metropolitan areas in person, peruse auction catalogues and follow the online auctions that are available to everyone through the Web."

"Swann Galleries was founded in 1940 by my grandfather and his nephew, Benjamin Swann, as a rare books auction house. They held their first auction in 1941, which was a long time before I was even born. When I was a child of five, and my brother was three, our father would take us to the auctions, and we would play and run around the podium during the sale.

"My mother was an expert in twentieth-century first editions, my father was an expert on autographs, and my grandmother was an expert on antique maps; but I really did not start to get seriously interested until I was in my mid-twenties."

NICHOLAS'S LEARNING TRAIL

"I graduated from college, spent some time in Europe, and after returning to this country began learning the business. I fell in love

The most important recommendation is: Learn to be objective about the things you own. Without that objectivity you tend to misinterpret any information you unearth. Also, at auctions, always get a catalog, and when items come up for sale, take a guess at the price they will bring. Then after they have sold, figure out why you were wrong—if indeed you were wrong. Learn from your mistakes, and when you find that you are right most of the time, you are ready to enter the current marketplace.

HOUSE CALLS

Ronald Bourgeault: Northeast Auctions, Portsmouth, New Hampshire

"We lived in Hampton, New Hampshire, where my mother's father had been the only doctor in town. My mother went on house calls with him and became friendly with everyone in town. Mother kept up these friendships and when I was young she would take me to visit these townspeople. I was fascinated by the old things in the homes and the owners would proudly tell me about their heirlooms or relics.

"All of this piqued my interest in history, and I became a dedicated collector of insurance calendars that had reproduction Currier and Ives prints on them. When I was eight years old I walked into Hyman Webber's antique shop [a local New Hampshire dealer]

with posters—and it really is true love and a lifetime commitment, not just a one-night stand."

Learning about posters—or any other field of collecting—can be really difficult work and it is hard work. "It is necessary to read a lot and currently there are no good general references for posters," Lowry said. "As I look at my library, I see books on war posters, travel posters, ski posters, drink posters, beer posters, health posters, sports posters, and posters featuring countries and cities—but there is no one book that covers them all."

Ronald Bourgeault began his antiques education when he was eight. In Tucson in 2006, he appraised this nineteenth-century chest of drawers for $4,000.

and asked for a job. He hired me for one dollar a day."

RONALD'S LEARNING TRAIL

"I ended up talking to anyone who had a lot of time (mostly the older ladies) and wanted to share their stories and knowledge. This pleased Mr. Webber, because I would often end up making a sale. During the auctions, Mr. Webber would have me auction some of the items that he would have trouble selling himself, because he knew that the people that I spent time talking to would buy from me—but not necessarily him. Mr. Webber frequently took me on house calls—partly to entertain me, and partly to teach me. Before we went into a house he would tell me, 'Remember, everybody has a price in mind'—a major lesson that I used throughout my career."

DIGGING UP THE PAST

Andrew Brunk: Brunk Auctions, Asheville, North Carolina

Andrew's interest in old things began early. "I grew up in the mountains of North Carolina and became involved in an archeological dig, a twelfth-century Native American village, which took place on my family farm. This was the beginning of my treasure-hunting. I loved unearthing things that had not been seen in centuries, and I remember picking a shard out of the dirt and seeing a thumbprint of the person who had made it eight hundred years ago. To this day I recall that almost electrical connection to a long-lost time.

"When I was young, my father was a woodworker and I worked in his shop and had my own little bench, making things from scraps. Along the way I learned how to identify types of wood and the fundamentals of furniture construction."

ANDREW'S LEARNING TRAIL

In 1983, Brunk's family started an auction gallery—"Good training for what I would become after I graduated from Guilford College [in North Carolina] where I majored in literature," he says.

In 1989, Andrew served an internship at MESDA (Museum of Early Southern Decorative Arts in Winston-Salem, North Carolina). "I was there when Frank Horton was still there. Frank was an icon in the field of Southern decorative arts. It was Frank L. Horton and his mother, Theo Taliaferro, who had the vision that led to the founding of MESDA in 1965."

He moved to New York City in 1990, right after the art market crashed.

"I needed to find a job with my only marketable skill—identifying 'stuff.' Fortunately, I was

Andrew Brunk explains the history and value of this beautiful nineteenth-century inlaid cherry corner cupboard. The owner purchased it for $600 in the 1940s. Today's value: $12,000–$25,000.

ANDREW BRUNK'S CHECKLIST FOR COLLECTORS

* **FOCUS**: Keep your eye trained on a particular part of the field and stick to it. For most appraisers, this concentrated study in one field can lead to a lifetime of ongoing learning and enjoyment. At some point, if you manage to learn one field well, you can always draw on the skills you acquired in mastering that subject and apply them to learning another.

* **SHARPEN YOUR EYE**: Make it your goal to look at images of as many objects as possible in your area of interest. Do this often. Look at auction catalogs and try to understand why one piece brought more than another. When you review books, scholarly works, and magazines, concentrate on each object. Look closely at masterpieces and see how they differ from the other items. A good visual memory will serve you well in the field of art and antiques.

* **MAKE FRIENDS WITH DEALERS AND COLLECTORS**: Seasoned professionals and passionate collectors are often extremely knowledgeable, and you will find many who are very generous with their knowledge. Successful dealers depend on their good judgment about antiques to make a living, and you can learn a lot from them very quickly. Many people who want to learn about antiques choose a savvy dealer to be a mentor and serve an apprenticeship if they can.

* **LOOK CLOSELY**: The devil is in the details. Forgetting to take the time to really look at an object is a serious mistake that even veteran dealers and collectors occasionally make.

  - How is an object constructed or formed?
  - What are the materials?
  - What is the style of the form?

  These are all observations that need to be made. Stand back and take an overall look, then step in and look as closely as you can for pertinent details. If possible, take the object apart. Get a portable bright light to help you see details, and then try to find out what everything you observe is trying to tell you (or hiding from you)—in many cases, common sense will help out. In American furniture, repairs can make for very big changes in value. Ask yourself questions such as, "Is one of the legs replaced?" "Has the top been off?" Learn the important questions to ask in your area of focus.

* **FINALLY, SPEND SOME MONEY**: There is an old adage in the field—you never forget your mistakes when your own money is on the line. Every dealer and collector has made missteps, and they never forget them and the lessons they taught. You will carry these incidents with you, and you always will remember the piece you should have bought, the piece you were tricked on, and the time you talked yourself out of believing in yourself.

  Remember, the most important factor in the marketplace is not age, condition or any other physical factor, but who wants it. It may be old and rare, but if no one wants it, it isn't worth anything.

hired by Lubin Galleries, an auction company on West Twenty-sixth Street where, in addition to cataloguing, I bought estates. I learned to walk into a place and assess the contents at a glance. If I bought the estate for Lubin Galleries, I got fifteen percent of the profit—if it made a profit. But if there was a loss, I had to absorb fifty percent of the loss. When I was wrong, it cost me a lot of money, a very painful lesson. I still remember my mistakes."

Andrew moved on to an internship at the Philadelphia Museum of Art and a fellowship at Winterthur Museum in Delaware. By 1998, he was back at the Philadelphia Museum of Art, this time as assistant curator of the Worldly Goods: The Arts of Early Pennsylvania 1680–1758. Jack Lindsey, curator of American decorative arts at the museum, became Andrew's mentor.

Two years later, he was at Christie's East, working his way up, in a mere two years, to become the head of Christie's American furniture department.

But even the cachet of Christie's couldn't keep Andrew from going back to North Carolina to join the family auction house. "Christie's was a plum job, but a regional auction house like the one owned by my family can really make things happen; we are lighter on our feet and have less hierarchy.

"My training over the years taught me how to look at objects and understand the factors that go to value. Just like in my early days," Brunk concluded, "I still sift and sort through things looking for items that 'sparkle.' The idea of finding a lost treasure and bringing it into the daylight still thrills me."

CRAZY ABOUT POTTERY

David Rago: Rago Arts & Auction Center, Lambertville, New Jersey

David Rago's path was a little different from that of many of his colleagues. When he was a college student, he happened to see a Roseville tea set in the "peony" pattern and his subsequent interest in American art pottery became "undeniable and unavoidable." Like Nicholas Lowry, Rago's interest in these items was a romance, a

DAVID RAGO'S SIX-STEP PROGRAM FOR COLLECTORS

1. **USE THE INTERNET**: The Internet offers free and easy access to nearly unlimited information. With the Internet you have the ability to learn more in a few years than previous generations were able to learn in a lifetime of searching for answers. Buy used books online. Join artnet or one of the other online information providers.

2. **SUBSCRIBE:** Read the trade magazines that reflect your specific interests. Just a few hundred dollars a year will keep you busy and your knowledge growing.

3. **ASK**: You are the reason online forums, auction house experts, *Antiques Roadshow* experts, and antiques show dealers are able to stay in business. While you have to be courteous, undemanding, and sensitive to others' availability and their need to do business, these dealers, specialists, and experts will take the time to answer your thoughtful and informed questions, because sharing their knowledge is an important part of what they do.

4. **THINK**: The questions that tend to get answered are the ones that are the fruit of reason and thought. If someone asks me what year George Ohr started potting, I think—hey—they could find that out in a book or online. If they ask me what compelled Ohr to make his marvelous creations over a thirty-year period and then simply quit, I am intrigued by the question and make time to talk to that person.

5. **REFLECT**: When you have done a combination of the previous four steps, kick back, and let it come together for you.

6. **REPEAT**: Steps one through five.

David Rago with fellow Pottery & Porcelain appraiser (and his wife!), Suzanne Perrault.

passion, and a compulsion to learn and understand all their complexities.

DAVID'S LEARNING TRAIL

"The timing for me was great," Rago remembered. "It was in the early 1970s and if my interest had developed later, I could not have afforded to buy what I liked. It was before the American art pottery craze had gotten into full swing, and there was very little information on the subject out there at the time. I had to learn it all on my own. I touched things, read books, and gathered knowledge whenever it made itself available."

He was on the forefront of the growing interest in American art pottery—and later mid–twentieth century and modern design. Interestingly, a Roseville peony pattern tea set would not impress Rago very much today.

IS THERE A DOCTOR IN THE HOUSE?

Wes Cowan: Cowan's Auctions, Inc., Cincinnati, Ohio

It is actually *Dr.* C. Wesley Cowan, because he has earned a PhD in anthropology from the University of Michigan and at one time taught in the Anthropology Department at the Ohio State University and was curator of archeology at the Cincinnati Museum of Natural History. Of course, archeology and antiques collecting are closely related; only the focus and goal differ.

Currently, Cowan owns his own prestigious auction house in Cincinnati and is one of the hosts of the PBS television series *History Detectives* as well as being a featured appraiser on *Roadshow*. Yet despite his many academic achievements, he traces his interest in antiques

Wes Cowan's love affair with antiques began when he was "just a boy with a bicycle."

and collecting back to the time when he was just a boy with a bicycle.

WES'S LEARNING TRAIL

Cowan is a native of Louisville, Kentucky, and remembers, "Like a lot of people, my interest in antiques started out as a kid. I grew up in a houseful of antiques and I went to auctions with my mother, who likes all things old. I became interested and would ride my bike around to the various antiques shops in my neighborhood in Louisville. I was interested in all sorts of things and saved my money to buy anything I liked that I could afford.

"My interest waned in high school, but while I was in grad school at the University of Michigan, I was looking for any excuse not to write my dissertation, and I started up with antiques again. As a student I had no money to speak of, but I became really interested in nineteenth-century photography. Most of the dealers I visited were not interested in photographs and I almost always ended up walking away with real treasures for just a little bit of money. I soon discovered there were other people who were as interested in photography as I was, and they would buy the photographs that I had found, so the next step was selling to supplement my income.

"Sometime in 1993 or 1994, I was asked to appraise a large collection in a Louisville estate. The law firm who commissioned the appraisal asked if I would buy the things I had appraised and I told them that would be unethical, but I did offer to represent their interests and sell it for them. I combined the photograph collection with other historical ephemera—manuscripts, autographs, political campaign memorabilia—got my auctioneer's license and had a very successful sale of historical Americana. After that, my business just exploded.

"People kept asking me when my next historical Americana auction would be, and wanted to con-

sign merchandise. There was a void to be filled in the marketplace for these types of auctions at the time and in 1995 I started my auction company."

WES COWAN'S ADVICE FOR COLLECTORS

"Over the years, I have had many mentors. Today I consider myself a generalist, with a specialty in nineteenth-and early twentieth-century photography. My advice for collectors, or anyone interested in antiques, is to seek out a person who is willing to share their knowledge and experience. I tell people who are interested in learning about photographs to start on the Internet, but then go to the library. Visit museums, join a collectors group, soak up as much information as you can! The reference librarians are dying to help you in your search and you may find some very valuable information just for the asking."

ALL BUSINESS
Richard Wright: Richard Wright Antiques & Dolls, Birchrunville, Pennsylvania

Our appraisers considered Richard Wright one of the most knowledgeable people in the business. Sadly, Richard passed away during the writing of this chapter. Respected and loved by all of us, he was eager to contribute to this book. He had provided us with his background, education, and advice. He was humble and it wasn't until after his death that I heard stories describing a striking young man, who in the 1960s cruised London in a 1920s Packard, buying antiques and had a stint as road manager for Fleetwood Mac.

RICHARD'S LEARNING TRAIL

It all started when Wright went with his parents to country auctions where they liked to buy their fruits and vegetables. "But I would take my allowance and go to the area where the household goods were sold, and buy whatever I could for twenty-five cents.

"I would buy just about anything that interested me and about a year later I decided to begin selling the things that I had bought. I opened my first antiques shop when I was ten years old in my father's furniture store. Eventually, I made more money than he did and he became my business partner when I was sixteen!

"Like so many other appraisers who I work with on *Roadshow*, I am largely self-taught. When you are buying and selling antiques for

Richard Wright; dolls were his passion.

YOU'RE A DOLL

"Not all that long ago, I was called to buy a collection of majolica and among the three hundred or so pieces there was a little leaf-shaped Etruscan majolica dish with a note on the bottom that said, *Bought from Richard Wright September 18, 1960*. Dolls are my specialty now, and my interest in dolls started when I bought a doll for one dollar, and sold it for five dollars. Years later, I bought it back for twelve hundred dollars."

your livelihood you have to get pretty savvy in a hurry."

RICHARD WRIGHT'S ADVICE FOR COLLECTORS

"People ask me to teach them about dolls, and I always say, 'No!' because you cannot learn antiques in a day. The truth is that it has taken me a long time to know what I know today and I still am learning all the time.

"Becoming knowledgeable in any area of antiques is a hands-on experience; you have to see it and touch it. Watching *Roadshow* is very helpful, but any knowledge that you pick up from the show has to be supplemented with personal experience. Those interested in learning need to talk to experienced and respected collectors and dealers—but once that conversation is over, the student needs to go out into the marketplace and test their knowledge."

CHINA TRADE
Lark Mason: iGavel Inc.,
New York City

Mason says, "I was bitten by a love of history in fourth grade. My mother opened up an antiques shop in Doraville, Georgia, in 1964 and my uncle owned an antiques business in Tallahassee, Florida. My uncle's business was located in a huge warehouse; he purchased all types of objects from single items to household contents and entire antiques shops. One year he bought a circus. As a ten-year-old boy, having an uncle whose job was selling wavy fun-house mirrors and even the circus wagons was hard to beat. What could be more exciting?

"My interest in history grew as I was allowed to touch and handle many of the objects that had a connection to the past."

LARK'S LEARNING TRAIL

Mason attended Georgia State University, the University of Tennessee, Knoxville, and Tennessee Technological University. He recalls, "In college I opened an antiques shop and hired fellow students to work for me. After two years, I learned what it meant to be a small-business owner, and in order to focus more on my studies, closed the shop and sold my inventory.

"After I graduated, my father gave me the best advice anyone could receive. He said I had a real skill and interest in art and antiques, and had a rare opportunity to align my future career

Lark Mason, sharing the good news in Grand Rapids, Michigan, as he discusses an eighteenth century Sino-Tibetan bronze that he valued at $5,000 to $8,000.

LARK MASON'S ADVICE TO ASPIRING COLLECTORS & APPRAISERS

* "Learning about Chinese art is complicated and challenging." He advises those interested to start by reading about China in general—religions, geography, history—and not focus right away on the artwork.

* After you have a general understanding of Chinese culture, go to museums and closely study the displays—reading the notations on the exhibits and really looking at the items being displayed. Take in and memorize every visible nuance. "It is very important to visually encounter these objects in person to begin to understand them."

* With diligence, you will start to develop an affinity for certain types of items and not for others. At that point, begin reading more books on these items, starting with general information and then specifics. This helps narrow your focus.

* "One of my favorite tricks," Mason confides, "is to sketch something that interests me. The sketching process forces me to look at the details and reinforces the image in my mind. This process creates a touchstone in my memory that can be referred to later and helps me in the identification and authentication process."

with my interests. I took his advice and applied to Sotheby's Works of Art Program in London, where I was one of the thirty American students selected from hundreds of applicants.

"After completing the program I was offered a job with Sotheby's in New York City. I was in the appraisals department for six years, and during that time developed a broad knowledge about many subjects and found I had an affinity for Chinese art. When an opening arose, I joined the Chinese department in 1985.

"By 1988, I had developed a working knowledge of the Chinese language and an expertise in Chinese furniture and export works of art. The former director of the Beijing Palace Museum wrote to Sotheby's requesting help with a book on Chinese furniture, and I took a six-month sabbatical from Sotheby's and moved to China. While in China, I visited countless workshops and collectors, improved my language skills,

finished translating the Chinese furniture book, and headed back to New York."

Lark Mason was a senior vice president and director of online auctions at Sotheby's New York until he founded his own company, iGavel, in 2003. He is an appraiser and advisor to museums and private collectors. He has curated shows on Chinese furniture, including one at the prestigious Asian Art Museum in San Francisco.

TOY MAN

Noel Barrett: Noel Barrett Antiques & Auctions Ltd., Carversville, Pennsylvania

Noel Barrett believes that the majority of people who are appraisers started out as collectors. "They have a passion for old things, and they enjoy discovering things that speak to them."

NOEL'S LEARNING TRAIL

Barrett began his career in antiques when he "found an old toy, like one I had as a kid. I bought it, put it on a shelf, and thought it looked neat. But it needed some 'friends' to keep it company, so I started collecting.

"What I started with was purely nostalgic, but it opened my eyes, and I started seeing things that I wanted to buy. A large percentage of the people who become appraisers have a kinship to the material they collect. Eventually, I became a dealer, which in my opinion is the only true path to becoming a serious appraiser."

Noel Barrett: "Learn by doing" is his best advice to aspiring collectors and appraisers.

NOEL BARRETT'S ADVICE TO ASPIRING COLLECTORS & APPRAISERS

"I learned from doing. I was never really a student per se, and when I started there were not many books on the subject. I remember a specialist in toys at the time who supposedly had all the books on the subject and they all fit on one shelf. There were maybe thirty books in all. Now a thousand books probably would not cover all the printed material that is available to collectors and appraisers on this subject.

"It is in the buying and selling over the years that you really learn, and generally you learn more from your mistakes—when you pay too much for something or shy away from buying something you should—those are the lessons that really stick with you. But you have to jump in to learn those lessons. You don't gain real knowledge by sitting on the sidelines."

GRANDMOTHER HAD IT

Catherine Baron: Catherine's Estates & Appraisals, Tucson, Arizona

Catherine Baron's interest began in her grandmother's attic in Cameron, Missouri. "I used to root around in Grandmother's two-story farmhouse. There was a sense of uncovering treasures that had a haunting familiarity, yet they were exotic and unknown. These became my playthings as a child."

CATHERINE BARON'S ADVICE TO COLLECTORS & APPRAISERS

"As a college student, I did not have two nickels to rub together. I furnished my dorm rooms and apartments with things I found in flea markets. I enjoyed touching the items and getting the tactile impression of what they were—the smell of things, the feel, how they actually are. I believe that in order to be an appraiser you have to have an intuitive interest in all these aspects so that you can really know the piece you are appraising."

CATHERINE'S LEARNING TRAIL

"Educationally, I took the scenic route. I studied a lot of foreign languages, but I actually majored in biology for my undergraduate work because I wanted to know how things work. I was introduced to the museum world as an undergraduate, when I worked in the Natural History Museum at the University of Kansas in Lawrence. Then I got a master's in art history—actually classical art history, with an emphasis on Greek and Roman art—an area that attracted me because the idealism and realism of classical art is the foundation for all the art that followed."

MUSEUM APPRAISING

"Later, I worked in the Memphis museum system doing such things as downtown walk-ing tours and tours of Elmwood Historic Cemetery." Baron also worked at the Mallory-Neely House and at the Magevney House, and sometimes she was asked by staff to do an appraisal in one of these houses. The Mallory-Neely House is a twenty-five-room Victorian mansion built in 1852 and has most of its original furnishings. The Magevney House is an 1830s cottage and one of the oldest homes still standing in Memphis.

"When I was asked to do an appraisal of a painting or a piece of furniture, I really enjoyed the research, and I always felt very fortunate to have the opportunity to handle these beautiful artifacts while determining their monetary value.

Catherine Baron from Tucson, Arizona took "the scenic route" on her path to becoming an appraiser.

"After graduate school, in 2001, I became the collections manager for the Arizona Historical Society and that was my first experience with *Roadshow*. The first day I was there, the *Roadshow* was considering taping the Historical Society's Murphy silver collection for one of their field segments. They decided to do the Pima Air and Space Museum instead. I was very disappointed.

"I started my own appraisal and estate business in 2003, joined the American Society of Appraisers, and got my auctioneer's license. I was truly in the trenches, building a business while continuing to learn about antiques and the process of appraisals. It has been an invaluable experience. When *Roadshow* returned in 2006 to tape for the 2007 season, I contacted them and asked if they needed another appraiser. The rest is history."

APPRAISERS' FAVORITE *ROADSHOW* MOMENTS

Our appraisers generously share their time and talent with us; many have been with *Roadshow* since the beginning. So we wanted to learn, why: "Why do you do this?" and "Do you have a favorite memory?" Here are their answers:

David Rago's Epiphany

"*Roadshow* changed my feelings about business—and my business life has never been the same. My favorite moment came during the show's third season, when I realized that I was actually working with an appraiser from a *competing* auction house. We were talking to each other and helping each other in earnest as we did our *Roadshow* work. What a surprise. I never expected that 'trench warfare' business competition could give way to collegial cooperation.

I haven't looked back since then."

Steven Dice's Impetuous Error

"When a guest laid an ivory folding ruler on my table that was signed *A. Stanley* for Augustus Stanley, I just lost it. The excitement of finding such a rare piece made me forget *Roadshow* schooling—that is, not to give away too much information. Because of my error, this wonderfully rare piece did not get on television. Despite my impetuous mistake, this was my favorite moment because the item was so unique and special."

John Buxton's True Tale

"I was sitting at the Tribal Arts table in Richmond, Virginia, when a couple approached me with a hand-painted wooden box. I told them I did not appraise that type of item, and they suggested that I needed to look inside. As I opened the little doors of the box it began playing 'Raindrops Keep Fallin' on My Head.' Inside there was a genuine shrunken head from the South American Jivaro tribe. It was the absolute real thing, and I was extremely excited. I immediately went to Aida Moreno, our executive producer at that time, so that it could be taped. 'John,' she said, 'do you know how many calls we get every time we put a piece of ivory [carved from elephant tusk] on the air? Just how many do you think we would get from something like that?' Of course the piece never made it to tape, but it's a story you just cannot make up."

Andrew Brunk's First Look

"I opened a miniature desk that a gentleman had brought into the 2008 Dallas event. Its cubbyholes and drawers were stuffed full of objects going back hundreds of years. The owner had never looked through the desk, and the great array of artifacts—some valuable, some not—had remained safely sealed away. The desk was an ark, carrying with it the complex history of a family; being the first one to see and delve into its contents was truly memorable."

John A. Delaney's Enthusiasm

"I enjoy the camaraderie among the appraisers, and I enjoy the interaction with the people as they come up to the table with their items. That's what *Roadshow* is all about for me."

James Callahan's Charmed and Surprised Moment

"A little girl and her two brothers brought in a Persian sword. I believe that I appraised it for around three thousand dollars. I wanted to tape it for television, but the two little boys would not go on the air. The little girl, on the other hand, stood right up and went before the cameras. During the on-air conversation it came out that their grandfather had given them the sword. I asked them if they knew how much he had paid for it. Not hesitating for a moment, the girl said, 'Knowing my grandfather, it could not have been much.'"

Gloria Lieberman's Love of Teaching

"My favorite *Roadshow* moment happens every time we tape a segment. It is when we are being miked, and the guest is nervous and asks questions that I try not to answer before we are taped. But I find that I am as impatient to answer questions as the guest is to ask them! It is at those moments that I realize how much I love to share knowledge and watch someone's eyes light up with the things they learn."

Jeni Sandberg's A Star!

"What I enjoy most about *Roadshow* is how genuinely excited people are to attend an event. I remember one lady in St. Paul who told me she just grabbed something out of her cupboard, knowing it didn't have any value, but she wanted a reason to come to *Roadshow*. Another time, in Spokane, the people were incredibly nice and they kept telling me they were so honored that we came to their city—I was even given a free cup of coffee at the local Starbucks when I told them I was with *Roadshow*. It made me feel like a star! These are the things that turn a very long day of *Roadshow* appraisals into an incredible experience."

ASPIRING COLLECTORS AND APPRAISERS—LEARN FROM THE EXPERTS

Learning about art and antiques takes years of devoted study, and the education never stops. Art and antique specialists must keep up with the marketplace by reading everything available concerning their field. They must keep their ear to the ground to stay aware of the constant changes and future trends in the marketplace, as well as what prices are going up and which are coming down.

An art and antiques appraiser must learn how to distinguish truth from myth and be able to locate and apply countless pieces of information that illuminates the history and the value of an object.

As diverse as their subjects and personalities, there is universal agreement among the art, antiques, and collectible appraisers on five important steps that will help you become an expert in your area of interest and to stay on top of the game. Professional or passionate collector, all agree that the joy in owning what you love is increased with what you know about the object.

- **Read whatever is available on your subject.** Subscribe to trade magazines, newspapers, and newsletters that reflect your specific interests, read books, scholarly works, and auction catalogs. Build your own library—and use it frequently.
- **Research on the Internet.** The Internet has it all—perhaps even too much! Search and bookmark any site that relates to your specific interests. Build a network of Internet pen pals that share the same interests and are willing to share their information (and excitement). Keep in mind that knowing the right questions is as important to building these relationships as finding the answers. Use your library. Reference librarians are happy to help you, and libraries often have access to, or can help you locate, copies of books that are out of print.
- **Observe at antiques shows, auctions, flea markets, museums.** Every visit can be a valuable lesson. Shows and flea markets are places where you can see an object, touch it, compare it, and even smell it—and it is a place to ask questions. Most dealers are happy to tell you what they know. At auctions and auction previews you can observe an item in detail and watch the marketplace in action. It can be thrilling to study an auction catalog in detail then see it for yourself. Museums are often the place to see the rare and valuable—usually supplemented by excellent research materials available from your local library.
- **Find a mentor, join collector clubs and associations that reflect your interests.** You will usually find people who are passionate about their collecting, and are very knowledgeable—and anxious and willing to share

what they know. Many people find an experienced dealer or appraiser to be their mentor. Either way, having a good mentor will increase your knowledge and confidence.

- **Enter the marketplace and buy something—something that you love, as well as something that is well-priced.** After all the reading, researching, observing, and talking, it is time to buy something for your collection. Testing your knowledge in the market-

{ LEARNING ABOUT ART AND ANTIQUES TAKES YEARS OF DEVOTED STUDY, AND THE EDUCATION NEVER STOPS. }

place is one of the most important ways to increase your confidence and skills—and, of course, have pride and enjoyment in a collection of things that you treasure.

FINAL THOUGHTS

If our guests and the wonderful objects they bring are the lifeblood of *Roadshow*, then our appraisers are our heart. Some of these highly skilled professionals are exceptionally charismatic, others dazzlingly learned, and still others are seasoned old pros, full of life stories to share. They are the bedrock on which *Roadshow* is built.

It is amazing how many of the appraisers seen on *Roadshow* started out when they were young children and maintained their interest in art and antiques throughout a lifetime. Conventional wisdom says that most children aspire to be firefighters, dog whisperers, ballerinas, rock stars, television reporters, or ballplayers. Yet there are kids who yearn to be antiques specialists. And for this we say: Thank goodness!

Landscape with an Obelisk, by Dutch artist Govaert Flinck (1615–1660) was stolen from Boston's Isabella Stewart Gardner Museum on March 18, 1990. This missing masterpiece's frame still hangs empty on the museum's wall awaiting its return.

MISSING MASTERPIECES

Did you know the halo of Christ was missing?

Well it is—sort of. It turns out that a physical halo, studded with precious and semiprecious stones, was stolen from a church in Honduras early in 2009. Also stolen from Honduras in 2009 was Madonna of the Sorrows, a carved figure that once graced the main altar of a church, but according to Interpol (the International Criminal Police Organization), they are nowhere to be found.

Interpol's list of missing items is staggering. There are rugs, bejeweled belts, a gold bracelet from Pompeii, a bronze sculpture of a chimpanzee, coins, Ottoman tombstones stolen from Turkey, ancient gold plaques from South America, clocks, books, pages from a Koran stolen from Tunisia, candlesticks, the pen of former Argentine president Roberto Ortiz, and the head of Julius Caesar, sculpted from basalt but missing Caesar's nose and part of his chin when last seen.

Think of it: The world is full of missing masterpieces! We define these as treasures that are master works of art that are valuable—culturally and artistically—and irreplaceable. And, as you will discover, a masterpiece means something different to each of us. Some missing materpieces were stolen. Some items were lost as a result of natural disasters while others vanished in the fog of war or are lost to time.

Still other masterpieces may be hidden in your attic or basement, or positioned in full view at any yard sale or flea market because they have fallen out of favor or fashion. Although they are not actually missing or lost, they are treasures no one recognizes. Of course, these are the most exciting finds for *Roadshow* fans.

STOLEN TREASURES

According to the FBI Art Theft Web site, "Art and cultural property crime—which includes theft, fraud, looting, and trafficking across state and international lines—is a looming criminal enterprise with estimated losses running as high as $6 billion annually." To understand this dollar amount, consider the following: In a 2006 account of the FBI's painting category alone, 166 Rembrandts, 167 Renoirs, 200 Dalís, and 175 Warhols are missing.

ROADSHOW DISCOVERS A PURLOINED TREASURE

Our most famous theft-recovery story begins innocently in Omaha, Nebraska, when a guest showed *Roadshow* appraiser Wes Cowan, of Cowan's Auctions, a daguerreotype portrait of Edgar Allan Poe (1809–1849). A daguerreotype represents the earliest photographic process with the picture printed on a copperplate. Cowan was very excited because only a few daguerreotypes of Poe are known to exist, and a new one would be an important historical find.

Our guest had purchased the piece for $96 from a shop in Walnut Grove, Iowa. Despite

MARSHA'S MUSINGS

When we began Season 13 in 2008, *Roadshow* became very proactive in uncovering stolen art. We teamed up with the Art Loss Register (artloss.com) to help find the sixty plein air (painted outdoors) oil paintings of collector Jim McCarty, who had had his entire art collection stolen from storage near Palm Springs, California.

We documented his missing paintings and publicized the theft during one of our episodes in a new segment called *Roadshow's Most Wanted!* As of this writing, Jim *did* recover one of his paintings.

In Season 14 in 2009, we proudly took this initiative to the next level. We now work with the FBI and local police in their efforts to uncover stolen treasures. Each season, law enforcement will try to provide us with the names of people who have been the victims of art theft. Our goal is to air as many "most wanted" stories as possible.

You can support our efforts. If you think you may be in possession of stolen art, contact your local authorities, or when appropriate, the FBI. If you think you have information about stolen art seen on our show, you may contact us at Roadshowstolenart@wgbh.org.

some damage—a diagonal smudge or scratch across the face—the circa 1847 photograph was appraised by Cowan for $30,000 to $50,000.

Shortly after leaving our *Roadshow* event, the wildly excited guest decided to sell the daguerreotype portrait. To do this, she needed to have it

The discovery of the theft of this rare daguerreotype of Edgar Allen Poe began when a guest brought it to the Nebraska *Roadshow* event.

positively authenticated, so she contacted the Edgar Allan Poe Society in Baltimore, and they in turn contacted Michael Deas, who had written the authoritative book *The Portraits and Daguerreotypes of Edgar Allan Poe.*

The society authenticated the daguerreotype as being one of Poe, but Deas recognized it almost immediately as being alarmingly similar to one he had examined in 1981 at the Hampden-Booth Theater Library, located in the Players, a private theatrical club in New York City. A quick check with the library confirmed that Deas's hunch was right: The Poe daguerreotype he had seen there was missing.

Meanwhile, the newly found portrait had been consigned to Cowan's Auctions for sale. Shortly after, the FBI entered the picture and took possession of the daguerreotype. After they authenticated it as the one belonging to the Hampden-Booth Theater Library, the historically important Edgar Allan Poe daguerreotype was returned to the library in November 2005.

LOST FOREVER

The Associated Press reported the case of Stéphane Breitwieser, a French waiter, who pilfered 239 objects from provincial museums throughout Europe from 1996 until his arrest in Lucerne, Switzerland, in 2001. His mother, attempting to protect her wayward son, determined that she needed to destroy the evidence. She chopped up the paintings, threw them into the trash and down the garbage disposal. She discarded other purloined objects into local canals. Shortly after, the French police recovered 102 objects from the mud, but many of them were irrevocably damaged—lost forever.

ALASKAN LEGACY STOLEN AND PARTIALLY FOUND

"Some stolen treasures rob us of the ability to connect to an important part our collective history—and sadly, these cultural treasures simply cannot be replaced. Such is the case with the Kilbuck collection that vanished from Ottawa University, Ottawa, Kansas, in July 1994," said John Buxton, a tribal arts expert from Dallas, Texas.

In 1885, John Kilbuck and his bride, Edith Romig, went to Alaska as part of the first group of Moravian missionaries. They were located among the Yup'ik people in Bethel, Alaska,

WORLD'S MOST WANTED

Art theft, a crime that crosses international borders, requires international cooperation. The FBI and Interpol frequently support and assist each other in facilitating the prevention of these crimes. The following are some of the items that both agencies consider most wanted:

* The 1727 violin made by Antonio Stradivari known as the Davidoff-Morini violin, stolen in 1995 and said to be worth $3,000,000.
* Caravaggio's *Nativity with San Lorenzo and San Francisco*, stolen in 1969 and worth $20,000,000.
* A wood, ivory, and gold statue, *Lion Attacking a Nubian*, circa 720 BC, stolen in 2003 from the National Museum of Iraq. Value not disclosed.
* *The Madman* by Francisco Goya, stolen in March 2008 from a Danish castle. Value not disclosed.
* *Portrait of Marie de Medici* by Peter Paul Rubens, stolen at the same time as Goya's *The Madman*. Value not disclosed.
* *Count Lepic and His Daughters* by Edgar Degas, stolen in February 2008. Value not disclosed.
* *A Cavalier* by Frans van Mieris, a small portrait, stolen in June 2007, and worth in excess of $1,000,000.
* *La Jardin du Luxembourg* by Henri Matisse, stolen from the Museu Chácara do Céu in Rio de Janeiro, Brazil, in February 2006. No value ascribed.
* Salvador Dalí's 1929 *Two Balconies*, Claude Monet's *Marine*, and Pablo Picasso's 1956 *Dance*, stolen with the Matisse painting. The value has not been determined.
* *Portrait of Rembrandt's Father* by Rembrandt, stolen in 2006 from a museum in Serbia and Montenegro. Experts now say this is a fake with a maximum value of 40 euros. The original still hangs in the Tirol Museum in Innsbruck, Austria, and is known as *Bust of Old Man in a Cap*.
* *Reclining Figure* (1968–1970) by Henry Moore (this piece weighs two and a half tons and was stolen using a crane). It is worth around $6,000,000. Museum officials fear that it was sold for the value of its metal as scrap.

RECENTLY RECOVERED: SUCCESS!

* *Poppies near Vétheuil* by Claude Monet, recovered February 2008. Found in the backseat of a white Opal Omega parked in the parking lot of a psychiatric clinic.
* Edvard Munch's *The Scream* and *Madonna*, both recovered in 2006, circumstances of the recovery were not disclosed.
* *Blossoming Chestnut Branches* by Vincent van Gogh, recovered February 2008, from the same vehicle as *Poppies near Vétheuil*.
* *The Portrait of Suzanne Bloch* by Pablo Picasso, stolen in 2007 and recovered in January 2008, valued at $50,000,000.
* *Statue of King Entemena of Lagash*, stolen from the National Museum of Iraq and recovered in July 2006.
* Pierre-Auguste Renoir's portrait of a nude woman, stolen in 1975 and recovered in 2008, when the painting was brought into an Italian art expert to be appraised.
* *View of the Sea at Scheveningen* by Vincent van Gogh. Stolen in 2002, the thieves were caught and convicted in 2003, but the painting was not recovered until 2005. Van Gogh's *Congregation Leaving the Church in Nuenen* was also recovered in 2005.

The Thinker by Auguste Rodin: A 28-inch bronze casting was found—and then lost again—amidst the tragedy of the World Trade Center.

pipe, all depicting the Eskimo culture of the time. Seventy-three years later, in 1994, these artifacts were stolen from the library.

The FBI has recovered most of the Kilbuck collection. Still missing is an ivory pipe, with extensive scrimshaw decoration, valued at $2,500 to $3,500.

DISASTERS

Political, cultural, and religious conflicts that resound throughout history have caused wrenching human suffering and the loss or total destruction of some of our greatest art treasures. These man-made disasters disconnect us from our past. What follows are two examples of monumental tragedy and their aftermath.

THE WORLD TRADE CENTER TRAGEDY

The crushing destruction of the World Trade Center in 2001 cost thousands of lives and caused the loss of countless art treasures. One of the saddest art losses was the disappearance of approximately 300 sculptures by the French artist Auguste Rodin (1840–1917), which were located in the offices of Cantor Fitzgerald. This prestigious firm, which lost over 650 employees in the catastrophe, occupied floors 101 and 103 through 105 of the North Tower.

Bits and pieces of the Rodin sculptures were found in the debris, but the firm's 28-inch bronze casting of *The Thinker* was found *intact* (although somewhat the worse for wear).

Rodin created *The Thinker* for the lintel on his Gates of Hell doorway that was inspired by

which is on the Kuskokwim River, about forty miles from the Bering Sea.

The Kilbucks quickly learned the Yup'ik language and established it as the official language of the Moravian Church in Alaska. Over time, John and Edith Kilbuck became an influential part of Alaskan life. In 1911, the Kilbucks sent a collection of artifacts to Ottawa University Library. The collection included boxes, ladles, fishing tools, sewing awls, hooks, harpoons, snowshoes, snow goggles, and at least one ivory

Dante's *Divine Comedy.* Originally entitled *The Poet,* this statue is one of the most famous pieces of sculpture in the world, and original castings, in various sizes, can be found in more than twenty museums around the world.

Then the unthinkable happened: After the 28-inch bronze casting of *The Thinker* was discovered in the rubble, it vanished once again. And it hasn't yet been recovered.

WAR'S AFTERMATH: THE NATIONAL MUSEUM OF IRAQ

Two years after the collapse of the World Trade Center, during the Iraqi war, an estimated 15,000 masterpieces and national treasures disappeared from the National Museum of Iraq. Known as one of the five greatest museums in the world, it housed the world's most complete history of early civilization, including irreplaceable vestiges of Mesopotamia, known as the cradle of civilization. At the beginning of the Iraqi war in 2003, the United States agreed not to bomb the museum, but Iraqi forces occupied the building and fortified the building's western side against American troops. The Americans remained reluctant to fire on the site because of the cultural treasures it contained.

The last of the museum staff left on April 8, 2003, and the looting began that day, and continued until April 12—reportedly by Iraqi nationals. They stripped the museum of its most valuable possessions, including the Sacred Vase of Warka, the Mask of Warka, and the Bassetki Statue (see boxed text on more information about these treasures). The museum remained closed for the next six years.

Thankfully, a number of masterpieces from the National Museum of Iraq have been returned—recovered by customs agents around the world, or stored safely and discovered in other locations. Many, however, were severely damaged, and about half have not yet been found and returned to the museum. Still, in February 2009, the Iraq Museum reopened its doors, devoting one hall to objects taken during the looting and since returned.

Archeologists discovered the Sacred Vase of Warka around 1934 in a temple complex devoted to the Sumerian goddess Inanna, in Uruk (a valley in the province of Baluchistan in Pakistan). Standing about three feet tall, it was a monumental piece made from alabaster. Looters of the museum forcibly wrenched the vase from its case, snapping it off the base. It was returned to the museum by men driving a pickup truck on July 12, 2003, during an amnesty for pillaged items.

The Mask of Warka, also known as the Lady of Uruk, is one of the earliest depictions of a human face. It is about 8 inches tall and most likely represents the goddess Inanna or one of her priestesses. It was recovered by Iraqi police service members, who received a tip from an informant. Armed with shovels, they unearthed the mask, which had been buried in a backyard in Baghdad. Both the mask and sacred vase are over 5,000 years old.

The Statue of Bassetki (named for the town where it was found in the 1960s) is 4,000 years old. This copper statue is a partial figure of a man—only the portion from the waist down survives. It was recovered—owing in large part to the efforts of the 812th Military Police Company—in a cesspool, covered with axle grease and human excrement.

Back in fashion: These beautiful Tiffany Studio lamps, ca.1905, were brought to the Palm Springs event in 2008 and valued at $130,000.

FALLING OUT OF FASHION CAN MAKE A MASTERPIECE DISAPPEAR

Every *Roadshow* appraiser has run into situations in which someone has inherited an item from a deceased loved one. The first person who inherits such a piece may remember that "Grandmother" loved it and said it was important—but subsequent owners are not exactly sure about the details. Then, as the heirloom is passed down again and again, the particulars about the object become more and more vague until the item is just an old piece of family clutter. Tiffany lamps and American Arts and Crafts furniture are good examples of this. During most of the second quarter of the twentieth century, people were simply not interested in Tiffany lamps, and they were considered by many to be out of style.

Large numbers of them were placed in attics and forgotten until the late 1950s when they were once again viewed as examples of fine American craftsmanship and artistic attainment. The same process happened to American Arts and Crafts furniture. When this style went out of fashion, large quantities were either discarded or stored in attics and barns, where they moldered until interest resurfaced in the late twentieth century.

These are just two examples. True tales abound of stunning treasures that were long forgotten and found in the oddest places! Read the stories that follow...you may not even realize what is hanging above a mantel near you.

A MASTERPIECE IN THE SPARE ROOM

In the 1960s, Jean Preston was working as a curator of historic manuscripts at a museum in Huntington, California. While living in America she found two small paintings. She did not realize what they were, but thought them "quite nice" and decided to buy them for her father before she returned home to England. She paid less than $300 for both. In 1974, her father died and she inherited the paintings. This retired Oxford resident lived an unassuming life, not realizing until 2006 that she had a fortune hanging behind the door of her spare room.

In 2005, a family friend and former head of the department of art history at the University of Bristol thought the paintings were worth researching and asked her permission to have them authenticated. They turned out to be missing medieval masterpieces, the work of early Italian Renaissance painter Fra Angelico. After Jean's death in November 2006, the paintings sold for close to $2 million!

OUR CUP RUNNETH OVER

A diminutive, 5½-inch-tall metal cup with two faces came into the possession of a British "rag and bone" man—or junk dealer—who had passed it on to his son at the time of his death. The son thought even less of the piece, but figuring it was made from either brass or bronze, he put the piece in a box and shoved it under a bed, where it stayed for many years.

When the son was getting ready to move, he came upon the cup again and examined it more closely. This time, he realized it was *not* made of brass or bronze, and sent it to the British Muse-

TOUCHED BY THE ANGELS

Fra Angelico (c.1400–1455), born Guido di Pietro, was a Dominican friar as well as one of the great artists of the Italian Renaissance. When he moved to the convent of San Marco in Florence in 1436, Cosimo de' Medici became his patron. At Cosimo's urging, Fra Angelico undertook the decorating of the new religious compound with numerous frescoes.

One of his most famous works was the altarpiece, which was composed of the image of the Virgin Mary surrounded by saints in a natural arrangement as if they were in conversation. During the Napoleonic Wars, this masterpiece was broken up into eight separate paintings and the paintings were scattered. Six of the paintings were recovered over time, but two had been missing until 2005.

um for an opinion. The experts there had never seen anything like it and sent it to Oxford University for testing. There, experts revealed the cup was made of gold—dating from the third or fourth century BCE!

The cup is believed to be from the Persian Achaemenid Empire, and the faces represent the Roman god Janus, the god of gates and doors who is associated with beginnings and endings. The month of January is named after Janus.

At auction in 2009, the cup sold for $100,000—a happy ending for the owner—and a masterpiece rediscovered!

ROADSHOW FINDS

Collectors and treasure hunters are always looking for the multi-million-dollar masterpiece to turn up in a yard sale or junk shop priced at a dollar—or even less. You may have heard stories of a Picasso masterpiece, worth $2,000,000, turning up in a Sarasota, Florida, thrift store, or an imperial Fabergé Easter egg that had been painted white when it was found in a Texas junk shop. Although some of these stories may be urban legends, *Roadshow* has showcased real discoveries of great significance over the years. Here's a best-of-the-best rundown, straight from the experts who appraised them.

A CHAIR TO DIE FOR—OR IN

Appraiser Wendell Garrett, with *The Magazine Antiques*, remembers a taping in Rochester, New York, in 1999. A guest brought in a rather macabre item: The chair in which John Quincy Adams had died—in the middle of giving a speech on the floor of the House of Representatives. It had been missing for 150 years!

Garrett tells the following story: It was February 1848, and Adams was impassioned, railing against the war with Mexico. At this point in his career, Adams, the sixth president of the United States, had been elected to the House of Representatives by the state of Massachusetts, after being defeated for reelection by Andrew Jackson. He served there for seventeen years.

Reportedly, Adams got so overwrought while speaking that he suffered a stroke and died. According to Garrett, the chair in which Adams breathed his last, "spooked everyone and no one would sit in it so the House Sergeant-at-Arms took it home with him." That chair descended in the family and reemerged in Rochester at

Roadshow. "It was not worth a great deal of money—maybe around two thousand dollars—but it had great historical interest."

A COUNTRY CLASSIC

Appraiser Ken Farmer of Ken Farmer Auctions in Radford, Virginia, vividly remembers a large Southern pottery face jug that turned up in Miami in 2001. Farmer first saw the jug lying on its side as a woman wheeled it onto the set. Initially, he was not sure whether it was an old piece or not, but "when she stood the jug up," Farmer remembered, "I knew it was unlike anything anybody was making today."

The jug was in the form of an African-American man wearing a waistcoat and with big hoop

The owner of this Southern redware face jug admitted that her family didn't particularly like the jug, but she probably loved the price that it later sold for at auction: $80,500!

earrings in his ears. The figure had fully detailed hair and articulated limbs, and was covered with a typical Southern alkaline glaze. The owner said that it had been passed down in her family and in each generation it had been taken on by one of the women—reluctantly.

It was not something the members of the family particularly loved. The owner added that the jug had spent the past few months in a closet, because it was receiving the unwanted attentions of a beloved family pet, who was using it as a bathroom. It is a bit hard to imagine such ignominy for a piece that was in fact an American masterpiece of ceramic art.

Farmer identified the piece as having been made by John Lehman, an artist of German descent, who worked in the mid–nineteenth century as a potter. For a time, Lehman worked in Randolph County, Alabama, which forms part of Alabama's border with neighboring Georgia. Lehman is thought to have worked in both Alabama and Georgia during the mid–nineteenth century, and since the current owner's family was from Alabama, it is thought that this particular jug was probably crafted in that state.

Valuing such a rare masterpiece is very difficult, since so few have been sold over the years, and initially Farmer suggested a rather conservative value, $25,000 to $35,000. However, when the jug sold at auction some time later, it brought an astounding $80,500, and Farmer speculated that this might be a record price for a so-called Southern face jug.

THE SUFFRAGETTE NECKLACE

Jewelry expert Joyce Jonas particularly remembers a woman who had brought in a suffragette necklace for her to evaluate.

It was from the English suffragette movement that is associated with "Mrs. Pankhurst"—also known as Emmeline Pankhurst—and her daughters Christabel, Sylvia, and Adelia. "The necklace was silver," Jonas related, "and it was beautifully enameled with the colors of the English suffragette movement—purple, green, and white.

"On the back," she continued, "there were enameled some of the abstract symbols of the suffrage movement. Among other things such as an arrow in a fence, there were bars to symbolize the prison bars that imprisoned them, and keys to symbolize the devices that released them from their cages.

A stunning English suffragette necklace, bought for five dollars fifteen years ago and brought to Baltimore in 2007. Appraiser Joyce Jonas originally thought it was worth between $6,000 or $7,000, but after more research, she considered it a missing masterpiece worth $30,000 to $35,000.

"The woman who owned it had bought it for five dollars, fifteen years before. It was black and discolored; she cleaned it up and did some research to find out about it. When it came into me, I knew it was very rare, but at the time I thought it might be worth six thousand to seven thousand dollars.

"Later research, however, proved that the piece was much rarer than I had previously thought. In fact, there was only one other known, and it was located in Glasgow, Scotland. This was indeed a missing masterpiece, and further thought suggests that the piece is more likely to be worth between thirty thousand and thirty-five thousand dollars—which is a lot of money for a piece of early twentieth-century silver and enamel jewelry."

THE ITALIAN CAMEO

Another incredible treasure Jonas recalls is an Italian shell cameo that dated to the sixteenth century. Many cameos come to *Roadshow* but this one was exceptional. According to Jonas, "It was an oval approximately five by four inches and it was carved with a representation of the Sistine Chapel frescoes by Michelangelo. The detail was simply exquisite. I examined it under a loupe, and besides seeing the finger of God touching Adam, I saw hundreds of other tiny figures doing all sorts of things. My oohs and ahhs of admiration attracted a lot of attention from the other appraisers as I studied the intricacy of the details and the beauty of the workmanship.

"It was so good that I thought for a moment that Michelangelo might have carved this piece himself, but I later discovered that he is thought never to have carved cameos. The piece, however, was done by the sixteenth-century Italian carver, Alessandro Masnago, who was active in Milan from approximately 1560 to 1620.

"The cameo," Jonas continued, "came to the current owner from a Dutch sale of old master paintings and objects that had once belonged to Marie Antoinette and the guest had the original catalogue from the sale in Holland."

As for the worth of this piece, Jonas says there was a difference of opinion among the cameo experts, and values ranged from a low of $10,000 to a high of around $25,000. She points out that it is often very difficult to price one-of-a-kind masterpieces such as this one, and it will bring what the market will bear when—and if—it is sold.

REVERBERATIONS FROM THE CIVIL WAR

As already mentioned, missing masterpieces do not always have extraordinary monetary value, but they do possess strong historical echoes that can send shivers up appraisers' spines. Rafael Eledge of Shiloh Civil War Relics in Shiloh, Tennessee remembers a Civil War–era sword, pistol, and a photo of the owner wearing both of these items that came into *Antiques Roadshow* in Spokane, Washington, in 2007.

There was also a canister ball with the collection. This projectile had wounded the owner of the other items at the Battle of Shiloh (April 6 and 7, 1862). More than 16,000 soldiers suffered severe injuries during this battle (also called the Battle of Pittsburg Landing). Eledge said, "The wounded man was taken to the transport boats on the Mississippi to be taken back to his home in either Illinois or Ohio, but he died on the way. If he had died at Shiloh," Eledge continued, "the gun and the sword would probably have been lost for all time."

Explaining further, Eledge said, "Those who were killed at Shiloh were just buried in mass graves, and the gun and the sword would either have been passed on to someone else for continued use in the war or just discarded. There was no name on either piece, so if they survived, there would have been no way to connect them to this particular soldier."

To Eledge, seeing these four items together—the gun, the sword, the photograph of the soldier, and the canister ball that killed him—is like holding history in your hand. These pieces transcend the romance and glory of cavalry charges, waving flags, and titanic forces clashing. They represent the crescendo and climax of a particular man's life during a pivotal time in American history. They depict the human devastation of war through one soldier's experience.

THE APPRAISERS' WISH LIST

America's hidden masterpieces are still out there! Here are some treasures our appraisers long to discover at a *Roadshow* event.

MAKE ME A MAP

Christopher Lane, co-owner of the Philadelphia Print Shop, hopes to find a copy of what he refers to as the "founding map," the most accurate map of America available at the time of the Revolution.

John Mitchell (1711–1768) was from a prosperous Virginia family. He went to Scotland to study at the University of Edinburgh and remained there until 1731. When he returned to

Scene from the Battle of Shiloh April 6 and 7, 1862 by Thure de Thulstrup.

FINDING THE FOUNDING MAP

* To enable Mitchell to prepare a detailed map of North America, Britain's Board of Trade and Plantations gave Mitchell access to all their records and geographic reports and asked the colonial governors to send new surveys to London.

* This led to the first printed edition of "A Map of the French and British Dominions in North America." It was engraved by Thomas Kitchin, a famous British engraver at the time, and contained a copyright date of February 13, 1755.

* A second edition was produced by Mitchell around 1757. This edition contained several changes in geographical detail, plus two large blocks of text were added in the middle of the Atlantic. The text was Mitchell's explanation of how he had gathered together the numerous provincial maps into the bigger frame of North America and his data sources.

* Mitchell died in 1768, and an updated third edition, published by the firm of Jefferys and Faden, came out in 1773.

* The fourth edition came out in 1775 and was retitled "A Map of British Colonies in North America"—which reflected the lessening of French influence in North America after the end of the French and Indian War.

* This fourth edition of Mitchell's map was used and annotated in 1782 by Richard Oswald at the Treaty of Paris, where peace was made with Great Britain and the new boundaries of the United States of America were established. Oswald used red ink to mark this line on the map. This "red line" map is now located in the British Library.

Virginia, he fell ill and returned to Great Britain to recover. It was during his recuperation there that he developed his interest in maps and map-making. Mitchell was inspired to draft "A Map of the British and French Dominions in North America" to help resolve the fear and conflict between Britain and France in North America.

The two great nations had differing interpretations of the boundaries, with the British claiming (approximately) the land from the Atlantic to the Mississippi and from the Gulf of Mexico to the Great Lakes. The French, on the other hand, said the British rights stopped at the Appalachian Mountains, and they owned everything west of that, in what would be modern Louisiana and Ohio.

Mitchell completed the first draft of his map in 1750, but no one knows if it still exists. There were four editions in total. Christopher Lane concludes, "These maps were generally made in two types: as wall maps—in which the paper was glued to a linen backing and attached to wooden rods for hanging, and saddlebag maps—which are folding maps about fifty-two by seventy-five inches. The wall maps are very rarely seen because they were too roughly used over the years. If either the wall map or saddlebag map were to walk into *Roadshow*, I would be speechless! In excellent condition, an example of Mitchell's founding map of the United States would be worth one hundred and eighty to two hundred thousand dollars."

TABLE THE NOTION

Andrew Brunk would like nothing better than to see the spectacular American tilt-top "pie crust" tea table that was pictured in Edward Wenham's *Collector's Guide to Furniture Design* (Collector Press, 1928). "After this book was published," Brunk said, "the table just vanished from public sight without a trace."

This missing masterpiece has beautifully carved leaves and scrolling on the "knees" and a turned pendant. It is nearly identical to the details carved on a table made for the Lee family of Stratford Hall, the birthplace of Robert E. Lee. However, the table photographed for Wenham's book is a bit fancier than the Lee table, and may be worth slightly more money on today's market.

This missing table is attributed to the workshop of Robert Walker (1710–1777). Walker worked in King George County, Virginia, from 1745 to 1755, where he made the pie crust tea table.

If the lost table were found, and subsequently sold, it would bring in excess of $1 million at auction—and possibly much more. Brunk noted that in late 2007, a Philadelphia table made in the 1750s and very similar to this one brought a record price of $6.7 million, so the Walker table that has gone astray might bring more than he envisions. Only the marketplace can set the price with absolute certainty.

A pie crust table is a modern term used to describe a table with a top that has a carved, raised, and scalloped border around the outer edge of the table's top. This feature is said to resemble the crimped edge of a pie crust—hence the name.

THE PLANE TRUTH

Independent appraiser Steven Dice of Federal Way, Washington, is passionately interested in tools and implements, and to him some early tools can indeed be works of art.

Dice speaks lovingly of tools with extraordinary design and clever execution and pieces that were made from exotic materials. One such piece is a humble plough or plow plane, an instrument designed to "plow" a groove in boards—usually for the fitting of drawer bottoms, cabinet backs, glass panels, or for doing molding work, among other things. Dice is particularly interested in a plough plane that was made from elephant ivory, with scrimshaw decoration that included representations of both the British and French flags. It has German silver mountings and was made by John Moseley & Son Company of London, circa 1850. It was exhibited at the 1855 Paris Exposition, and is considered one of the finest artistic examples of the toolmaker's trade.

This plough plane has disappeared, and no one knows where it has gone. "Someday," Dice says, "it will probably be discovered in somebody's basement, and to have it turn up at a *Roadshow* event would be monumental!" As for the value, Dice thought it was worth between $30,000 and $50,000.

CHASING CHIPPENDALE

When it comes to missing pieces of American furniture, Michael Flanigan dreams of a

THOMAS AFFLECK
(1740–1795)

Affleck had apprenticed as a cabinetmaker in Edinburgh, Scotland, and worked in London before coming to Philadelphia in 1763, where he opened a workshop. The tables in the suite described in this page are attributed to Affleck by bills of sale but the chairs are attributed to Benjamin Randolph, according to Andrew Brunk in his article in the 2007 edition of *American Furniture*. The suite was made between 1770 and 1771. These pieces are now considered to be the finest examples of Philadelphia-made Chippendale furniture, and while several of the components of the set are well-known, others are still missing.

Roadshow sighting of a piece from the suite of Chippendale furniture made for the Cadwalader family. "You would see the appraisers with their jaws on the floor just gaping it at."

General John Cadwalader (1742–1786) was a prosperous Philadelphia merchant who became a brigadier general in the Pennsylvania Militia during the Revolutionary War. In 1768, he married Elizabeth Lloyd of Maryland, one of the wealthiest women in America. A year later, Cadwalader and his bride purchased a house in Philadelphia, and began extensive renovations. They commissioned five family portraits from Charles Wilson Peale for display in the new parlor, plus a suite of furniture to be made by Thomas Affleck.

The two commode card tables in the suite are in the Philadelphia Museum of Art and seven (of the twelve) hairy paw foot chairs from the front parlor set are in either museums or well-known private collections. Four of the missing five chairs are known but unavailable and only one is unaccounted for. Why are the other pieces missing? It is all because of forbidden love.

It seems that one of General Cadwalader's descendents, Charles Cadwalader, married the family's young housekeeper and earned himself the cold-shouldered disapproval of Philadelphia's society.

Incredibly intricate eighteenth century Chippendale style armchair with distinctive "hairy paw" ball and claw feet is part of the Cadwalader furniture suite—some of which is still missing.

In response, Charles closed the house and sold the Cadwalader furniture at an auction held in Philadelphia in 1904. Examples of the set have been discovered in this country and in at least two European nations (Italy and Ireland)—but there are still prime examples (such as two sofas) that are missing—and waiting to be found—perhaps on *Antiques Roadshow*.

One of the missing pieces from the Cadwalader grouping, such as one of the missing chairs from the presumed set of twelve, would be worth a $1 million at auction, while a sofa would fetch $3 million to $5 million.

GET THE PICTURE?

Appraiser Wes Cowan yearns to find at least one daguerreotype from a collection of pictures of the Gold Rush taken by Robert H. Vance.

In the 1840s, the daguerreotype became all the rage in America. Everyone loved the idea that they could have both an inexpensive and accurate portrait of themselves or a loved one.

There were many daguerreotype artists around the country at that time, but one artist who was relatively unknown beyond the West Coast was Robert H. Vance (1825–1876). Born in Maine, Vance arrived in San Francisco at the height of the Gold Rush. This City by the Bay grew in two years from a town of just 812 people in 1848 to a bustling city of 25,000 in 1850. A skilled photographer, Vance was inspired by this new civilization to take more than 300 images of life in the gold mining camps, forming a priceless documentation of this chaotic, explosive era that became so iconic in American history.

Vance is one of the first documentary photographers. He knew there was a great deal of interest back East in the California Gold Rush and it occurred to him that people might pay to see

PRACTICAL PHOTOGRAPHY

Practical photography was invented in 1837 by Louis-Jacques Mande Daguerre working with Joseph Nicéphore Niépce. While not the first photographic process, it was the first that proved to be *practical* for making portraits, because it had a shorter exposure time. The French Academy of Sciences announced the Daguerre process on January 9, 1839 (Niépce had died, so Daguerre got the credit), and on August 19, 1839, the French government announced the invention was "free to the world."

That same year, 1839, an Englishman named William Fox Talbot invented a different photographic process, using paper rather than metal plates. This new process was enthusiastically received, especially in the United States, where many artists learned the technique and opened studios and galleries around the country.

his photos of the gold mining areas. With this in mind, Vance decided to house his photographs in rosewood frames and take them to New York City for display. Arriving in New York in June 1851, Vance opened his exhibition on the second floor of 349 Broadway, and although it was enthusiastically reviewed in a newly established photographic journal, it was a total and complete failure as few came to see his magnificent pictures.

He returned to San Francisco, leaving his photographs behind. In 1853 he advertised them,

Daguerreotypes come in a variety of sizes depending on the dimensions of the copper plates employed by the photographers. Most of these images are in smaller sizes, either sixth plate (2¾ by 3¼ inches) or smaller—with the smallest being sixteenth plate, which were 1⅝ inches by 2⅛ inches. Vance's photos of the men, mines, and camps associated with the Gold Rush were whole plate, which at 6½ by 8½ inches was the largest size made—and probably the rarest.

stating that they had cost him $3,000 to make, $700 to frame, but he was willing to take $1,500 for the whole lot. The collection was finally sold to St. Louis photographer John H. Fitzgibbons, who retired in 1877. From that day on, no one has seen or heard about the collection.

"Today, it would be hard to know what Robert Vance's photographs of the California Gold Rush are worth," says Wes Cowan. "One Vance whole-plate daguerreotype, which was not from this Gold Rush series, sold five years ago for one hundred and thirty thousand dollars. Using this figure as a base, that would mean the collection would be worth in excess of thirty million dollars! If this collection was unearthed, it would be considered one of the great finds in the history of the American West."

A CANNON TO DIE FOR

To some collectors—and especially to Rafael Eledge of Shiloh Civil War Relics of Savannah, Tennessee—a masterpiece may be something as ungainly as a rusty old cannon.

A cannon can be rare—and the ones made by the Singer, Nimick Company of Pittsburgh, Pennsylvania certainly qualify. To put this in perspective, the Phoenixville Iron Company of Chester County, Pennsylvania, produced well over 1,000 cannons for the Union, but Singer, Nimick made only six: two are at the Chickamauga battlefield near Chattanooga, Tennessee, one is at Gettysburg—and three are lost.

Most cannons are made from cast iron but the ones made by Singer, Nimick Company were cast steel and cost $626 when new. Only six were made because the cast-iron cannons made by other factories cost about half as much and worked just as well.

A big, heavy cannon should be hard to lose—yet it is not uncommon for a cannon to go missing. Many times, if capture was imminent, artillery companies buried their cannons rather than have them fall into enemy hands. During the Great Depression and World War II, Civil War cannons were sold as scrap, which means that they may be missing forever—or they could turn up.

HOW TO SPOT A SINGER, NIMICK CANNON

These missing cannons are easy to spot, shares Eledge. "They have big *US* on top of the barrel and are marked *Singer, Nimick, Cast Steel, 1862* on the trunions—which are the cylindrical protrusions on the cannon where it is fitted into its gun carriage."

"I hope, after reading this, someone will call me and tell me they have one of the missing Singer, Nimick cannons—or know where one is. To me that would be a missing masterpiece found."

WHAT A DOLL

Before his death, appraiser Richard Wright told us that he hoped to find a Kämmer and Reinhardt 131 googly-eye doll with black, or possibly mulatto, coloration—something he had never seen or been able to find.

Kämmer and Reinhardt went into business in Waltershausen, Thuringia, Germany, in 1886. When they made this elusive doll between 1916 and 1920, Kämmer and Reinhardt did not own a porcelain factory so they had to buy the dolls' heads from other manufacturers—in particular, Simon and Halbig, a porcelain factory in Grafenhain, Thuringia that they purchased in 1920.

To identify the Kämmer and Reinhardt 131 googly-eye doll look for a doll that:

- Is bisque and has a closed mouth
- Comes in several sizes—the smallest was 8½ inches, the intermediate size was 13 inches, and the largest was 16 inches
- Is marked with *Simon & Halbig* above a *K* with a star of David (with an ampersand in the middle) and an *R* for Kämmer and Reinhardt, the German manufacturer (Simon and Halbig made the bisque heads). Below that is the mold number 131. The number *131* signifies a doll's head that has "googly-eyes," and that this model was made sometime between 1916 and the early 1920s.

A "googly-eyed" doll is one that has large, often round eyes with irises glancing off to the side. Some collectors also call this type of ocular oddity in dolls "goo-goo" or roguish eyes. According to Wright, "The fashion for this sort of eyes on dolls really originated with Rose

O'Neill's Kewpie dolls, which had these sort of eyes. Kewpies were introduced in 1913 and were so popular that other makers sometimes copied the googly-eyes. The Caucasian version of the 131 turns up with some regularity and is worth about six thousand to seven thousand dollars, but the black and mulatto skin tones are out there somewhere, waiting to be found, but as yet have not turned up."

Wright valued this doll at at least $40,000.

GUITAR MAN

When asked what item he would like to see walk through the doors of *Antiques Roadshow*, Jim Baggett of Mass Street Music in Lawrence, Kansas did not hesitate to answer: "It would be a Martin OM-45 Deluxe guitar. I have been collecting Martin Guitars for thirty years and I have only seen one of these."

The OM-45 Deluxe originated in 1929 with the initials standing for *orchestra model*. According to Martin historian Mike Longworth, this series came about because banjoist Perry Bechtel, who was making the transition from the

C F. Martin Guitar Company has been in business since 1833 and has been located in Nazareth, Pennsylvania since 1838. The firm was founded by Christian Frederick Martin, a German immigrant, and in 2008 celebrated its 175th anniversary. Incredibly, it is still being run by a Martin, C. F. (Chris) Martin IV—the great-great-great-grandson of the original founder.

There is one very special OM-45 guitar, and that is the one made for Leonard Slye—or Roy Rogers, as he is better known. This particular instrument is even more elaborate than the other OM-45 Deluxe examples, with a more ornate floral pickguard inlay and headstock motif. This guitar is now on display at the Roy Rogers-Dale Evans Museum in Branson, Missouri.

plectrum (or four-string) banjo to the guitar, wanted Martin to create an instrument that had the neck join the body at the 14th instead of the 12th fret.

The OM-45 Deluxe was the fanciest standard flattop guitar offered by Martin. The back and sides are made of the finest quartersawn Brazilian rosewood. The top is select Adirondack spruce. The bridge and fingerboard are select ebony with inlaid snowflakes of mother-of-pearl. The entire border of the body is inlaid with abalone. Additionally, the Deluxe has a beautiful wreath-style mother-of-pearl inlay in the pickguard that makes it instantly recognizable. Only fourteen were made and it is thought that fewer than ten still exist—the whereabouts of perhaps only five are known. Baggett says that if a Martin OM-45 Deluxe guitar, in pristine condition, were to come into *Roadshow*, not only would he be ec-static, but he would value it at $350,000.

AFRICAN HUNT

"I would love to see an extraordinary Kongo nail fetish come into *Roadshow* for appraisal,"

reveals John Buxton. "These unique examples of African art could be worth as much as five million to eight million dollars."

A Kongo nail fetish is a powerful wooden fig-ure that is imbued with a spiritual force that is to some extent under human control. These figures often contain grave dirt or medicine and are of-ten embellished with shells, as well as nails, blades and/or spikes that have been driven into the body.

The primary purpose of these figures was to pursue and expose witches, thieves, adulterers, and other wrongdoers. The statues were hand-carved for use by tribal diviners, healers, and adjudicators, and did not start out studded with all the iron implements. These were added—for example, a nail might have been driven into the figure to seal an agreement with a vow; or if someone was accused of a crime, a nail would be hammered into the figure, and the accused would be asked to remove it with his or her bare hand. If the accused could not do this, they were believed guilty of the crime.

These figures are considered to be very power-ful, but when they are perceived to have lost their power, they are discarded or sold. So Buxton's dream of finding a truly old and authentic exam-ple of a lost (or discarded) Kongo nail fetish will happen—especially if all of us join in the hunt.

ROW YOUR OWN BOAT

Once upon a time, there was a palace in China called the Yuan Ming Yuan—or Garden of Gardens. It was the summer palace for the emperors of China. Victor Hugo, the French novelist, described it as "an unparalleled, aston-ishing, masterpiece of arts."

Over the years, the Yuan Ming Yuan became filled with Chinese and Western art treasures. But in another tragic example of man-made disaster, English, French, and Chinese soldiers sacked the

Summer Palace during the Second Opium War of 1860. In 1860 the British High Commissioner to China, Lord Elgin, ordered the destruction of the compound in retaliation for the torture and execution of twenty European and Indian soldiers who had been sent under a flag of truce to negotiate an end to the conflict. The soldiers looted as they burned the compound, but they left many treasures to be consumed in the fires. Works were dispersed to England and France and to local Chinese collectors.

Lark Mason's holy grail is one of the lost masterpieces of the Yuan Dynasty (1271–1368) —a large dragon head filled with mechanical figures, which sailed on one of the palace's lakes. "No one knows where it is—or if it still exists," Mason says. "Many of the details are rather vague, but I imagine that it might have been gilded bronze and wood, and sailed across the lake on its own, using some sort of clockwork motor. Had it survived, it would have been one of the treasures kept in the Yuan Ming Yuan complex. As for the monetary value, that would be hard to say, because no one living has actually seen the boat. But still, if by some miracle this masterpiece was found in excellent condition, its value would be quite extraordinary."

WHAT'S YOUR SIGN?

Lark Mason wants another masterpiece that went missing during the sacking of the Chinese imperial summer palace: The twelve bronze heads of zodiac animals that were part of the *Haiyantang* or zodiac water clock fountain. Part of its design was bronze-headed sculptures of the Chinese zodiac animals that spouted water to tell the time. When this exquisite fountain was destroyed, the bronze heads were detached and shipped to Europe. In recent years some of these heads have begun to turn up.

The recovery of the heads has become a pri-

GARDEN OF GARDENS

This vast compound of palaces, gardens, temples, towers, galleries, pavilions, bridges, lakes, and ancient trees, was eight times the size of the Vatican and five times the size of the Forbidden City. It was located just five miles from the Forbidden City and the initial construction began in 1707 under the reign of the Emperor Kangxi, who was building it as a gift for his fourth son, later to become the Emperor Yongzheng.

In 1725 Yongzheng began an expansion of the compound and added the waterworks—the lakes, the streams and the ponds. Later in the eighteenth century, another emperor embarked on further expansion, constructing stone palaces in the European style to satisfy his taste for the exotic.

ority for the Chinese government, and the heads of the ox, the tiger, the horse, the monkey, and the pig have all been recovered during the early years of this century. They are now housed in a Chinese museum, and Mason himself found the first two of these—the monkey and the pig, which were subsequently sold at auction.

In 2009, two other zodiac heads surfaced in the estate of French fashion designer Yves Saint Laurent: the rat and the rabbit. The Chinese government is disputing their ownership with Christie's, the auction house that is selling them, and the estate, represented by the cofounder of the

Yves Saint Laurent couture house, Pierre Bergé.

When the two bronze heads sold in late February 2009, controversy and international drama still plagued them. In 2007 the horse head from this group brought $8.9 million, but when the two figures from the Yves Saint Laurent estate sold, they brought approximately $20 million each!

However, Cai Mingchai, the Chinese gentleman who purchased them, refused to pay, saying that it was his patriotic duty not to. Pierre Bergé said that if he did not pay, he would not get the bronzes. This saga continues, and the final resolution is in doubt at the time this is being written.

CLOSING THOUGHTS

Every one of us at *Roadshow* is passionate about our collectibles. Like you, we are inveterate treasure hunters, always on the lookout for the next great discovery, always expanding our search and our knowledge about antiques, and along with these objects, the history of humankind. The scope of articles that fascinate us is infinite—and the more rare the object, the more ardent the chase. What joy we experience when we bring our treasures and spread them on an appraisal table to have them admired! This is a *Roadshow* moment; this is why we are here.

Two of the bronze fountain heads—a monkey and a pig—part of the zodiac water clock looted from the Chinese imperial summer palace in 1860. Some of the twelve heads have been recovered and have sold for many millions of dollars. Others are still missing.

Marked "Harley and Carll, Ohio Stoneware, Alexander Manufacturer, Centennial 1876," this impressive stone jug changed the owner's life after it sold for $110,000!

THE FINAL REALITY

What happens to all the items seen each year

on *Roadshow*? Of course, some treasures are sold. (Although no matter what the value, most are not!) Some pieces go home with their owners to be cherished and perhaps get passed on to the next generation. And some items are donated to a museum. Our curiosity is piqued: Are sellers happy with the price they ultimately receive? Do they find the task of selling antiques daunting? Do our guests enjoy their treasures *more*, after they learn about their history and value at *Roadshow*? We followed several stories to uncover what happens to some of the unique pieces you have seen on television after *Roadshow* leaves town. And for those who decide to authenticate or sell their precious items, at the end of the chapter we provide helpful guidelines to simplify the process for everyone.

One thing we conclude with great pride: We *have* changed people's lives. Join me on this journey toward the final reality.

MARSHA'S MUSINGS

If you bring an item to *Roadshow* for evaluation, remember to document what you have learned. It's easy to forget details, but if you write them down, you will have a record for posterity. We even provide a page in our event guide to make it easy for our guests. However you record your notes, store that record in a safe place and you will ensure its value for the next generation. One suggestion is to keep information with the item itself: inside the clock, attached to the back of the painting, etc. Even better, take a photo of your treasure, attach it to the item's description and its value, and save them in a safety deposit box. Some people create scrapbooks, photo-album style, listing their valuables and their provenance, which is also an excellent method of record keeping.

JUGBUG

"The owner thought the piece might be worth five hundred to a thousand dollars, but we told him that, even before doing further in-depth research, the retail value would be closer to sixty-five thousand to eighty-five thousand dollars," recalls Allan Katz, a specialist in American folk art. "It was an absolutely monumental piece of American stoneware and one of the greatest pieces I had ever seen!"

The story began during Katz's first *Roadshow*, in St. Paul, Minnesota in 2004. A man came to his table, pulling a red wagon that held a huge pot that was decorated in cobalt blue. It was close to two feet tall and weighed over eighty pounds. The owner had received this jug from his mother. He loved it, and innocent of its great value, he used it as an umbrella stand.

"It was lying facedown so that the decoration was not fully visible when he approached the table," Katz remembers. "But when he turned it over, it blew us all away. When we went to tape the appraisal, my heart sank when the guest picked up this heavy piece by its handles and put it on the table. The handles on this jug had been applied when the piece was made, and there was a very real possibility that they might detach and send this treasure of Americana crashing to the floor!"

The jug had a lot of writing on it, "Harley & Carll, Ohio Stoneware, Akron, Alexander, Manufacturer, Centennial 1876," and also a magnificent peacock drawn in cobalt blue slip that appeared on the jug's center. Katz recalls, "The bottom portion, where there was a hole for a spigot, had a high relief representation of the jug itself in miniature. At the time, we did not know who Harley and Carll were, and research had to be done. It turned out that John Alexander, the maker of this piece, actually won a gold medal at the Philadelphia Centennial Exposition in 1876, celebrating the hundredth birthday of our nation, but we had never seen this particular pot in any of the pictures of the items exhibited at the fair."

After hearing Katz's estimate of the jug's worth, the owner suddenly became very uneasy. He asked if we were sure of the value, and Allan replied that he was being conservative. After that, he explained that the piece was not insured and, in fact, he typically did not even lock his doors… and his first thoughts were of all the things that could have happened. But his initial apprehension quickly gave way to pure excitement.

When he returned home, and after much thought, the owner put the jug on consignment, and it went to a large antique show in Philadelphia where it sold for $110,000.

"He sent me a picture of the day the check arrived, and told me what he had done with the money. First, he set up a fund for his daughter's education, and then he bought a used Volkswagen bug and got license plates that read JUGBUG!"

WHAT'S THE PUNCH LINE?

Jeni Sandberg, a specialist in twentieth-century decorative arts at Christie's in New York City, remembers an important American art pottery punch bowl brought into Christie's in 2006. The consigner said that she had taken it to *Antiques Roadshow* in 1997, and it had appeared on television. Now she wanted to sell.

The bowl was glazed stoneware and the interior was decorated with images of poppies, butterflies, and the inscription: "Some Friends will wish you Happiness & Others wish you Wealth, but I will wish you best of all Contentment blest with Health."

Along with the bowl came an adorable photograph of the owner as a little girl ladling punch from the bowl.

The bowl had been made in 1901 by Susan Stuart Goodrich Frackelton, who was a china decorator, writer, and the founder of a pottery works. Frackelton was born in Milwaukee, Wisconsin in 1848, attended finishing school in New York City, and later studied art under Heinrich Vianden in Milwaukee.

From just after the end of the Civil War to 1891, Frackelton ran a shop specializing in glass, china, and stoneware, and taught china decorating. She exhibited her wares at the 1893 World Columbian Exposition in Chicago, the

THE FRACKELTON LETTER

The Old College
614 Milwaukee
November 27 1901

My dear Friends,

I send you a Thanksgiving bowl with Poppies. If you do not like this wax finish as well as the high glaze and duller blue, it shall be sent to the Pottery and refired.

A council of war had been held. Dora, Emma Damon, and Emma Hooker, Sarah, Cornelia, Alice and Anna. They voted this finish and color. It is the result of what is called a smothered kiln and is rather the vogue of present.

I hope that you and your friends may have a "cup of kindness"— and many a good salad from it with all the good times that come with them.

Wesa's cup will have to wait till a little later.

With much love
Yours
S. Frackelton

1896 Centennial Exposition in Philadelphia (where she won an award), and at the 1900 Paris Exhibition. She also invented a gas-fired kiln suitable for home use, which allowed women of the day to take up pottery making as a hobby.

Most of Frackelton's work was made from brick clay or gray and blue stoneware and dec-

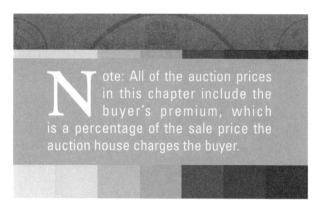

Note: All of the auction prices in this chapter include the buyer's premium, which is a percentage of the sale price the auction house charges the buyer.

orated with relief designs or under glaze blue decorations. This particular piece was created for Ansel and Mary Temple of Muskegon, Michigan. Mary Temple was from Wisconsin, and family tradition said that she and Frackelton were childhood friends. This is given credence by a letter from Frackelton that accompanied the bowl when it sold (see boxed text).

The bowl had been valued at *Roadshow* and subsequently by Christie's for $10,000 to $15,000, but when the bidding was over on December 19, 2006, it had more than doubled the highest figure. The bowl brought a very respectable $33,600, which includes the buyer's premium. This was a good two cups of kindness for the seller!

KATRINA, KATRINA

We have had a least one guest who came to *Roadshow* in urgent need of a financial helping hand. This woman lived on Florida's Gulf Coast and owned a home that was severely damaged by Hurricane Katrina. She came to us in Mobile, Alabama in 2006, hoping that items she had salvaged might be worth *something*, so she could pay to repair part of the damage.

This woman brought two sperm whale teeth elaborately decorated with scrimshaw, she explained how she had purchased the teeth years before at a tag sale for 10 cents each. Ron Bourgeault of Northeast Auctions in Portsmouth, New Hampshire, did the verbal appraisal, giving her an estimate of $25,000 for the two pieces. The guest was both shocked and thrilled at the same time. The two pieces never made it to television because we had taped a segment on scrimshaw earlier in the season.

Our guest was eager to sell them, and they appeared in Bourgeault's August 2006 marine sale. Bourgeault determined that it would be advantageous to sell the teeth separately—and as it turned out, this was excellent advice.

Lot 812 was the tooth with a drawing depicting an American eagle clutching a Union shield

This pair of sperm whale teeth is decorated with scrimshaw designs. The original owner's twenty cents' investment helped her recover from the devastation of Hurricane Katrina when the pair sold for $35,960.

over a fully rigged American ship under sail on the front. On the back was the image of a man on horseback (possibly Andrew Jackson). This sperm whale tooth brought $17,400.

Lot 813 was the tooth with an American eagle clutching a "Universal Liberty" banner over a fully rigged American ship under sail on the front and crossed British and American flags on the back, with images of cannon and anchors plus "Unity" over a brig with an owner's flag marked B.H. This piece brought $18,560. The seller was ecstatic! Not long afterward, a Tallahassee newspaper ran a story about the sale and how the proceeds helped the woman get her life back together after the devastation of Hurricane Katrina.

CIVIL WAR TREASURES— YOUR NAME IS MUDD

According to Wes Cowan, timing is a significant consideration when selling an antique or collectible. For instance, a piece from the mid-1800s that came to *Roadshow* in 2000 and sold in 2005, might have brought a higher price if it was auctioned just a few years later. Here's that story:

The original owner's name of the artifact really *was* Mudd—Dr. Samuel Mudd—and he was fatefully caught up in John Wilkes Booth's plot to assassinate President Abraham Lincoln. Whether Mudd was an innocent accessory or a guilty coconspirator is open to historical debate, but he was the doctor who set Booth's leg—injured when Booth jumped from the theater balcony to the stage—after murdering Lincoln on April 14, 1865.

As described in Cowan's auction catalog, "Samuel Mudd was born on a plantation and was a supporter of slavery. Around 4:00 in the morning after the assassination, John Wilkes Booth and David Herold arrived at Mudd's home, and the doctor removed Booth's boot and set his broken leg."

APPRAISAL MATTERS

On *Roadshow*, we give a "verbal approximation of value," and if this assessment is high ($2,500 or up) or historically important, it may be worth paying for a *written* appraisal at some point after you leave the *Roadshow* event. This investment can pay future dividends by protecting your asset and providing formal authentication, thereby establishing both monetary and historical value, important for both you and future generations.

In addition, written appraisals will enable you to insure the item for loss owing to theft or destruction. In most instances, insurance companies *require* written appraisals of individual items that are worth $2,500 or more.

I do know of at least one instance when an insurance company accepted the tape of a *Roadshow* on-air appraisal in lieu of a written appraisal. But many—if not most—times, the guest with a valuable object still needs a written appraisal from a qualified appraiser in order to get a fine-arts rider for their homeowner's insurance policy or a separate fine-arts insurance policy. Read more about appraisals at the end of this chapter.

Mudd supplied crutches made for Booth and sent him on his way. When the military investigator tracking Booth found Mudd, the doctor claimed not to have known the identity of the injured man. But Mudd's wife

This beautiful inlaid box was made by Dr. Samuel Mudd while he was imprisoned. Mudd was implicated in the plot to assassinate Abraham Lincoln.

is a lift-out shelf with seven compartments. There is an inlaid ribbon in the center of the lid with the name *Bertha* in black-stained wood. Inside the lid, under glass, is a pressed seaweed wreath inscribed *This wreath was made of pressed seaweed at Fort Jefferson, in the Dry Tortugas in 1867, by Dr. Mudd, imprisoned there as one of the conspirators in the assassination of President Lincoln.* "This is the sort of artifact that can send chills down your spine," said Cowan when he first saw it at the Denver *Roadshow* in 2000. At the time, Cowan valued it at $15,000 to $20,000. In 2005 the owner sold it for $12,075. Cowan adds that the box might have sold for a much higher price four years later, when interest in Abraham Lincoln reached a fever pitch because of the bicentennial of Lincoln's birth and the election of Barack Obama.

handed over the boot that had been cut off Booth's leg and inside was written, *J Wilkes*. Mudd was subsequently prosecuted as one of the conspirators and found guilty. Sentenced to life in prison, he escaped death by only one vote. He served his sentence in Fort Jefferson, in the Dry Tortugas, a group of seven desolate islands about seventy miles west of Key West, Florida.

In 1867, an epidemic of yellow fever hit the prison, killing the prison's doctor, and Mudd took over his duties. Andrew Johnson pardoned him in 1869, partly for his humanitarian acts during this epidemic. While an inmate at Fort Jefferson, Mudd is reported to have made small boxes decorated in different woods. The particular box that came into *Roadshow* was one of these.

The box, 12 by 7¾ by 4½ inches, is inlaid with a parquetry design (*parquetry* is a geometric inlay, while *marquetry* is pictorial). Inside

FROM RUSSIA TO ALASKA TO *ROADSHOW* WITH LOVE

In Spokane, Washington, in the summer of 2007, Doyle New York's Elaine Banks Stainton saw a painting by Russian artist Klavdiy Vasilievich Lebedev (1852–1916) that had once been part of the Dodge estate (probably Anna Thomson Dodge) in Detroit, Michigan. The gentleman who owned it at the time had flown, with the painting, from Anchorage, Alaska, just to have it appraised at *Roadshow*. Stainton saw the small 12½ by 15⅞–inch painting entitled *Threshing Floor* and wanted very much to put it on television because she had valued it at a very respectable $50,000 to $70,000. But the owner knew too much about the painting, and we decided that the segment would not be compelling for viewers. The man from Anchorage had purchased it for $10,000 from the Dodge estate in the mid-1990s. After his trip to *Roadshow*, he consigned it to Doyle's to sell, which the auction house did in 2007. It brought $67,000, which was just shy of Stainton's high estimate.

ROCK AROUND THE CLOCK

Mike Gutierrez, consignment director, Heritage Galleries of Dallas, Texas, recalls the sale of an iconic item from the early rock 'n' roll era that was appraised at the San Antonio, Texas, taping of *Roadshow* in 2007. The piece was a Buddy Holly and the Crickets British tour souvenir program that had been autographed twice by the legendary rock 'n' roll stars.

During their all-too-brief career in the late 1950s, Buddy Holly and his band, the Crickets, were a great success both in the United States and in England. The group went to Great Britain in 1958, and this tour inspired John Lennon and Paul McCartney of the Beatles, the Rolling Stones, and others who would shortly be at the forefront of the British rock scene.

This autographed program was collected by a young American woman visiting Liverpool with her family, where her father was a member of the armed forces. She was lucky enough to have special permission to sit on the stage through-

The iconic early rock-and-roll group, Buddy Holly and the Crickets. Souvenirs from one of their 1958 concerts in Great Britain turned into cash for the lucky owner—$14,340 to be exact.

out the Buddy Holly performance, and after the concert she was invited backstage where Holly, along with Jerry Allison and Joe Maudlin, signed the back cover of her souvenir program.

The program itself is a rarity for the tour, and it was also signed by Holly and Des O'Connor (from the supporting act) on the interior pages. The program, with its autographs, survived the years very well, and all the autographs were large, clear, and in good condition.

It was appraised for just a few dollars over $4,000 ($4,050 to be exact), and it sold at Heritage Galleries for $14,340—which did not include a smaller signed photograph included in the *Roadshow* appraisal.

POE PEOPLE

In chapter 7, I discussed the stolen Edgar Allan Poe daguerreotype that came into *Roadshow* and was subsequently returned to the rightful owner, the Hampden-Booth Theater Library in New York City. According to Wes Cowan, who was originally chosen to sell the piece, "Shortly after its return, the library decided to sell it. "It was consigned to Sotheby's where it brought a surprising one hundred and fifty thousand dollars on October 17, 2006. This far exceeded the thirty thousand to fifty thousand dollars that both *Roadshow* and Sotheby's had projected."

SOMETHING OF A FAMILY MATTER

Wes Cowan's great-great-grandfather was a member of John Hunt Morgan's cavalry—better known as Morgan's Raiders, a group of Confederate cavalrymen under the command of General John Hunt Morgan. During the Civil War, this group created a great deal of turmoil for the United States Army as well as tremendous losses and fear among Indiana and Ohio residents.

The real Andersonville prison, officially known as Camp Sumter, was the largest Confederate military prison during the Civil War and became notorious for its hellhole conditions. Approximately one-third of the 45,000 Union prisoners imprisoned there—on twenty-six acres with a swamp in the middle—died from starvation and disease. After the war, many in the North considered these deaths to be war crimes perpetrated by the Confederate army on the Union soldiers. The site of the prison is now Andersonville National Historic Site in Andersonville, Georgia.

Cowan's great-great-grandfather was captured with Morgan in Ohio, and was sent to Camp Douglas—a prison camp in Chicago known as the North's Andersonville.

In a moment that has an element of serendipity to it, a distressed photograph album with twenty-two *carte de visite* photographs came to *Roadshow* in Bismarck, North Dakota to be appraised by Wes Cowan. Ten of these images were of Morgan's Raiders, which included Wes Cowan's great-great-grandfather. Cowan appraised them for $10,000 to $16,000, but when they actually sold at Cowan's in Cincinnati, they brought a slightly more modest $7,700.

HOME IS WHERE THE ANTIQUE IS

You've heard true tales from our appraisers about pieces that guests decided to sell. Some items brought prices at auction above the estimates received at *Roadshow* and beyond their owners' wildest dreams. How fortunate! Others did not. But what about the guests who brought their cherished items for evaluation and decided to take them home—for the long term? I talked to some of these guests too. We identify them only by initials in order to respect their privacy.

WRIGHT OR WRONG

"When our great-grandmother and her husband were planning to build a house, they chose Frank Lloyd Wright," said *Roadshow* guest P.C., recounting her story to *Roadshow* appraiser Ken Gloss. "Unfortunately, Great-grandmother felt that Mr. Wright just did not really have a grip on what he was doing, and did not seem to adapt to what she wanted in her home. She was not shy about telling him so," in the letters she wrote to the man whom many now consider the preeminent architect of the twentieth century.

"After protracted discussion, Great-grandmother (Great-granddad was just the money man) decided that the house Wright had in mind would be too expensive to build, and not what she wanted because there were not enough bedrooms and closets. She decided to build it herself, acting as her own general contractor, based on the Wright designs. The prairie-style house she built still stands in the Midwest."

Wright's letters, and a number of his drawings, were preserved and have descended in the family to this day, inherited jointly by the three great-grandchildren who brought them into the Omaha *Roadshow* in 2004. In the car on their way to the event they had a spirited conversation about their value: P.C.'s sister thought it would be wonderful if the set of plans and twenty to thirty letters were appraised for $5,000. P.C. replied, "Oh, come on now! If we are dreaming, why not make it ten thousand dollars!"

Little did they know that, later that day, Ken Gloss would evaluate these items between $100,000 and $125,000 for the lot! P.C. and her siblings are still a little flabbergasted over that number, and they have placed the letters in a vault for now. "We were shocked," P.C. said, "we had never dreamed they would be anywhere near that valuable. We may consider selling them someday, but right now they are just locked up."

THE "LUCKY SECRETARY" REVISITED

You may remember the "lucky secretary" story from chapter 2. A charming, sprightly woman, M.L., who says she is "ninety-two going on ninety-three," brought us her treasured bookcase-desk; we valued it at $15,000 to $25,000. She shared a fascinating tale of how this piece probably saved her mother's life by postponing her voyage on the *Titanic*. What happened to the lucky secretary after *Roadshow* was over?

M.L. says that *Roadshow*'s careful and considerate furniture transporters returned it to her house and placed back where it had always been. It will remain there until it is time for it to be passed on to another member of M.L.'s family.

Who will that be? When M.L. first spoke to appraiser Leslie Keno, she told him that her grandmother had won the piece in a family auction. It seems there were nine children involved at the time—and one was in Australia. The lawyer told the family there was no way the secretary could be divided, so the offspring would just have to bid on it, and the highest bidder would pay the money into the estate.

M.L.'s grandmother won the bidding and it has been in M.L's branch of the family ever since. When asked what would happen when the time came for the bookcase to be passed on again, M.L.

said, "My kids want it, but I do not know whom to choose, so they may have to bid on it, just the way my grandmother did all those years ago."

I'M THE ONE WHO IS LOVING IT

There was a running joke between *Roadshow* fan J.A. and her mother. J.A. kept insisting that someday she was going to find something in the attic and take it to *Antiques Roadshow* to be evaluated. J.A.'s mother never failed to remind her that since her house was only five years old, it was unlikely that anything would turn up in her attic that would interest *Roadshow* appraisers.

One day, a large package arrived at the door. It contained a painting bought by J.A.'s aunt at an auction. She thought it was Late Italian Renaissance and had always cherished it. J.A. shared her aunt's admiration. Her aunt was moving to a smaller home and decided to pass on the piece to her niece. J.A. immediately called her mother and said, "Oh my goodness! It's the painting—I'm going to *Roadshow*!"

"I never planned to sell the piece," she says, "but I wanted to know its history." At the 2005 *Roadshow* event in Providence, Rhode Island, Alan Fausel was totally overwhelmed by the piece. "This is a Florentine Madonna. When it was restored, unfor-

tunately, somebody wrapped it up in Bubble Wrap. There are little dots here where the varnish was still wet. At some point, you may want to redo that varnish. But here you have a great painting. Do you have any idea of what it's worth?"

J.A. confessed that she didn't but told Fausel "there was a dollar amount on the paper when I received it in the mail—fifteen thousand dollars—but I figure that was just for insurance purposes."

A gift from the owner's aunt turns out to be a painting by Franciabigio (1482–1525), one of the great masters of the High Italian Renaissance.

Then Fausel dropped the bombshell: He announced that the painting was potentially better, *way better,* than her aunt had imagined—*High* Italian Renaissance rather than *Late* Italian Renaissance.

"If this painting were *attributed* to Franciabigio—meaning we aren't quite sure—it is worth about fifteen thousand dollars. But if we could prove that it's *really,* truly by Franciabigio by showing it to the proper scholar in Italy, which I believe it is, it's worth sixty thousand to eighty thousand dollars. It's one of the best old master paintings I've seen come into *Roadshow.*"

Currently, J.A. is considering taking some photos to the director of the Worcester Art Museum, who specializes in European art. But until she does, she says, "I drink my coffee with my painting every morning." As for the future, J.A. says it is her job to pass the painting along to someone who will love it as much as her aunt did—and as much as she does. "But at the moment, I am the one who is loving it."

CHANGING PLACES AND LIVES: THE BEADED BLANKET

Some of our guests decide to share cherished treasures with larger audiences by donating them to museums or other repositories. Here's a story of a family heirloom that found a new home and inspired new interests.

In St. Paul, Minnesota, R.J. brought a beaded blanket made by her great-great-grandmother, Jane Dixon LaFrambois. R.J. knew the piece was important to the history of her family, but little else. It was a cherished heirloom, and R.J. admitted, "I had not really thought about the value of the piece in advance. I took it to *Roadshow* because I wanted to know exactly what it was. However, by the time appraiser Donald Ellis began talking about money, I knew it was going to

WHAT'S IN A NAME?

Franciabigio was an Italian painter of the Florentine Renaissance, whose paintings hang at the Getty Museum in Malibu, California, the Pitti Palace in Florence, Italy, and the Dresden Gallery in Dresden, Germany.

No one is sure what Franciabigio's (1482–1525) real name was. The son of a Milanese linen weaver (or, some sources say, he was born in Florence)—his real name is thought to be Marcantonio Franciabigio, or Francia Bigio, or—as others insist—Francesco di Cristofano. Regardless, this artist is best known as Franciabigio. When it comes to Italian High Renaissance paintings, which were very seldom signed by the artist, attribution is everything.

be a lot, just from the way he spoke about it."

Ellis told R.J. that the piece, which was a woman's blanket, shawl, or dance blanket, was worth $60,000 to $75,000 and was made circa 1840. It required a bit of conservation and needed to be handled with great care in the future.

After *Roadshow* left town, Mr. Ellis helped negotiate a deal with the Minneapolis Institute of the Arts, where it was exhibited behind an acrylic shield and with a dark piece of cloth hung behind it, so the holes in the fabric were not as visible.

R.J. said that the blanket was featured in several newspapers. She did presentations on its history to various groups, among them sev-

PRESERVE AND PROTECT

Please take to heart the words handle with care when you store or showcase your fine antiques and collectibles. Here are some top to-dos and don'ts from our appraisers:

PRINTS, MAPS & FINE ART ON PAPER:

* Remove the print from the frame and gently release it from the wooden backing. Over time, wood releases an acid that is damaging to paper. Consult with a professional framer to determine a safe way to reframe—possibly using the original backing with the addition of an acid-free barrier between the wood and the picture.

BRONZE, PEWTER AND SILVER:

* Bronze—dust carefully. Do not polish.
* Pewter—wash and dry thoroughly. Do not polish.
* Silver—do not over-polish. Use an abrasive-free polish that will not wear down the ornamentation or the silver mark.

eral historical societies. In addition, the blanket sparked her desire to dig more deeply into that side of her family's history. Now, she is busy recording her research and someday hopes to compile it into a book.

NEXT STEPS: WISE WORDS ON APPRAISALS AND SALES

You've returned home from a *Roadshow* event with good news, or you've been inspired by these pages to look more closely at the treasures around you. Now what?

First, Find an Appraiser

As we mentioned earlier in this chapter, we strongly advise getting a written appraisal for your valued items, even if you choose to hold onto them. Helaine Fendelman, past president of Appraisers Association of America and contributing editor of *Country Living* magazine, suggests that you consider the following:

- Find an appraiser who specializes in and is qualified to evaluate your object. Antiques have categories, and the field is too wide for any one appraiser to be knowledgeable across all categories. In other words, do not hire a jewelry appraiser to value furniture.
- Make sure the appraiser is a member of a professional, not-for-profit, appraisal organization. (See Appendix for listing and contact information.)
- Ask the appraiser for credentials or references.
- Understand that fees range from $75 to $400 per hour depending on the area of the country and the individual appraiser. The hourly fee will be for on-site time. Find out in advance if there are additional charges, such as a rate for research and report-preparation times. Ask if there is a separate, additional fee for travel time to your home for the appraisal. Obtain a written agreement detailing the services to be performed and the fees to be paid.
- Never pay or expect to pay a percentage of the value of the item or items being appraised; that is illegal.

Second, Prepare for the Appraisal

- Have any prior appraisals, bills of sale, exhibition history, or other documents related to the item available for the appraiser to examine.

- Prepare a list of the items to be appraised and make sure all items are readily available for inspection, unboxed, etc.

Third, Review the Appraisal Report

- The final written appraisal document should include a photograph and an accurate, complete description of the item, detailing the date, country of origin, physical condition, and measurements.
- The appraisal report must clearly state the purpose of the appraisal (replacement value, fair market value, insurance value, etc.), the date the items were examined, the date/s they were valued, and the effective date of the document.
- A good appraisal presents impartial and confidential information. A professional appraiser does not both appraise and then try to buy the object.

LEARNING HOW TO SELL

Selling antiques and collectibles successfully, especially those valued at $2,000 or more, can be a daunting experience. Many people simply do not know where to begin. We are here to help.

According to Elaine Banks Stainton, senior vice president, executive director, painting department, Doyle New York, "There is always a cost to selling antiques and collectibles. I advise people that many of the items we see of lesser value can be sold successfully online, or in a yard sale, and therefore sellers will avoid unnecessary costs and commissions involved in selling them through antiques dealers or at auction."

You can sell your valuables in three ways: On consignment through your local antiques dealer; by contacting a relevant collectors' organization and offering your item to a specialized audience of online readers; and selling through a reputable auction house with a proven track record in the same category as your item, such as jewelry, furniture, toys, and so on.

PRESERVE AND PROTECT

GLASS:

* Gentle washing is the ideal way to show the true beauty of glass. Line your sink with a towel to provide a cushion and use warm water, not hot, which may cause cracking.

QUILTS:

* Do not store in a plastic bag. Do not fold unless you are willing to refold the quilt in a different way every few months as textiles that have been folded will eventually "break" along the fold line. The ideal way to store a quilt is by covering a tube with acid-free tissue and then rolling the quilt on the tube. Use more tissue between layers of the quilt. Then store the quilt in a dye-free muslin bag.

ANTIQUE & COLLECTIBLE TOYS MADE OF WOOD & METAL:

* Do not repaint an area where the surface decoration has worn off.

PAPER, PAINTINGS, TEXTILES, AND WOOD FURNITURE:

* Keep out of direct sunlight, which causes fading and reduces value.

BRINGING YOUR TREASURE TO A DEALER OR TO AUCTION: A BEGINNER'S GUIDE

If you have pieces valued in excess of $2,000, our appraisers recommend that you consider selling them to a reputable dealer or at auction. The object, the market, region, and timing can all make a difference. The best advice: Just like when you consider selling your house, get several estimates and compare before you decide. Sometimes a dealer is your best bet and sometimes an auction is the way to go. Following are basic guidelines on each, followed by some insider, "just between us"

thoughts and tips, first from dealer Arlie Sulka and then from David Rago.

When selling to a dealer:

Keep in Mind

It is important to find a dealer with expertise and credibility, who specializes in the item or items being offered. Prior to going to a dealer you should have an appraisal for fair market value, which is the amount to expect if you have a willing seller and a willing buyer for your item (see boxed text Words For the Wise).

You can sell your item directly to the dealer. You will receive half of retail value, but it is a guaranteed sale. Some dealers will agree to sell your

Auction in action–The thrill of bidding draws crowds to *Roadshow* appraiser and auctioneer Ken Farmer's outdoor auction.

item on consignment. In this case, dealers will negotiate a percentage of the selling price as a fee.

When consigning to an auction house: Keep in Mind

Auction houses generally follow the following process:

- **Evaluation:** Most large auction companies require you to bring in your item for an on-site evaluation. The evaluation is usually free. You will receive an estimate of the price your item may bring at auction. Sometimes, you can send good quality photographs by mail. However, this may get you only a preliminary auction estimate and the evaluation by mail may take four to six weeks. If you want an appraiser to come to your home, the cost can be steep.
- **The decision to sell**: After evaluation, the auction company's expert will decide if your item is appropriate for sale in their venue. You, the consigner, must now decide if this is what you want to do. Take into consideration the auction estimate, the auction house's quoted commission rate, the cost of shipping the item to the auction house, cataloging fees, and other costs associated with selling that are the consigner's responsibility (see the section Just Between Us/Insider Tips, page 171). The higher the value of the item, the more likely some of these costs may be negotiable.
- **Shipping**: Items that have to be shipped to the auction house need to be packed by the consignor or his agent. Large auction companies often have a shipping department that can help you with this process, and if the consignment is large and the value potentially high, they may come and retrieve it—but first, ask if there is a fee.
- **The reserve price**: This is the minimum price that an item must bring in order to sell—sometimes called a reserve. This price

WORDS FOR THE WISE

Auction Value: Most often, the term refers to a fair market value (see following), but it also can be used to indicate the highest price that a piece will realize in any marketplace.

Fair Market Value: The amount of money a willing seller can expect to receive from a willing buyer.

Insurance Replacement Value: The amount of money it would take to replace a lost, stolen or destroyed item within a reasonable time and from an appropriate market (see following).

Appropriate Marketplace: A retail source similar to where the item was purchased. For instance, a diamond ring from Tiffany or Cartier cannot be replaced with a purchase from a mass-market discounter. That would not constitute an appropriate marketplace.

Retail Value: The price of an item sold to the general public by a vendor who has bought the item from a wholesale source and has added a markup.

Provenance: Derived from the Latin for *to come forth*, the term refers to the provable history (photographs or letters, for instance) of where an object has been and to whom it has belonged over the years.

should be agreed upon between you and the auction house beforehand. If the item you are trying to sell fails to reach the reserve or minimum price, it will not be sold—but you may incur charges anyway. Find out.

- **The contract:** Read it over very carefully, noting the commission charges and the list of other charges you might incur, such as catalog photographs and insurance.
- **Payment**: A check will generally be mailed to you within thirty to thirty-five days after the sale is over. It will be the hammer price (the price at which the auctioneer's gavel falls that indicates the final bid for the object) minus commission and fees. Checks will not be issued until after the buyer has paid his bill in full.

Just Between Us:

Reasons for Selling to a Dealer

Arlie Sulka, managing director of Lillian Nassau in New York City says, "Depending on the circumstances, selling to a dealer can be the best choice." She cites some of her reasons:

- **Seasoned dealers who are specialists in a particular field are familiar with the marketability of an item in their area of expertise and know what a fair purchase price should be.** Unlike auctioneers, they are willing to risk their own money to buy an item—and in order to be successful, they need to be right most of the time.
- **When dealers buy inventory, they pay immediately**. If an item is consigned to auction for a specialty sale, the auction house may only hold a couple of sales a year in that specialty category, thereby making a seller wait for four to six months for the sale to occur. Payment is usually made thirty to forty-five days after the date of the sale. If for some reason the auction buyer pays late for the item, the seller may not receive monies within the designated time period. And, if the buyer backs out of the sale, the seller may not be paid at all and will have to

either re-consign the object or find another way to sell the piece.

- **When a dealer sells an item, the buyer does not have to pay an additional commission (buyer's premium).** Using an example hammer price (see page 169—Words For the Wise) of $40,000, if a buyer successfully bids that amount at auction, the buyer can actually pay as much as $50,000 with the additional buyer's premium added on top of the hammer price. Although the buyer has paid $50,000 for the object, the seller is compensated based on the hammer price of $40,000, from which usually a commission is deducted as well as an insurance fee and photography fee, leaving the seller with a net price of around $35,000. Also while the above item may have a presale estimate of $40,000 to $60,000, the reserve, or the minimum price, for which the seller has agreed to sell the item may be less than the minimum estimate—say $35,000. If the object sells only for the reserve price, the seller may only net around $30,000. Lastly, if the object fails to reach its reserve price and is unsold, the seller sometimes has to pay a buy-in fee, and insurance and photography charges. In this worst-case scenario, the seller may end up responsible for expenses incurred on an item that did not sell.
- **Selling to a dealer does not carry any fees that must be paid without having received any proceeds.** There is no risk that an item may be sold for significantly less than expected, because selling to a dealer means that the object has been sold.
- **Selling to a dealer is not a gamble.** If an object fails to meet a reserve at auction, the piece might be considered "burned." Auction buyers have good memories and may recognize that the piece didn't sell for years.

This may negatively impact the owner's ability to sell the item in another venue. Issues may be raised about why the piece didn't sell. Was the reserve too high? Were there condition problems? Even if no issues existed, the piece may no longer be considered "fresh."

- **Dealers do not have a minimum value for items that they buy and sell**. Today, many of the major auction houses do have a minimum amount per lot, and that cuts out a significant amount of objects that owners may want to sell.

Just Between Us:
Insider Tips for Selling at Auction

David Rago offers the following pointers on the auction sale experience, especially for first-time auction consigners:

- **Pick specialty auction houses for specialty goods or a major auction house that has a number of specialty departments and expertise.** Rago says, "In short, why consign material to an auction house that does not know or understand the material being offered? This is especially true for twentieth-century goods."
- **Understand the terms the auction house is giving you**. Auction houses quote their commission rates, but are often less forthcoming about other charges that might be incurred. Important questions to ask include: What does a photo cost in the catalog? Will it be in color or black-and-white? What size will the picture be? Will it be on the cover? (You should be so lucky!) What is the placement of the item in the order of sale? Who pays for insurance? What is the level of insurance coverage?
- **Agree on the reserve price for the item**. What do you pay if the piece fails to sell? You have to be a proactive seller, as no two

auction houses have exactly the same terms or offer the same services.

- **Be realistic about what you have to sell**. Negotiating a better commission rate, getting free catalog photos and so forth is just not likely to happen unless you have an item worth more than $3,000. If you have a piece worth $50,000 to $100,000 or more, you probably will be able to set your own terms. Expect to pay no commission and pay nothing else for additional services such as photos for the catalog or insurance. The auction house will make its money from the commission the buyer pays, and that is usually about 20 percent or more.
- **Take into account the prevailing economic conditions**. If an item was worth $4,000 last year, it might be worth less this year—or perhaps more in future years. Consider the economic and political climate of the time.

DECISIONS, DECISIONS, DECISIONS: A RECAP

Deciding to sell is your first decision. If you do choose this route, we can't stress enough how important it is to remember that there is always a cost to selling. It may be in the form of a commission paid to an auction house, advertising cost paid to a magazine or newspaper, or the fair-market value you may have to take when you sell an item to an antiques dealer. Your next steps are: Obtaining a good fair-market appraisal; getting estimates from reputable (well-known and respected) dealers and auction houses; and researching the marketplace through local collectors and online. Armed with all this information, you are ready to make an informed decision of when and where to sell that will give you the best opportunity for success in the marketplace.

Good luck!

MARSHA'S FINAL MUSING

As we complete our behind-the-scenes tour of *Antiques Roadshow*, I realize that this book has been as much a learning experience for me as it has been for you. It provided me with a rare opportunity to look back and review all the exciting people, events, and artifacts that have been part of my life for many years.

In each episode, we all learn so much from our appraisers. We share intimately in the guests' discoveries: We grow joyously excited when they get a surprising or financially rewarding appraisal and feel their disappointment when they receive news that is not what they wanted to hear. Nonetheless, whether an item is worth $500 or $500,000, there is always some-thing new to learn. Watching *Antiques Roadshow* inevitably becomes an education in our country's rich and varied history, wrapped up in a weekly, edge-of-your seat treasure hunt. Every day, I have the privilege of working toward creating programming that makes a difference in people's lives—*and* having so much fun doing it. I collaborate with a superb team. When we are on the road, what a pleasure I have meeting people who live in and around the cities we visit. Their warmth and enthusiasm for the show make all the hard work a true labor of love.

So please keep sharing your special treasures with us so we can continue to provide you with great television each week. And thank you for allowing us into your homes and hearts.

See you on Monday nights!

Mark L. Walberg and Marsha Bemko, a winning team, at the Emmy Awards. Without you viewers we wouldn't be here!

CONTACTING OUR APPRAISERS

Our appraisers are our best resource. To contact them, please visit our Web site, pbs.org/antiques, and click on *appraisers*; you will find them listed alphabetically and by their area of expertise.

REFERENCE BOOKS FROM THE ROADSHOW LIBRARY

ART

Benezit, E. *Dictionaire Des Peintures, Sculpteures, Dessinateurs, et Graveurs, Vol 1–14*. Paris, France: Grund, 2009

Mason, Lark E. Asian Art. Easthampton, MA: Antique Collectors Club, 2003

Moneta, Howard. *Davenport Art Reference & Price Guide*. Phoenix, AZ: LTBGordonsart, Inc., 2009

Wood, Jeremy. *Hidden Talents: A Dictionary of Neglected Artists Working 1880–1950*. Billingshurst, England: Jeremy Wood Fine Art, 1994

CERAMICS

Godden, Geoffrey. *Encyclopedia of British Pottery and Porcelain Marks*. London, England: Barrie & Jenkins, Random House, 1991

Irvine, Louise. *Royal Doulton Series Ware*, Vols. 1–4. Kensington, England: Richard Dennis, 2007

Lang, Gordon. *Miller's Pottery and Porcelain Marks*. New York: Sterling Publishing, 1995

Opie, Jennifer. *Scandinavia Ceramics and Glass in the 20th Century*. London, England: V&A Publications, 1989

Rago, David. *American Art Pottery*. New York: Knickerbocker Press, 2001

Rontgen, Robert. *Marks on German, Bohemian and Austrian Porcelain 1710–Present*. Atglen, PA: Schiffer Publications, 1981

CLOCKS

Bull, Simon. *Antiques Roadshow Clocks and Watches*. Coventry, England: BBC Books, 1995

Shenton, Alan. *Pocket Watches 19th and 20th Century*. Woodbridge, Suffolk, United Kingdom: Antique Collector's Club, 1996

COLLECTIBLES

Hake, Ted. *Hake's Price Guide to Character Toys*. New York: House of Collectibles, 2004

Hake, Ted. *Toy Premiums*. Paducah, KY: Collector Books, 1996

Lambrou, Andreas. *Fountain Pens Vintage and Modern*. London: Philip Wilson Publishers, 2006

Overstreet, Robert. *Overstreet Comic Book Price Guide*. New York: Avon Books, 1997

White, Karl T. *Fishing Tackle: Antique and Collectible Vol. 1–3*. Luther, OK: Hollis Enterprises, 2002

FURNITURE

Andrews, John. *Victorian and Edwardian Furniture Price Guide*. Woodbridge, Suffolk, England: Antique Collector's Club, Ltd., 1986

Beckerdite, Luke. *American Furniture*. Lebanon, NH: University Press of New England, 1998

Bly, John. *Antiques Roadshow Small and Decorative Furniture*. Coventry, England: BBC Books, 1995

Payne, Christopher. *19th Century European Furniture*. Woodbridge, Suffolk, England: Antique Collector's Club, Ltd., 1986

Pina, Leslie. *Fifties Furniture with Values*. Atglen, PA: Schiffer Publishing, 1996

Pina, Leslie. *Classic Herman Miller*. Atglen, PA: Schiffer Publishing, 1998

GLASS

Arwas, Victor. *The Art of Glass*. Winterbourne, Berkshire, United Kingdom: Andreas Papadakis Publishers, 1999

Luther, Louise. *Miller's Art Glass*. London: Mitchell Beazley, 2006

Van Den Bossche, Willy. *Antique Bottles*. Woodbridge, Suffolk, United Kingdom: Antique Collector's Club, 2001

MUSICAL INSTRUMENTS

Sadie, Stanley. *The Grove Dictionary of Musical Instruments, Vol. 1–3*. New York: Oxford University Press, 1985

METALWORK AND SILVER

Kjellberg, Pierre. *Bronzes of the 19th Century Dictionary of Sculptures.* Atglen, PA: Schiffer Publishing, 1994

Morrill, Penny. *Mexican Silver 20th Century Handwrought Jewelry and Metalwork.* Atglen, PA: Schiffer Publishing, 2007

Morris, Alastair. *Antiques from the Garden.* Woodbridge, Suffolk, United Kingdom: Antique Collector's Club, 2001

Pickford, Ian. *Jackson's Silver and Gold Marks of England, Scotland & Ireland.* Woodbridge, Suffolk, United Kingdom: Antique Collector's Club, 2007

Rainwater, Dorothy. *Encyclopedia of American Silver Manufacturers.* Atglen, PA: Schiffer Publishing, 2003

Wyler, Seymour. *The Book of Old Silver.* New York: Crown, 1974

TEXTILE

Middleton, Andrew. *Rugs & Carpets: Techniques, Traditions & Designs.* London: Mitchell Beazley, 1966

Sherrill, Sarah B. *Carpets and Rugs of Europe and America.* New York: Abbeville Press, 1996

OTHER BOOKS OF INTEREST

ART

Falk, Peter Hastings, ed. *Dictionary of Signatures and Monograms of American Artists.* Madison, CT: Sound View Press, 1988

Falk, Peter Hastings, ed. *Who Was Who in American Art, 1564–1975.* 3 vols. Madison, CT: Sound View Press, 1999

Lipman, Jean and Tom Armstrong, ed. *American Folk Painters of Three Centuries.* New York: Hudson Hills Press, 1980

Mayer, Ralph, *A Dictionary of Art Terms and Techniques.* New York: Harper & Row, 1969

CERAMICS

Bushell, Stephen W., *Oriental Ceramic Art.* New York: Crown, 1980

Cushion, John and Margaret. *A Collectors History of British Porcelain.* Woodbridge Suffolk, Antique Collector's Club, 1992

Evans, Paul. *Art Pottery of the United States.* New York: Feingold & Lewis, 1987

Godden, Geoffrey A. *Godden's Guide to European Porcelain.* London: Barrie & Jenkins Ltd., 1993

Greer, Georgeanna H. *American Stonewares: The Art & Craft of Utilitarian Potters.* Atglen, PA: Schiffer Publishing, 1996

Kirsner, Gary. *The Mettlach Book.* Coral Springs, FL: Glentiques Ltd., 1994

Kovel, Ralph and Terry. *Kovel's New Dictionary of Marks.* New York: Crown, 1986

Lage, Chad. *Pictorial Guide to Pottery & Porcelain Marks.* Paducah, KY: Collector Books, 2004

Lehner, Lois. *Lehner's Encyclopedia of U.S. Marks on Pottery, Porcelain & Clay.* Paducah, KY: Collector Books, 1988

Lewis, Griselda. *A Collector's History of English Pottery.* London: Barrie & Jenkins, Ltd., 1969

Roerig, Fred and Joyce Herndon Roerig. *The Collector's Encyclopedia of Cookie Jars.* Paucah, KY: Collector Books, 1991

Rosson, Joe L. *Official Price Guide to Pottery and Porcelain.* New York: House of Collectibles, 2005

CLOCKS

Korz, Frederick W. *Official Price Guide to Collecting Clocks.* New York: House of Collectibles, 2003

Swedberg, Robert and Harriett. *Encyclopedia of Antique American Clocks.* Iola, WI: Krause Publications, 2001

COLLECTIBLES

Bowen, Glen Benton. *Collectible Fountain Pens.* Gas City, IN: L-W Book Sales, 1992

Guernsey's. *Elvis The Official Auction Catalogue.* New York: Harry N. Abrams, 1999

Hake, Ted and Russ King. *Price Guide to Collectible Pin-Back Buttons 1896–1986.* Iola, WI: Krause Publications, 1991

Luscomb, Sally C. *The Collector's Encyclopedia of Buttons.* Atglen, PA: Schiffer Publishing, 1997

Mackley, William J. *American Bird Decoys.* New York: E.P. Dutton, 1965

Miller, Steve. *The Art of the Weathervane.* Atglen, PA: Schiffer Publishing, 1984

Olman, John M. and Morton W. *The Encyclopedia of Golf Collectibles.* Florence, AL: Books Americana, Inc., 1985

Russo, Thomas A. *Mechanical Typewriters: Their History, Value, and Legacy.* Atglen, PA: Schiffer Publishing, 2002

Thompson, Helen Lester. *Sewing Tool & Trinkets.* Paducah, KY: Collector Books, 1997

FURNITURE

Dubrow, Eileen and Richard. *American Furniture of the 19th Century.* Atglen, PA: Schiffer Publishing, 1981

Fairbanks, Jonathan L. and Elizabeth Bidwell Bates. *American Furniture 1620 to Present.* New York: Richard Marek, 1981

Fales, Dean A., Jr. *American Painted Furniture 1660–1880.* New York: E.P Dutton, 1972

Fitzgerald, Oscar P. *Four Centuries of American Furniture.* Iola, WI: Krause Publications, 1995.

Fredgant, Don. *American Manufactured Furniture.* West Chester, PA: Schiffer , 1988

Greenberg, Cara. *Mid-Century Modern Furniture of the 1950's.* New York: Harmony Books, 1995

Hayward, Helena. *World Furniture.* New York: McGraw-Hill, 1965

Hurst, Ronald L. and Jonathan Prawn. *Southern Furniture 1680–1830.* New York: Harry Abrams, Inc., 1997

Kassy, John. *The Book of American Windsor Furniture.* Amherst: University of Massachusetts Press, 1998

Kates, George N. *Chinese Household Furniture.* New York: Dover Publications, 1948

Miller, Judith and Martin. *The Antiques Directory Furniture.* New York: Portland House, 1985

Rago, David. *The Collector's Guide to Arts and Crafts.* Layton, UT: Gibbs Smith, 2005

Sack, Albert. *The New Fine Points of Furniture, Early American.* New York: Crown, 1993

Safford, Frances Gruber. *American Furniture in the Metropolitan Museum of Art. Vol. 1, Early Colonial Period: The Seventeenth-Century and William and Mary Styles.* New York: Metropolitan Museum of Art; New Haven, CT: Yale University Press, 2007

Stimpson, Miriam. *Modern Furniture Classics.* New York: Watson-Guptill, 1997

Wills, Geoffrey. *English Furniture 1550–1760.* New York: Doubleday, 1971

Viel, Lyndon. *Antique Ethic Furniture.* Des Moines, IA: Wallace-Homestead, 1983

GLASS

Bacri, Clotilde. *Daum Masters of French Decorative Glass.* New York: Rizzoli, 1993

Edwards, Bill and Mike Carwile. *Standard Encyclopedia of Carnival Glass.* Paducah, KY: Collector Books, 1998

Gardner, Paul V. *The Glass of Freerick Carder.* New York: Crown, 1971

Grover, Ray and Lee. *Carved and Decorated European Art Glass.* Rutland, VT, Charles Tuttle Company, 1970

Hajdmach, Charles R. *British Glass 1800–1914.* Woodbridge, Suffolk, England: Antiques Collector's Club, 1991

Jackson, Lesley. *20th Century Factory Glass.* New York: Rizzoli, 2000

Jargstorf, Sibylle. *Paperweights.* West Chester, PA: Schiffer Publishing, 1991

Marcilhac, Felix. R. Lalique. *Catalogue Raisonne del' Oeuvre de Verre.* Paris: Les Editions de L'Amateur 1989.

McKearin, George S. and Helen. *American Glass.* New York, Crown, 1968

Newman, Harold. *An Illustrated Dictionary of Glass.* New York: Thames and Hudson, 1987

Pina, Leslie. *Fifties Glass.* Atglen, PA: Schiffer Publishing, 1993

Pullin, Anne Geffken. *Glass Signatures, Trademarks, and Tradenames.* Radnor, PA: Wallace-Homestead, 1986

Reilly, Darryl and Bill Jenks. *Early American Pattern Glass.* Iola, WI: Krause Publications, 2002

Revi, Albert Christian. *Nineteenth-Century Glass.* New York: Galahad Books, 1967

Sloan, Jean. *Perfume and Scent Bottle Collecting.* Radnor, PA: Wallace-Homestead, 1989

Truitt, Robert and Deborah. *Collectible Bohemian Glass 1880–1940.* Kensington, MD: B&D Glass, 1995

METALWORK AND SILVER

Coffin, Margaret. *The History and Folklore of American Country Tinware 1700–1900.* Camden, NJ: Thomas Nelson & Sons, 1968

Jackson, Sir Charles James. *English Goldsmiths and Their Marks.* New York: Dover, 1964

Kauffman, Henry J. *Early American Ironware Cast and Wrought*. Rutland, VT: Charles E. Tuttle Company, 1966

Kauffman, Henry J. *American Copper and Brass*. New York: Bonanza Books, 1968

Laughlin, Ledlie Irwin. *Pewter In America: Its Makers their Marks*. New York: American Legacy Press, 1981

Rainwater, Dorothy T. and H. Ivan. *American Silverplate*. Nashville, TN: Thomas Nelson, 1968

TEXTILES

Aleshire, Liz and Kathleen Barack. *Official Price Guide to Quilts*. New York: House of Collectibles, 2003

Blum, Dilys E. *The Fine Art of Textiles, Philadelphia*: Philadelphia Museum of Art, 1997

Black, David, ed. *The Atlas of Rugs and Carpets*. London, England: Tiger Books, 1994

Bolton, Ethel Stanwood and Eva Johnston Coe. *American Samplers*. New York: Dover, 1973

Farady, Cornelia Bateman. *European and American Carpets and Rugs*. Woodbridge, Suffolk, England: Antiques Collector's Club, 1990

Ford, P.R.J. *Oriental Carpet Design*. London: Thames and Hudson, 1989

Johnson, Frances. *Collecting Household Linens*. Atglen, PA: Schiffer Publishing, 1997

Milanesi, Enza. *The Bullfinch Guide to Carpets*. New York: Little, Brown and Company, 1992

Ring, Beth. *Childhood Embroidery—American Samples and Pictorial Needlework 1650–1850*. New York: Alfred A. Knopf, 1993

Safford, Carleton and Robert Bishop. *America's Quilts and Coverlets*. New York: Bonanza Books, 1985

Schlosser, Ignaz. *The Book of Rugs: Oriental and European*. New York: Bonaza Books, 1968

Scofield, Elizabeth and Peggy Zalamea. *20th Century Linen and Lace*. Altglen, PA: Schiffer Publications, 1995

ASSOCIATIONS

Any one of the associations below will refer you to a qualified appraiser in your area.

American Society of Appraisers (ASA)
http://asainfo@appraisers.org or
http://www.appraisers.org

Antiques Dealers' Association of American, Inc.
http://www.adadealers.com

Appraisers Association of America (AAA)
http://www.appraisersassoc.org

Appraisers National Association
http://www.ana-apraisers.org

International Society of Appraisers (ISA)
http://isa-appraisers.org

International Vintage Poster Dealers Association
http://www.ivpda.com

The National Antiques & Art Dealers Association of America
http://www.naadaa.org

ASSOCIATIONS AND COLLECTOR CLUBS

Membership in these clubs often includes subscription to a newsletter.

Abingdon Pottery Collectors' Club
http://abingdon.net/~aacc/content/pottery.html

American Cut Glass Association
http://www.cutglass.org

American Hatpin Society
http://americanhatpinsociety.com

Antique Glass Salt and Sugar Shaker Club
http://www.antiquesaltshakers.com

Antique Telephone Collector Association
http://atcaonline.com

Automatic Musical Instrument Collectors' Association
http://amica.org

Belleek Collectors International Society
http://info@belleek.com

Blue and White Pottery Club
http://blueandwhitepottery.org

Bookend Collector Club
http://ikuritzky@aol.com

Candy Container Collectors of American
http://www.candycontainer.org

Cane Collectors Club
http://liela@walkingstickworld.com

Coca-Cola Collectors Club
http://cocacolaclub.org

Cody Firearm Museum at the

Buffalo Bill Historical Center
http://bbhc.org

Coin Operated Collectors Association
http://www.coinopclub.org

Coleman International Collector's Club
http://www.colemancollectorsclub.com

Custard Glass Collectors Society
http://www.custardsociety.com

Early Typewriter Collectors Association
http://etcetera@writeme.com

Fenton Art Glass Collectors of American, Inc.
http://www.fagcainc.wirefire.com

Fostoria Glass Society of America, Inc.
http://www.fostoriaglass.org

Frankoma Family Collectors Association
http://www.frankoma.org

Friends of Old Quimper (Les Amis de Vieux Quimper)
http://www.oldquimper.com

Hager Pottery Collectors of America
http://www.lanette-clarke@msn.com

Hammered Aluminum Collectors Association
Dannie Woodward
PO Box 1346
Weatherford, TX 76086

Homer Laughlin China Collectors Association
http://hlcca.org

International Carnival Glass Association, Inc.
http://internationalcarnivalglass.com

International Club for Collectors of Hatpins and Hatpin Holders
Audrae Heath
PO Box 1009
Bonners Ferry, ID 83805-1009

International Map Collectors Society
Membership Secretary
104 Church Road
Watford, WD17, 4 QB
United Kingdom

International Match Safe Association
http://www.matchsafe.org

International Nippon Collectors Club
http://www.nipponcollectorsclub.com

International Perfume and Scent Bottle Collectors Association
http://www.perfumebottles.org

Kate Greenaway Society
http://www.postcardclassics@juno.com

Majolica International Society
http://www.majolicasociety.com

Marble Collectors' Society of America
http://blockglas@aol.com

National Association of Avon Collectors
Connie Clark
PO Box 7006, Department P
Kansas City, MO 64113

National Cambridge Collectors, Inc.
http://www.cambridgeglass.org

National Cuff Link Society
http://cufflink.com

National Depression Glass Association
http://www.ndga.net

National Graniteware Society
http://www.granitware.org

National Greentown Glass Association
http://www.greentownglass.org

National Imperial Glass Collectors' Society, Inc.
http://www.imperialglass.org

National Milk Glass Collectors' Society
http://nmgcs.org

Train Collectors Association
http://www.traincollectors.org

National Valentine Collectors Association
Nancy Rosin
PO Box 1404
Santa Ana, CA 92702

National Association of Watch and Clocks Collectors, Inc.
http://www.nawcc.org

Newspaper Collector's Club of American
http://historybuff.com

North Dakota Pottery Collectors Society
http://www.ndpcs.org

Novelty Salt and Pepper Shakers Club

http://dmac925@yahoo.com

Occupied Japan Club
http://www.ohclub.com

Pen Collectors of America
http://pencollectors.com

Schoenhut Collectors Club
Pat Girbach, Secretary
1003 W. Huron St.
Ann Arbor, MI 48103-4217

Shawnee Pottery Collectors' Club
PO Box 713
New Smyrna Beach, FL 32170-0713

Society of Inkwell Collectors
http://www.membership@soic.com

Southern Folk Pottery Collectors Society
http://www.sfpcs@rtmc.net

Stangl/Fulper Collectors Club
http://www.stanglfulper.com

Still Bank Collectors Club of America
http://www.stillbankclub.com

Toaster Collectors Association
http://www.toastercollectors.org

Wallace Nutting Collector's Club
http://www.wallacenutting.com

Warwick China Collectors Club
http://www.warwick@ntsource.com

Westmoreland Glass Society
http://www.westmorelandglass.org

White Ironstone China Association, Inc.
http://whiteironstonechina.com

COLLECTOR PUBLICATIONS

ABC Collectors' Club Newsletter
http://www.drjgeorge@nac.net

Antiques & Fine Art Magazine
http://antiquesandfineart.com

Antiques and the Arts Weekly
http://www.antiquesandthearts.com

Antiques Roadshow Insider
www.antiquesroadshowinsider.com

American Cut Glass Association, The Hobstar
http://acgakathy.com

Antique & Collectors Reproduction News
http://acrn@reponews.com

Antique Advertising Association of America, Past Times
http://www.pastimes.org

Antique Bottle & Glass Collector magazine
http://glswrk@enter.net

Antique Radio Classified
http://antiqueradio.com

Antique Trader
http://antiquetrader.com

Antiques & Collecting Magazine
http://www.acmagazine.com

Art & Antiques Magazine
http://www.artandantiques.net

Art + Auction
http://www.artinfo.com/artandauction

ARTnews
www.artnews.com

Autograph Collector
http://DBTOG@aol.com

The Carousel News & Trader
http://www.carouseltrader.com

Collector Glass News (Glass Collectors Association promotional)
http://glassnews.com

Collector's Life
http://toystorenet.com

Fiesta Collectors Quarterly Newsletter
http://chinaspecialties.com

Fine Art Connoisseur
www.fineartconnoisseur.com

Hall China Collector's Club Newsletter
Virginia Lee
PO Box 360488
Cleveland, OH 44136

Kovels on Antiques and Collectibles
http://www.kovelsonlinestore.com

National Blue Ridge Newsletter
Norma Lily
144 Highland Drive
Blountville, TN 37617

NM (Nelson McCoy) Express
www.mccoylovers.com

Paper & Advertising Collector's Marketplace
http://www.pcmpaper.com/

Paper Pile Quarterly (paperweights)
http://www.info@paperweight.org

Maine Antiques Digest
http://www.maineantiquesdigest.com

Old Stuff
http://oldstuffnews.com

Pepsi-Cola Collectors Club Express
Bob Stoddard, editor
PO Box 817
Claremont, CA 91711-0817

Purinton News and Views
Joe McManus, editor
PO Box 153
Connellsville, PA 15425

Rosevilles of the Past
http://www.rosepast@worldnet.att.net

The Magazine Antiques
http://www.themagazineantiques.com

Tins and Signs
PO Box 440101
Aurora, CO 80044

Toy Shop
Mark Williams, publisher
700 E. State Street
Iola, WI 54990-0001

Vetri: Italian Glass News
Howard Lockwood, publisher
PO Box 191
Fort Lee, NJ 07024

Vintage Fashion and Costume Jewelry Newsletter
http://www.vfck@aol.com

Westmoreland Glass Collector's Newsletter
PO Box 143
North Liberty, IA 52317

Willow Review
PO Box 41312
Nashville, TN 37204

WEB SITES OF INTEREST

GENERAL

liveauctioners.com
http://www.liveauctioners.com
An invaluable general listing of the prices at which a huge variety of items sold for at auction.

abebooks.com
http://abebooks.com
A site listing the booksellers, their books, and prices (well over 100,000 titles).

artfact.com
http://artfact.com
A pay site that provides auction prices for art and antiques. Covers a wide variety of international artists.

askart.com
http://www.askart.com
A pay site that lists artists and the prices their works sold for. Emphasis is on American artists.

Association of Collectors Clubs
http://collectors.org/
Maintains directory of collectors clubs—5,654 of them!

artdaily
http://artdaily.org
Online-only newspaper

artnet.com
http://www.artnet.com
A pay site that provides a survey of the art market and its current pay trends for both dealers and buyers.

artprice.com
http://www.artprice.com
Additional pay sites listing artists and the prices their art has brought at auction.

The Collectors Weekly
http://www.collectorsweekly.com
An informational site for collectors of antiques and vintage items. Covers everything from old beer steins to Eames chairs.

priceminer.com

http://priceminer.com

An online pricing guide for art, antiques, and collectibles. Culls its data from eBay and other online auction sites.

replacements.com

http://www.replacements.com

A site retailing china, silver, and collectibles and a site to use for researching silver flatware and china patterns.

tias.com

http://tias.com/

An auction site devoted solely to antiques and collectibles.

Today's Vintage

http://todaysvintage.com

The online accompaniment to the hardcopy magazine, this site offers articles on everything vintage.

SPECIFIC

The Baghdad Museum Project:

http://www.baghdadmuseum.org/looting/

This Web site is tracking the identification and return of the looted art objects.

FBI Art Theft Program

http://www.fbi.gov/hq/cid/arttheft/arttheft.htm

The Hermitage Museum (St. Petersburg, Russia)

http://www.hermitagemuseum.org/html1_1_167.html

On this Web site there is a section devoted to the details of the recently discovered theft of 221 pieces from their collection in 2006.

Interpol

http://www.interpol.int/Public/WorkofArt/Default.asp or
http://www.interpol.int/Public/WorkofArt/statistics/StatObject2000.asp

The National Museum of Iraq

http://the.iraq.musuem

This site contains information about the impact of the 2003 looting.

Antiques Roadshow Image Credits

All photographs by Jeff Dunn for WGBH except for the following:

Photograph on page 3 by Bob Birkett
Photograph on page 14 by Betsy Bassett for WGBH
Photograph on page 18 courtesy of Gloria Lieberman
Photograph on page 22 by Image WGBH
Photograph on page 31 by Larry Canale for Antiques Roadshow Insider
Photographs on pages 39 and 59 courtesy of Richard Crane
Image on page 42 by Jill Giles and Chas Norton
Photograph on page 49 courtesy of the National Archives
Photograph on page 51 by Amanda Clarke for WGBH
Map photographed on page 53 © GeoNova Publishing, Inc
Photographs on page 53 and 78 by Sam Farrell for WGBH
Photographs on pages 56 and 57 courtesy of Dorothy Harris
Photographs on page 72 and 73 by Jeff Dunn
Photograph on page 77 (upper) by WGBH
Photograph on page 77 (lower) by Jeff Cronenberg for WGBH
Photograph on page 134 courtesy of Isabella Stewart Gardner Museum
Photograph on page 138 by Katie Feiereisel
Photograph on page 145 courtesy of Library of Congress
Photographs on pages 148 and 154 courtesy of Christie's
Photograph on page 158 courtesy of Northeast Auctions
Photograph on page 168 by Ken Farmer
Photograph on page 172 courtesy of Mathew Imaging

Explore ROADSHOW's Video Archive, send us your stories, see exclusive slideshows from tour events, and more...

pbs.org/antiques

Don't forget to watch the show!
Mondays at 8/7C on PBS